Conversations with Christian

Film Theory in Media History

Film Theory in Media History explores the epistemological and theoretical foundations of the study of film through texts by classical authors as well as anthologies and monographs on key issues and developments in film theory. Adopting a historical perspective, but with a firm eye to the further development of the field, the series provides a platform for ground-breaking new research into film theory and media history and features high-profile editorial projects that offer resources for teaching and scholarship. Combining the book form with open access online publishing the series reaches the broadest possible audience of scholars, students, and other readers with a passion for film and theory.

Film Theory in Media History is published in cooperation with the Permanent Seminar for the History of Film Theories.

Conversations with Christian Metz

Selected Interviews on Film Theory
(1970–1991)

Edited by
Warren Buckland and Daniel Fairfax

Amsterdam University Press

Cover ilustration: Christian Metz. Photo: Sylvie Pliskin
Cover design: Suzan Beijer
Lay-out: Crius Group, Hulshout

Amsterdam University Press English-language titles are distributed in the US and Canada by the University of Chicago Press.

ISBN 978 90 8964 825 9
e-ISBN 978 90 4852 673 4 (pdf)
DOI 10.5117/9789089648259
NUR 670

Contents

Acknowledgements

Warren Buckland's acknowledgements. Conceived as a sequel to my first edited collection of translations *The Film Spectator: From Sign to Mind* (Amsterdam University Press, 1995), *Conversations with Christian Metz* has taken more than a decade to complete. It is thanks to the intervention of Daniel Fairfax, who translated over half of the interviews, that the volume has finally been finished. Friends, colleagues, and associates also assisted along the way, including Edward Branigan, Elena Dagrada, Cormac Deane, Thomas Elsaesser, Delphine Evenou, Vinzenz Hediger, Santiago Hidalgo, Martin Lefebvre (who forwarded to me several invaluable unpublished essays), Alison McMahan, Adrian Martin, Jeroen Sondervan, Francesco Sticchi, Meryl Suissa, and Corin Willis. I would also like to thank the interviewees, who responded to my queries: Raymond Bellour, Michel Fano, André Gardies, André Gaudreault, Jean Paul Simon (who responded to many queries), Daniel Percheron, and Marc Vernet. Finally, I would also like to thank Paul Whitty, Research Lead at the School of Arts, Oxford Brookes University, who agreed to cover copyright clearance costs.

Daniel Fairfax's acknowledgements: Thanks, above all, go to Warren Buckland for taking the initiative on this project, and being an attentive and generous collaborator. I would also like to acknowledge Vinzenz Hediger and Trund Lundemo for their work in getting the book series 'Film Theory in Media History' off the ground, Dudley Andrew, Francesco Casetti, John Mackay and Thomas Elsaesser for their general guidance and wisdom, and Jean-Louis Comolli, Jean Narboni, Raymond Bellour, and Jacques Aumont for taking the time to discuss Metz's work and his influence on their own thinking. Finally, my warmest thanks goes to Michelle (for everything).

A note on the translations

In this book '*sémiologie*' is translated as 'semiology' not 'semiotics' (this latter term evokes the Anglo-American work of C.S. Peirce). In his interview with André Gardies (see Chapter 12), when asked if he prefers '*sémiologie*' or '*sémiotique*' (semiotics), Metz says: "I prefer *sémiologie*. Because '*sémiologie*' means Roland Barthes, Saussure, the European tradition, which does not separate semiology from philosophy, from general culture, from the literary tradition."

The reader will find enclosed in square brackets [ ] information added by the translators, as well as the original French terms that have been translated.

Publication details

Chapter 1. 'Sémiologie, linguistique, cinéma. Entretien avec Christian Metz'. René Fouqué, Éliane Le Grivès et Simon Luciani. *Cinéthique* 6 (January–February) 1970, pp. 21–26. Translated by Daniel Fairfax.

Chapter 2. 'Cinéma et sémiologie. Sur la 'specificité'. Entretien avec Christian Metz'. Jean-André Fieschi. *La Nouvelle Critique*, 36 (September, 1970), pp. 48–53. Translated by Daniel Fairfax.

Chapter 3. 'Entretien sur la sémiologie du cinema'. Raymond Bellour et Christian Metz. *Semiotica*, 4, 1 (1971), pp. 1–30. Reprinted by permission of Walter De Gruyter Publishers. Translated by Daniel Fairfax.

Chapter 4. 'Entretien avec Christian Metz'. Daniel Percheron and Marc Vernet. *Ça-Cinéma* 7/8 (1975), pp. 18–51. Reprinted with the permission of Daniel Percheron and Marc Vernet. Translated by Meryl Suissa.

Chapter 5. 'Théorie du cinéma. Table ronde'. Christian Metz, Michel Fano, Jean Paul Simon, and Noël Simsolo. *Cinéma* 221, April 1977, pp. 49–61. Reprinted with the permission of Jean Paul Simon and Michel Fano. Translated by Warren Buckland.

Chapter 6. 'Conversation sur *le Significant imaginiare* et *Essais sémiotiques*'. Jean Paul Simon, Marc Vernet, and Christian Metz. *Ça-Cinéma,* 16 (January 1979), pp. 5–19. Reprinted with the permission of Jean Paul Simon and Marc Vernet. Translated by Daniel Fairfax.

Chapter 7. 'The Cinematic Apparatus as Social Institution: An Interview with Christian Metz'. Sandy Flitterman, Bill Guynn, Roswitha Mueller, and Jacquelyn Suter. *Discourse,* 1 (Fall, 1979), pp. 1–35. Reprinted with the permission of Wayne State University Press.

Chapter 8. 'A Seminar with Christian Metz: Cinema, Semiology, Psychoanalysis, History'. Chaired by Rick Thompson. Published in *Media Centre Papers* 16, introduced and edited by John L. Davies (Bundoora, Victoria: La Trobe University, 1982), pp. 16–46.

Chapter 9. 'Réponses à *Hors Cadre* sur *Le signifiant imaginaire*'. Christian Metz. *Hors Cadre* 4 (1986), pp. 61–74. Reprinted with the permission of Presses Universitaires de Vincennes. © PUV, Saint-Denis, 1986. Translated by Daniel Fairfax.

Chapter 10. 'Entretien avec Christian Metz'. Michel Marie and Marc Vernet. *Iris,* 10 (1990), pp. 271–296. Translated by Daniel Fairfax.

Chapter 11. 'Christian Metz. Entretien'. André Gaudreault. *24 Images* 49 (1990), pp. 63–65. Reprinted with the permission of André Gaudreault. Translated by Warren Buckland.

Chapter 12. 'Une ethique de la sémiologie. Entretien avec Christian Metz'. André Gardies. *CinémAction* 58 (1991), pp. 76–94. Reprinted with the permission of André Gardies. Translated by Daniel Fairfax.

The editors have made every effort to seek permission from copyright holders. A few holders could not be traced, and a few others did not respond.

Introductions

The international reputation of the work of Christian Metz, translated into more than twenty languages, justifies the homage paid here to the founder of a discipline: film semiology.
(Michel Marie, speaking of the conference 'Christian Metz and Film Theory', held at the Cerisy Cultural Centre in 1989).

Modern film theory begins with Metz.
(Constance Penley, *Camera Obscura*)

A Furious Exactitude: An Overview of Christian Metz's Film Theory

Warren Buckland

Buckland, Warren and Daniel Fairfax (eds), *Conversations with Christian Metz: Selected Interviews on Film Theory (1970–1991)*. Amsterdam: Amsterdam University Press, 2017.

DOI: 10.5117/9789089648259/INTRO1

Abstract
This first Introduction to *Conversations with Christian Metz* presents a brief and basic overview of Metz as writer and researcher, focusing on the key concepts that influenced him (especially from linguistics, semiology, and psychoanalysis), and those he generated, supplemented with some of the issues he raises in the interviews.

Keywords: Christian Metz, film theory, semiology, psychoanalysis, interviews

> Those who know Metz from the three perspectives of writer, teacher, and friend are always struck by this paradox, which is only apparent: of a radical demand for precision and clarity, yet born from a free tone, like a dreamer, and I would almost say, as if intoxicated. (Didn't Baudelaire turn H. into the source of an unheard of precision?) There reigns a furious exactitude. (Roland Barthes)[1]

From 1968 to 1991, Christian Metz (1931–1993), the pioneering and acclaimed film theorist, wrote several influential books on film theory: *Essais sur la signification au cinéma, tome 1 et 2* (volume 1 translated as *Film Language: A Semiotics of the Cinema*); *Langage et cinéma* (*Language and Cinema*); *Le signifiant imaginaire. Psychanalyse et cinéma* (*Psychoanalysis and Cinema: The Imaginary Signifier*); and *L'enonciation impersonnelle ou le site du film* (*Impersonal Enunciation or the Place of Film*).[2] These books set the agenda of academic film theory during its formative period. Throughout universities around the world, Metz's ideas were taken up, digested, refined, reinterpreted, criticized, and sometimes dismissed, but rarely ignored.

This volume collects and translates into English for the first time a series of little-known interviews with Christian Metz. In these interviews, Metz offers summaries, elaborations, and explanations of his sometimes complex and demanding theories. He speaks informally of the most fundamental concepts that constitute the foundations of film theory as an academic discipline (concepts from linguistics, semiology, narratology, and psychoanalysis). Within the interview format, Metz discusses in elaborate detail the process of theorizing – the formation, development, and refinement of concepts; the need to be rigorous, precise, and to delimit the boundaries of one's research; and he talks at great length about the reasons theories are misunderstood and derided (by both scholars and students). The interviewers act as inquisitive readers, who pose probing questions to Metz about his influences and motivations, and seek clarification and elaboration of his key concepts in his articles and books. Metz also reveals a series of little-known facts and curious insights, including: the contents of his unpublished manuscript on jokes (*L'Esprit et ses Mots. Essai sur le Witz*); the personal networks operative in the French intellectual community during the sixties and seventies; his relation to the filmology movement, cinephilia, and to phenomenology; his critique of 'applied' theory; the development of a semiology of experimental film; his views on Gilles Deleuze's film theory; the fundamental importance of Roland Barthes to his career; and even how many films he saw each week.

Roland Barthes mentions three ways he knew Metz: writer, teacher, and friend. Barthes characterizes Metz's disposition as a 'furious exactitude.' This was not only manifest in his writing; Maureen Turim mentions Metz's 'incredible intensity' as a teacher: "He talks for three hours, breaking only in the middle to retreat with his students to a café, *'boire un pot'*, and gossip. But in the seminar itself, the lecture is given with minute precision, no pauses, no stumbling, with few notes, mostly from an articulate memory."[3] But Metz's exactitude also allowed for "a free tone," an issue he discusses with Daniel Percheron and Marc Vernet in Chapter 4 of this volume. Metz tells them that his policy in tutorials involved being "ready to speak to people (to listen to them especially), to give people space to talk about their research, to let them speak, give the freedom to choose one's topic of interest, etc. .... It is rather a 'tone', a general attitude ...." Metz emphasized the need to speak to students as individuals, to express a genuine interest in their ideas, rather than simply rehearse a pre-formulated (empty) speech when responding to their research. With regard to supervising theses, Martin Lefebvre notes in a conversation with Annie van den Oever that "[a]n almost entire generation of [French] scholars was either supervised by [Metz] or had him sit as a jury member for their doctoral defense. [...] For several years he was literally at the center of the field and therefore had a large role in shaping it."[4]

In the following pages, I present a brief and basic overview of Metz as writer and researcher, focusing on the key concepts that influenced him and those he generated, supplemented with some of the issues he raises in the interviews.[5]

Foundations: Structural Linguistics

> Cultural meanings are inherent in the symbolic orders and these meanings are independent of, and prior to, the external world, on the one hand, and human subjects, on the other. Thus the world only has an objective existence in the symbolic orders that represent it.[6]

Christian Metz's film semiology forms part of the wider structuralist movement that replaced the phenomenological tradition of philosophy prevalent in France in the 1950s and early 1960s. Phenomenology studies observable phenomena, consciousness, experience, and presence. More precisely, it privileges the infinite or myriad array of experiences of a pre-constituted world (the given) that are present in consciousness. In contrast, structuralism redefines consciousness and experience as outcomes of structures that are not, in themselves, experiential. Whereas for phenomenology meaning originates in and is fully present to consciousness, for structuralists meaning emerges from underlying structures, which necessarily infuse experience with the values, beliefs, and meanings embedded in those structures. A major premise of structuralism, and its fundamental difference from phenomenology, is its separation of the *surface level* (the infinite, conscious, lived experiences of a pre-given world) from an *underlying level* (the finite, unobservable, abstract structure, which is not pre-given and not present to consciousness). The two levels are not in opposition to one another, for structuralism establishes a hierarchy whereby the surface level, consisting of conscious experience, is dependent on the underlying level. Structuralism does not simply add an underlying level to the surface phenomenological level, it also redefines the surface level as the manifestation of the underlying level. A fundamental premise of structuralism is that underlying abstract structures underpin and constitute conscious lived experiences.

Metz's work is pioneering in terms of reconceiving film within the framework of structuralism – or, more precisely, its derivative, semiology. From a semiological perspective, film's properties cannot be studied as a conscious aesthetic experience or be defined as a sensory object. Instead, this sensory object is reconceived as a form of signification – as the manifestation of a non-observable, underlying abstract structure. To analyze film as signification therefore involves a fundamental shift in perspective, from the study of film as an object of experience in consciousness to the study of film's underlying structures, which semiologists call systems of codes.[7]

This shift in perspective is largely attributable to the foundational text of structural linguistics, Ferdinand de Saussure's *Course in General Linguistics* (first published in 1916). Saussure redefined meaning internally, by locating it within language itself, conceived as an underlying finite system, rather than in the referent or in the experiences of language users. This relocation of meaning has profound consequences for the way language (and other systems of signification) is conceived. The term 'meaning' within this theory is defined narrowly: it is synonymous with 'signification' (the signified), rather than 'reference' or 'lived experience'. Signification is an internal value generated from the structural differences between codes. This is one of the foundational principles of semiology: it replaces an external theory of meaning, which posits a direct, one-to-one causal correspondence or link between a sign and its referent, with an internal theory, in which the meaning is based on a series of differential relations within language: "In language, as in any semiological system," writes Saussure, "whatever distinguishes one sign from the others constitutes it."[8] Saussure identified two fundamental types of relation within semiological systems: syntagmatic and paradigmatic (what he called associative) relations. 'Syntagmatic' refers to the relation of signs present in a message, while 'paradigmatic' refers to signs organized into paradigms – classes of comparable signs that can be substituted for one another. Paradigms are systems of available options, or a network of potential choices, from which one sign is chosen and manifest. The sign manifest in a message is not only syntagmatically related to other signs in the message, but is also structurally related to comparable signs in the paradigm that were not chosen. Signs are therefore defined formally, from an intrinsic rather than extrinsic perspective, and holistically, as a network of paradigmatic and syntagmatic relations. A sign in a message does not embody one fixed meaning predetermined by its link to a referent, and cannot therefore be interpreted by itself in isolation. Instead, it gains its meaning from its structural relations to other signs.

Structural linguistics is founded upon the hierarchy between *langue/parole*, the linguistic equivalent of the structuralist hierarchy between surface and underlying level. *La parole* refers to language's phenomenological level (the conscious, experiential level of speech), whereas *la langue* refers to the underlying language system of codes. *La parole* is simply the manifestation of *la langue* and is reducible to it. Saussure described *la parole* as infinite and heterogeneous, and *la langue* as finite and homogeneous. Generating an infinity of speech utterances with finite means is possible by recognizing that all utterances are composed from the same small number of signs used recursively in different combinations. This principle – the principle of economy – is another founding assumption of semiology: all the infinite surface manifestations can be described in terms of the finite system underlying them. The structural linguist André Martinet explained this principle of economy via the concept of double articulation.[9] The first articulation involves the minimally meaningful units, which Martinet calls 'monemes'. These monemes, in turn, are composed of non-signifying significant units (phonemes), which constitute the second level of articulation. Meaning is generated from the recursive combination of the small number of phonemes to generate a large number of monemes, and then by the recursive combination of monemes to generate potentially infinite number of sentences. This is how double articulation accounts for the extraordinary economy of language, which is, according to Martinet, language's unique, defining characteristic. The meaning of monemes is generated from the structural relations between phonemes, rather than from a referent. The phonemes are autonomous from reality (they do not 'reflect' reality, but are arbitrary); meaning emerges out of non-meaning – from the selection and combination of phonemes into monemes.

These basic semiological principles – meaning is defined intrinsically, as sense rather than reference; meaning derives from syntagmatic and paradigmatic relations; the principle of economy, in which an infinite number of messages can be reduced to an underlying finite system that generated them – presents to film and cultural theorists a framework in which to study and analyze the 'symbolic order': the realm of language, discourse, and other systems of signification (literature, film, fashion, gestures, etc.). Structural linguistics and semiology oppose positivism, behaviorism, phenomenology, and existentialism, which remain on the surface, on the level of lived experience. Structural linguistics analyzes the underlying codes of verbal language, and semiology employed its methods to analyze the underlying codes of additional systems of signification.

Employing the methods of structural linguistics to analyze additional systems of signification does not entail a reduction of these other systems to verbal language, despite Roland Barthes' reversal.[10] Although Saussure worked out his method of analysis via verbal language, he did not restrict this method to verbal language, but conceived it at the outset as a part of semiology; verbal language is just one system of signification among many. Film semiology conceives film not as a language but as a coded medium, a system of signification that possesses its own specific underlying system of codes, which can be studied using general structural methods that have been developed in structural linguistics. Metz makes this point clear in his interviews with Raymond Bellour (Chapter 3) and André Gardies (Chapter 12). He tells Bellour that: "In no case is it a matter of exporting to semiology those linguistic concepts that are linked to language [*langue*] alone." He then gives an example: "'Paradigm' and 'syntagm', such as they have been defined by Martinet, are legitimately exportable concepts [...]. [They are] in no way linked to the specificity of language systems." The semiologists' study of film is therefore made, not via any direct resemblance between film and verbal language, but by studying film within the general context of signification. The question 'Is film a language?' is ill-formed and not very interesting; it is a terminological quibble. Linguistics becomes relevant *on methodological grounds*: film's specific, underlying reality can be reconstructed by a set of "legitimately exportable concepts" developed by structural linguists. At least from this methodological viewpoint, film semiologists were justified in using structural linguistics to study film, because this discipline is the most sophisticated for analyzing a medium's underlying reality, its system of signification. Therefore, David Bordwell's critique of film semiology is entirely misplaced when he writes: "Despite three decades of work in film semiotics, however, those who claim that cinema is an ensemble of 'codes' or 'discourses' have not yet provided a defense of why we should consider the film medium, let alone perception and thought, as plausibly analogous to language."[11] This mistaken view is what Metz calls (in the same interview) a reflex response, a conceptual blockage. "If a notion was emphasized by a writer who was a linguist by occupation, it is once and for all [mistakenly perceived as] 'purely linguistic', prohibited from being exported." When Metz (or his interviewees) uses the term 'film language', he uses it in the sense of 'filmic signification'.

Metz's Key Works in Film Theory

Metz's film theory contributes to the foundations of semiology as conceived by Saussure. Studying film from a structural-semiological perspective involves a fundamental shift in thinking: rather than study film 'in general', in all its heterogeneity, Metz instead studied it from the point of view of one theory, a prerequisite for adopting a semiological perspective according to Barthes:

> To undertake this research, it is necessary frankly to accept from the beginning (and especially at the beginning) a limiting principle. [...] [I]t is decided to describe the facts which have been gathered *from one point of view only*, and consequently to keep, from the heterogeneous mass of these facts, only the features associated with this point of view, to the exclusion of any others.[12]

The researcher's focus is deliberately limited to the relevant (pertinent, essential) traits of the object under study while filtering out all other traits. What is relevant is dependent on or defined by one's theoretical perspective. Semiology focuses on the underlying system of signification while excluding the heterogeneous surface traits of phenomena. Similarly, D.N. Rodowick characterizes the rise in structuralism and semiology in the 1960s as "a stance or perspective on culture that is [...] nothing less than the imagination of a new conceptual and enunciative position in theory."[13] That new position comprises a singular unifying perspective: "theory must rally around a method, which can unify synthetically from a singular perspective the data and knowledge gathered within its domain."[14]

This new position does not analyze pre-given experiences, behavior, or facts in the manner of phenomenology, behaviorism, and positivism. Instead, as soon as the analyst moves beyond the pre-given and the self-evident, he/she must *construct* the object of study – the virtual underlying system that generates and confers intelligibility on behavior, facts, and experiences. The 'underlying reality' of systems of signification is not an empirical object simply waiting to be observed. Instead, it is an abstract object that needs to be modeled: "One reconstitutes a double of the first [original] object," writes Metz, "a double totally thinkable since it is a pure product of thought: the intelligibility of the object has become itself an object."[15] This new, virtual object of study places theory centre stage, for it is via theory that this abstract object becomes visible. And each theory constructs its abstract object differently in accordance with its own concepts. This non-empirical mode of analysis necessitates a reflexive attitude toward theoretical activity. Rodowick calls this the metatheoretical attitude: "a reflection on the components and conceptual standards of theory construction."[16] Metz not only foregrounds this metatheoretical attitude in his published research, he discusses it extensively in the interviews published in this volume. For example, in his 1986 "Responses to *Hors Cadre* on *The Imaginary Signifier*" (Chapter 9), he dispels the notion that one simply 'applies' concepts from one domain to another:

> I have not applied anything, I have placed the cinema within more all-encompassing ideas, which fully concern the cinema just as much as they concern other objects: the general mechanisms of signification (whence the use of the term 'denotation', etc.), or of the imaginary subject, with ideas that have come from psychoanalysis but that are today, as with their predecessors, circulating far beyond their place of origin. (Metz, "Responses to *Hors Cadre* on *The Imaginary Signifier*")

In other words, he argues that he studies film within the conceptual spheres it already belongs to (including signification); it is therefore incorrect to think he applies to film concepts foreign to it.[17]

In addition to theorizing film within the parameters of one set of theoretical concepts, Metz explicitly defined his method of analysis, which he derived from Saussure. Semiological analysis names a process of segmentation and classification that dismantles all types of messages (speech, myths, kinship relations, literary texts, films, etc.) to reveal their ultimate components and rules of combination. These components and rules constitute the underlying codes that enable these messages to be produced. Metz therefore attempted to reconceive film according to the semiological principles presented above – meaning is intrinsic; it is generated from syntagmatic and paradigmatic relations; and infinite messages can be reduced to an underlying finite system that generated them. He aimed to develop a precise, delimited study of one aspect of film, its level of signification, illuminated and explained from one theoretical perspective.

New Objects and Problems of Study: 'Cinema: Language or Language System?'

In his first essay on film semiology, 'Cinema: Language or Language System?'[18] (initially published in 1964), we encounter Metz's exact, rigorous, and reflexive academic approach, one that aims to clarify his theoretical terms and problems. He asked if there is a filmic equivalent to *la langue*/language system in film. Metz's background assumption in this essay is that film must possess an equivalent to *la langue* to be defined as a language (*langage*). Not surprisingly, the results were negative: he concluded that cinema is a language (*langage*) without a language system (*langue*). Much of his description involves documenting how the underlying reality of film does *not* resemble *la langue*. The negative results are not unexpected, for the semiological language of film does not possess the same system specific as verbal language. Metz's failure to establish the semiology of film in this essay is due to two factors: under the influence of Barthes, he analyzed film in terms of the *result* of a structural linguistic analysis of verbal language. Secondly, he was unable to define film (the filmic image) as a symbolic order independent of, and prior to, the external world. In other words, he could not locate a system of syntagmatic and paradigmatic relations in the filmic image. This means he was unable to analyze the potentially infinite number of filmic images in terms of a finite system of underlying codes. He could not, therefore, define the meaning of images intrinsically, but had to fall back on the pre-semiological referential theory. Despite the limited success of his results in 'Cinema: Language or Language System?,' Metz established a new object of study, new problems to address, and a new methodology with which to approach film. Francesco Casetti argues that Metz's 1964 essay "introduces a shift in the approach to the filmic phenomenon and in the kind of topics leading to this approach. A new research *paradigm* is born, as well as a new *generation* of scholars."[19] The new object of study was the unobservable, latent level of filmic signification or codes that makes filmic meaning possible and which defines its specificity. Metz explored this new level of filmic reality in subsequent work.

Identifying Film's Paradigmatic Axis: 'Problems of Denotation in the Fiction Film'

In 'Problems of Denotation in the Fiction Film'[20] Metz employed the semiological method of segmentation and classification to identify an internal level of signification in film, a level of meaning generated by the filmic text, not by the filmed events. He discovered a finite set of syntagmatic types – different sequences of shots identifiable by the specific way each structures the spatio-temporal relations between the filmed events. Metz detected eight different spatio-temporal relationships in total, which constitute a paradigm – a code – of different forms of image ordering. Metz called the resulting 'paradigm of syntagmas' the *grande syntagmatique* of the image track. These image syntagmas form a code to the extent that they offer eight different ways of reconstructing filmed events, which indicates that each syntagmatic type gains its meaning in relation to the other seven types. Metz outlines all eight syntagmas and discusses the need to refine them in his interview with Raymond Bellour (Chapter 3), where he emphasizes that the syntagmatic types are primarily manifest in classical narrative cinema.

Cinematic Codes and Filmic Textual Systems: *Language and Cinema*

Metz's reconceptualization of film as a semiological object reached its zenith in *Language and Cinema*. He achieved this by introducing a series of theoretical distinctions: between cinema/the filmic/the cinematic (where 'the cinematic' designates a subset of the filmic – codes specific to film); between cinematic codes (common to all films)/cinematic sub-codes (cinematic codes common to some films); and, most importantly, between codes/singular textual systems (underlying abstract systems/the totality of filmic and cinematic codes combined in a single film). As Metz explains in more detail in the first two interviews published here, but especially in 'Cinema and Semiology: On 'Specificity'' (Chapter 2), within this more expansive study, the cinematic language system, or cinematic specificity, is defined as a *specific combination* of codes and sub-codes. Defining specificity as specific combination of codes has several implications for film semiology: (1) cinematic codes cannot be studied in complete isolation as abstract paradigmatic systems, but can only be studied from a joint syntagmatic-paradigmatic perspective: that is, in terms of a combination of codes specific to film; (2) codes are not unique to one semiological system, but belong to several systems: and (3) codes can only be studied in relation to their substance, not purely in terms of an underlying abstract formal system.

By emphasizing substance, Metz followed the work of Danish linguist Louis Hjelmslev, who divided language into an expression plane (the signifier) and content plane (signified), and divided each plane into material, form, and substance, yielding the six-fold distinction:

	Material (or purport) of expression
Signifier	Substance of expression
	Form of expression
	Material (or purport) of content
Signified	Substance of content
	Form of content

Material is the amorphous unformed continuum upon which form is projected, segmenting the material into distinct units. The material so organized is the substance. That is, material + form = substance. The material of expression in verbal language refers to amorphous sounds. The form of expression refers to an abstract system imposed on those amorphous sounds, which yields the substance of expression, or phonemes (structured sounds). The material of content in verbal language refers to an amorphous mass of thoughts. The form of content refers to an abstract system imposed on those thoughts, yielding the substance of content, or structured concepts.[21] Metz concedes that film semiology cannot operate only in the abstract realm of pure form – the form of expression and form of content. Instead, he emphasized the need to include the substance of expression – that is, "the action of the form in the material."[22] Metz's expanded conception of film semiology therefore challenged his previous assumptions – that specificity can be defined in terms of one code (the *grande syntagmatique*), and that specificity can be defined in terms of an abstract underlying system.

In several interviews (Chapters 1, 2, 3, and 7), Metz discusses Emilio Garroni's *Semiotica ed Estetica*.[23] Garroni thought the attempt to define filmic specificity a spurious activity. Following Hjelmslev, he divorced codes from material of expression, claiming that codes should be defined formally, in abstract terms. This, in effect, implies that codes are not tied to or manifest in the material of expression of any particular language and are not, therefore, specific to any language; a code is pure form and can therefore be manifest in the material of expression of multiple languages. Metz agrees with Garroni that a language consists of multiple codes, but disagrees that all codes are formal, not related to material of expression. For Metz, some codes are specific – are tied to film's material of expression – and some are non-specific. But Garroni rejects the attachment to the immediate material qualities of media, and instead defines a shared system of codes. That is, Metz's film semiology attempts to create a 'disembodied' abstract theory of formal codes – disembodied in terms of their separation from the material of expression; but, in the end, he defined film in terms of a specific combination of formal and manifest codes, whereas Garroni argued that all codes are formal, non-manifest, and abstract.

In their interview with Metz, Daniel Percheron and Marc Vernet (Chapter 4) interrogate Metz in depth over the difficulties of *Language and Cinema*. They express the experiences of many film scholars when confronted with Metz's excessively cautious approach in this book – his incessant return to previous positions to restate, refine, or update them; the abstract nature of his concept of the code; and the lack of any firm enumeration of cinematic codes. Metz's response in the interview is to say that such a level of abstraction is common in other disciplines such as linguistics, and that he really needs to write a second volume, for whereas *Language and Cinema* cleared the groundwork, the second volume (never written) needs to categorize and list the various codes in detail.

Nonetheless, the enriched film semiology presented in *Language and Cinema* contributed to the transformation of three long-held theories of film: auteurism, realism, and film as narrative. The assumption behind auteurism is that meaning is located in the individual(s) in control of the production. Within semiology, the underlying system of finite codes determines meaning, not the code user; the code user does not 'express' himself or herself – does not convey some authentic experience; instead, his/her intervention simply involves selecting from a pre-existing system of codes. The code user therefore submits to the code, to its meanings and limits (or submits to the law of the signifier, in Lacan's terms). Film semiology challenged theories of realism by relocating meaning within film. The assumption behind realism is that meaning is located in film's recording capacity – in its 'direct', 'naturalistic' referential relation to reality. In *Language and Cinema*, Metz successfully challenged this assumption by relocating meaning within the filmic text itself, for he reconceived films as complex textual phenomena consisting of a specific combination of codes. Within semiology, what we traditionally call 'reality' is redefined as an effect or impression of codes, as Metz discusses in some detail in the first interview published in this volume (Chapter 1). Finally, in *Language and Cinema* Metz redefined his *grande syntagmatique* as just one contingent code manifest in films.

Psychoanalysis and Semiology: 'The Imaginary Signifier'

Metz extended his semiological analysis of film in his essay 'The Imaginary Signifier' (first published in 1975).[24] Although he appears to have abandoned semiology and replaced it with psychoanalysis, he argues in his opening part that "the psychoanalytic itinerary is *from the outset a semiological one*."[25] Later, he argues that linguistic-inspired semiology focuses on secondary processes of signification (mental activity and logical thinking), while psychoanalysis focuses on primary processes of signification (unconscious activities that Freud identified, such as condensation, displacement, symbolization, and secondary revision).[26] For Metz, psychoanalysis (especially Lacan's structural linguistic reinterpretation of Freud) addresses the same semiological problematic as linguistics, but on a deeper level, the primary subterranean forces that drive language, film, and other symbolic systems. These forces continually modify, displace, and transform signifiers, necessitating a reconceptualization of the object of study (verbal language, film, etc.) as a process or activity, not as a static object. The symbolic order is thereby expanded to include primary as well as secondary systems of signification, and is reconceived as a dynamic system.[27]

The wellspring of subterranean primary forces that drive film is absence, the absence of referents from the space of the filmic image, and the psychological consequences of this absence. Absence generates the spectator's desire for the absent object, thereby bringing into play the role of human subjectivity, especially phenomenological accounts of conscious lived experiences, in the generation of intrinsic filmic meanings. In 'The Imaginary Signifier' and in his response to the editors of the journal *Hors Cadre* (Chapter 9), Metz attempted to reveal how the imaginary (in Lacan's sense of the term) and desire operate on the level of the filmic signifier. He argues that the function of the imaginary in the cinema is to fabricate two structurally related impressions: the impression of reality (the sense of a coherent filmic universe) and a subject position for the spectator to occupy (the impression of psychic unity).

Confining himself to the analysis of the imaginary status of the filmic signifier, Metz discovered that the image on screen and the image in the mirror have the same status – both are inherently imaginary because both offer the spectator a dense, visual representation of absent objects (the objects photographed are absent from the space of the screen and the objects reflected in the mirror are absent from the mirror's virtual space): "In order to understand the film (at all), I must perceive the photographed object as absent, its photograph as present, and the presence of this absence as signifying."[28] It is because of the filmic signifier's lack, its limitations in representing the absent events, that a theory incorporating the spectator becomes necessary to explain the production of meaning in filmic discourse, for the spectator temporarily fills in the lack. That is, the image, structured upon a lack (the absence of the filmed events), requires the spectator to fill in meaning and 'complete' the image. Here, we see Metz combining semiology with a psychoanalytically-inflected phenomenology, for the cinema's impression of reality attempts to disavowal from the consciousness of the spectator the inherent lack in the filmic signifier. This is only achieved when it transforms the spectator's consciousness – that is, displaces his/her consciousness away from the material surface of the screen and toward the fictive, imaginary elsewhere of the film's diegesis.

Beginning from the premise that the filmic signifier represents absent objects, Metz proceeded to define the spectator's position in relation to the filmic signifier in terms of voyeurism and disavowal. The conditions that constitute the pleasures associated with voyeurism are 'mirrored' in the semiological structure of the filmic signifier. The voyeur, removed from the space of his object of vision, experiences visual mastery and pleasure over that object through this secure and superior spatial position. Similarly, in the spectator's perception of the filmic signifier: the filmed events exist in a different space (and time) to the spectator; there is no reciprocal relation between spectator and filmed events, for these events are absent, represented in effigy by the filmic signifier. For Metz, the filmic signifier therefore locates the spectator in a position equivalent to the space of the voyeur, and confers upon him the same pleasures and resulting illusory, transcendental psychic unity.

Yet, Metz did not sufficiently take into account the argument that the function of the imaginary (and the impression of reality) is, primarily, to act as a defense against the 'problems' feminine sexuality poses to the masculine psyche. It is precisely when the imaginary successfully acts as a defense against feminine sexuality that it is able to constitute an illusory, transcendental *masculine* psychic unity. Any analysis of the imaginary (and the impression of reality) must therefore begin with the problematics of sexual difference and identity. But in his attempt to disengage the cinema object from the imaginary, Metz ended up constructing his own imaginary discourse, a fetish that elides questions of sexual difference (but see Chapter 7, where he directly addresses sexual difference). Analysis of the problematics of sexual difference in the cinema is the primary object of study of second-wave feminist film theory. Laura Mulvey's foundational essay 'Visual Pleasure and Narrative Cinema' is representative of this work.[29] She shifted film feminism to the study of images as a semiological form of discourse, rather than a transparent window on to a pre-existing reality. The image was conferred its own materiality, its own signifying power. Mulvey also expanded the object of study: not just a critique of the image, but also the unconscious ideological-patriarchal nature of the cinematic apparatus – its semiological *creation* of a male gaze, of gendered (masculine) subject positions, and patriarchal (Oedipal) narrative forms that regulate desire, defining it as masculine: "Playing on the tension between film as controlling the dimension of time (editing, narrative) and film as controlling the dimension of space (changes in distance, editing), cinematic codes create a gaze, a world, and an object, thereby producing an illusion cut to the measure of [male] desire."[30]

Primary Forces and Secondary Codes: 'Metaphor/Metonymy, or the Imaginary Referent'

> [In] the long piece on metaphor and metonymy, you see that [Metz is] not really interested in these terms, "metaphor" and "metonymy," *per se*. What interests him is the *deep semantic and logical structure* they stand for, a structure which is independent of their surface manifestation in rhetoric or verbal language. A deep structure that seems to manifest itself also in dreams (according to psychoanalysis) and in films. This is why his isn't an attempt to "map" linguistics or classical rhetoric *onto* film.[31]

Metz's essay on metaphor and metonymy constitutes the next stage of his constant investigation of filmic signification.[32] In this long essay, he does not so much search for local metaphors and metonymies (or other figures and tropes) in the manner of the classification schemes of the eighteenth and nineteenth centuries, but instead seeks the deep semantic and logic structure of filmic discourse. This parallels his study of film language, which was not a search for local analogies between film and verbal language, but an attempt to define the conditions of possibility of filmic signification in terms of codes and their structural relations.

In 'Metaphor/Metonymy,' Metz characterizes signification in terms of primary (unconscious) forces or pressures, rather than exclusively secondary codes and structures; or, more accurately, codes and structures are driven by unconscious forces such as desire. This task requires Metz to tread a fine line between two positions he rejects: (1) positing that the primary and secondary are separate; and (2) positing that they need to be merged. With regard to position (1), Metz does not uphold an absolute opposition between primary and secondary processes. Instead, he argues that we cannot know these primary forces in themselves, for we only encounter them once they have been represented on the secondary level. And inversely, codes and structures are not purely secondary, but are driven by primary processes. With regard to position (2), Metz develops the ideas of Jakobson and Lacan in pursuing the *parallels* between unconscious processes (condensation and displacement), linguistic processes (paradigm and syntagm) and rhetorical processes (metaphor and metonymy), without collapsing the three sets of terms into each other. In his interview with Jean Paul Simon and Marc Vernet (Chapter 6), Metz acknowledges the frustration that readers and seminar participants express when he adds complexity to his model of filmic rhetoric by refusing to collapse the three levels into each other:

> Deep down, I know very well, from the numerous discussions I have had with very diverse audiences, that what anxious readers expected was for me to say: 'On the one side, we have metaphor = paradigm = condensation = découpage, and on the other side we have metonymy = syntagm = displacement = montage'. The only thing is that this does not hold water, it is a caricature of semiology.

Here, again, we encounter Metz's exactitude in refusing to simplify the complexity of the filmic and semiological phenomena he is studying.

Filmic Reflexivity: Impersonal Enunciation

The final three interviews published in this volume (Chapters 10, 11, 12) all took place around the same time, during the seminal conference 'Christian Metz and Film Theory', held at the Cerisy Cultural Centre in 1989.[33] Several issues recur: Metz's absence from research for a number of years (the first half of the 1980s), his return to research with an essay and book on impersonal enunciation, and his homage to his teacher and mentor Roland Barthes. It is only in his interview with André Gaudreault (chapter 11) that Metz directly reveals that Barthes' death in 1980 had a profound effect upon Metz.

Before developing his theory of impersonal enunciation in the late 1980s, Metz discussed enunciation in his short essay 'Story/Discourse (A Note on Two Types of Voyeurism).'[34] The linguistic concept of enunciation refers to the activity that results in the production of utterances, or discourse. Emile Benveniste further distinguished between two types of utterance, *histoire* (story) and *discours* (discourse). For Benveniste, *discours* in natural language employs deictic words such as personal pronouns (*I, you*) that grammaticalize within the utterance particular aspects of its spatio-temporal context (such as the speaker and hearer), whereas *histoire* is a form of utterance that excludes pronouns. *Discours* and *histoire* therefore represent two different but complementary planes of utterance: *discours* is a type of utterance that displays the traces or marks of its production, its enunciation, whereas *histoire* conceal the traces of its production. In his 'Story/Discourse' essay, Metz transferred Benveniste's two forms of utterance to a psychoanalytical theory of vision. He identifies exhibitionism with *discours* and voyeurism with *histoire*. The exhibitionist knows that she is being looked at and acknowledges the look of the spectator, just as *discours* acknowledges the speaker and hearer of the utterance, whereas the object of the voyeur's gaze does not know that she is being watched. The voyeur's look is secretive, concealed, like the marks of the speaker and hearer in *histoire*. Metz argued that classical narrative film is primarily voyeuristic, hence *histoire*, for it conceals its own discursive markers (the spectator's look).

Returning to filmic enunciation in *Impersonal Enunciation or the Place of Film*, Metz emphasized its impersonal status. That is, he acknowledged that film bears the traces of its production-enunciation, but that those traces are not analogous to personal pronouns. Instead, the traces of the process of enunciation are reflexive – they refer back to the film itself. In interview 10, Metz identifies two variants of reflexivity – reflection and commentary: "Reflection: the film mimes itself (screens within the screen, films within the film, showing the device, etc.). Commentary: the film speaks about itself, as is the case with certain 'pedagogical' voiceovers about the image [...] or in non-dialogue intertitles, explicatory camera movements, etc." One consequence of defining enunciation impersonally is that it can become a general concept close to narration, a point Metz makes at length in the same interview. It is with the concept of impersonal enunciation that Metz returns to the roots of semiology and its theory of signification, where meaning is defined as an internal value generated by the film itself.

Notes

1. Roland Barthes, quoted in D.N. Rodowick, *Elegy for Theory* (Cambridge, MA: Harvard University Press, 2014), p. 168.
2. Christian Metz, *Essais sur la signification au cinéma, tome 1et 2* (Paris: Klincksieck 1968; 1972); volume 1 translated as *Film Language: A Semiotics of the Cinema*, trans. by Michael Taylor (New York: Oxford University Press, 1974). *Langage et cinéma* (Paris: Librairie Larousse, 1971); *Language and Cinema*, trans. by Donna Jean Umiker-Sebeok (The Hague/Paris: Mouton, 1974). *Le signifiant imaginaire. Psychanalyse et cinéma* (Paris: Union générale d'éditions, 1977). *Psychoanalysis and Cinema: The Imaginary Signifier*, trans. by Celia Britton, Annwyl Williams, Ben Brewster, and Alfred Guzzetti (London: Macmillan, 1982); also published as *The Imaginary Signifier: Psychoanalysis and Cinema* (Bloomington, IN: Indiana University Press, 1982). *L'enonciation impersonnelle ou le site du film* (Paris: Méridiens Klincksieck 1991); *Impersonal Enunciation or the Place of Film*, trans. by Cormac Deane (New York: Columbia University Press, 2016).
3. Maureen Turim, 'Film Study in Paris', *Sub-Stance* 9 (1974), pp. 195–196.
4. Martin Lefebvre and Annie van den Oever, 'Revisiting Christian Metz's 'Apparatus Theory' – A Dialogue', in *Technē/Technology: Researching Cinema and Media Technologies – Their Development, Use, and Impact*, ed. by Annie van den Oever (Amsterdam: Amsterdam University Press, 2014), p. 243.

5. This introduction draws upon my previous discussions of Metz's work: Warren Buckland, 'Film Semiotics', in *A Companion to Film Theory*, ed. by Toby Miller and Robert Stam (Oxford: Blackwell, 1999), pp. 84–104; *The Cognitive Semiotics of Film* (Cambridge: Cambridge University Press, 2000); *Film Theory: Rational Reconstructions* (Abingdon: Routledge, 2012); and 'Semiotics of Film', in *The Routledge Encyclopedia of Film Theory*, ed. by Edward Branigan and Warren Buckland (Routledge, 2014), pp. 425–429.
6. Simon Clarke, *The Foundations of Structuralism: A Critique of Lévi-Strauss and the Structuralist Movement* (Brighton: Harvester Press, 1981), p. 2.
7. However, for an account of the influence of phenomenology on Metz's early work, see Dominique Chateau and Martin Lefebvre, 'Dance and Fetish: Phenomenology and Metz's Epistemological Shift', *October* 148 (2014), pp. 103–132. Similarly, Lefebvre presents a case for the role of aesthetics in Metz's film semiology: "I shall endeavour to show that the break with aesthetics signalled by Metz's semiology was not as thorough or absolute as it has often been made out to be." He examines the role of aesthetics via three concepts: expressiveness, stylistics, and poetics. 'Christian Metz and Aesthetics' (forthcoming).
8. Ferdinand de Saussure, *Course in General Linguistics*, trans. by Wade Baskin, ed. by Perry Meisel and Haun Saussy (New York: Columbia University Press, 2011), p. 121.
9. André Martinet, *Elements of General Linguistics*, trans. by Elisabeth Palmer (London: Faber and Faber, 1964), pp. 22–24.
10. Saussure argued that "linguistics can become the master-pattern for all branches of semiology although language is only one particular semiological system" (Saussure, *Course in General Linguistics*, p. 68). For Barthes, "we must now face the possibility of inverting Saussure's declaration: linguistics is not a part of the general science of signs, even a privileged part, it is semiology which is a part of linguistics: to be precise, it is that part covering the *great signifying unities* of discourse. By this inversion, we may expect to bring to light the unity of the research at present being done in anthropology, sociology, psychoanalysis and stylistics round the concept of signification" (Roland Barthes, *Writing Degree Zero and Elements of Semiology*, trans. by Annette Lavers and Colin Smith [London: Jonathan Cape, 1984], p. 79).
11. David Bordwell, 'Contemporary Film Studies and the Vicissitudes of Grand Theory', in *Post-Theory: Reconstructing Film Studies*, ed. by David Bordwell and Noël Carroll (Madison, WI: University of Wisconsin Press, 1996), p. 18.
12. Barthes, *Writing Degree Zero and Elements of Semiology*, p. 154 (emphasis in the original).
13. Rodowick, *Elegy for Theory*, p. 137.
14. *Ibid.*, p. 167.
15. Metz, quoted in Rodowick, *Ibid.*, pp. 183–184.
16. Rodowick, *Elegy for Theory*, p. 156.

17. Metz briefly takes up this issue of 'application' in his interview with Daniel Percheron and Marc Vernet, under the subheading 'You never 'apply' anything' (see Chapter 4). Raymond Bellour has commented:
    In this statement [you never apply anything], it is understood that:
    - this work is not applied in the elaboration of his own work
    - each work, therefore, implies, whether it be aware of the fact or not, the quest for its own program: it will therefore be singular, irreducible to comparison, which is what (eventually) defines it as a work;
    - Metz himself does not apply linguistics or psychoanalysis, but makes them work as reference spaces, 'programmes de vérite', historically determined, in order to elaborate his own program. (Bellour, 'Cinema and ...,' *Semiotica* 112, 1/2 [1996], p. 218).

    In his response to *Hors Cadre*, Metz is developing the third meaning of 'application'.
18. Metz, 'Cinema: Language or Language System?', in *Film Language*, pp. 31–91.
19. Francesco Casetti, *Theories of Cinema*, trans. by Francesca Chiostri and Elizabeth Bartolini-Salimbeni, with Thomas Kelso (Austin, TX: University of Texas Press), p. 91 (emphasis in the original).
20. Metz, 'Problems of Denotation in the Fiction Film', *Film Language*, pp. 108–146.
21. Metz discusses Hjelmslev's six-fold distinction in *Language and Cinema*, pp. 208–212.
22. *Ibid.*, p. 253.
23. Emilio Garroni, *Semiotica ed estetica. L'eterogeneità del linguaggio e il linguaggio cinematografico* (Bari: Laterza, 1968).
24. Metz, 'The Imaginary Signifier', *Screen* 16, 2 (1975), pp. 14–76; reprinted in *Psychoanalysis and Cinema*, pp. 1–87.
25. *Psychoanalysis and Cinema*, p. 3; emphasis in the original.
26. *Ibid.*, p. 18.
27. Metz briefly considered film as a dynamic textual system in the Conclusion to *Language and Cinema* via the concept of 'filmic writing': "writing is neither a code nor a set of codes, but a working of these codes, by means of them and against them, a work whose temporarily 'arrested' result is the text, i.e., the film" (*Language and Cinema*, p. 285). But this dynamic account of meaning remains on the secondary level of signification.
28. *Psychoanalysis and Cinema*, p. 57.
29. Laura Mulvey, 'Visual Pleasure and Narrative Cinema', *Screen* 16, 3 (1975), pp. 6–18.
30. *Ibid.*, p. 17.
31. Martin Lefebvre and Annie van den Oever, 'Revisiting Christian Metz's 'Apparatus Theory' – A Dialogue', p. 255.
32. Metz, 'Metaphor/Metonymy, or The Imaginary Referent', in *Psychoanalysis and Cinema*, pp.149–314.

33. The conference proceedings were published under the title 'Christian Metz et la théorie du cinéma', ed. by Michel Marie and Marc Vernet, *Iris* 10 (Paris: Meridiens Klincksieck, 1990).
34. Metz, 'Story/Discourse (A Note on Two Types of Voyeurism)', in *Psychoanalysis and Cinema*, pp. 89–98.

Christian Metz and the Constellation of French Film Journals in the 1960s and 1970s

Daniel Fairfax

Buckland, Warren and Daniel Fairfax (eds), *Conversations with Christian Metz: Selected Interviews on Film Theory (1970–1991)*. Amsterdam: Amsterdam University Press, 2017.

DOI: 10.5117/9789089648259/INTRO II

Abstract
This second Introduction to *Conversations with Christian Metz* presents Metz's interaction with and contributions to French journals dedicated to film criticism. This introduction surveys Metz's engagement with a number of publications during the 1960s and 1970s, including *Cahiers du Cinéma, Cinéthique, La Nouvelle Critique* and *Ça-Cinéma.*

Keywords: Christian Metz, film theory, semiology, psychoanalysis, film journals

In addition to providing new insight into Christian Metz's thinking on the cinema and its evolution over the course of nearly three decades, the interviews included in this book shed valuable light on another aspect of Metz's theoretical activity, namely, his interaction with French journals dedicated to film criticism. During the 1960s and 1970s in particular, Metz freely engaged with a number of publications, including *Cahiers du Cinéma, Cinéthique, La Nouvelle Critique* and *Ça-Cinéma*. The resulting interventions take the form not only of the interviews published below, but also various articles, chapters, and letters, in addition to the personal relations Metz forged with the critics and editors who worked for these journals. Although his contributions were not entirely free of partisan considerations, Metz was never affiliated with any one journal in particular, and the theorist adopted a broadly ecumenical approach toward organs that were otherwise renowned for their internecine, often bitter disputes with each other. Such an approach was reflected in the consideration his work was given by these same journals, which often combined admiration and critique in equal measure. Notably, the often-venomous tone that characterized these journals' polemical jousts with each other contrasts markedly with the generally respectful and amicable nature of the interviews conducted with Metz, even when differences in position were being thrashed out. This stands as a testament, above all, to the calming effect of Metz's patient, methodical temperament.

In the 'constellation' of journals that marked French film culture during this period, Metz can thus be seen as something of a shooting star: periodically making fulgurant appearances in unpredictable locations before receding once more into the darkness. Moreover, the nature of his interventions, and the reception he was given by the journals with which he interacted, were overdetermined by the broader social context of the time: as the political status quo in France was irrevocably shaken by the uprising of May 1968 and its aftermath, so too did French film culture undergo tumultuous transformations in the late 1960s and 1970s, which inevitably had profound implications for the response to Metz's ideas. Importantly, too, Metz's periodic collaboration with the major French film journals of this time had a pronounced effect on his theoretical approach toward the cinema. The more radical conclusions of *Langage et cinéma* from 1971 and, later, the adoption of a psychoanalytic framework in *The Imaginary Signifer* (1977), served to bring his work closer to the concerns of publications like *Cahiers du Cinéma* and *Cinéthique* than his earlier more strictly semiological project. We can therefore posit a relationship of reciprocal influence between the theorist and the constellation of film criticism that surrounded him, one where they entered into a dialogue with each other, pushed and critiqued each other, and, ultimately, shaped each other's ideas about cinema.

Cahiers du Cinéma

By far the most prolonged, regular, and theoretically fertile collaboration Metz had with a film journal during this time was with *Cahiers du Cinéma*, although, strangely, he was never interviewed by the journal. Founded by André Bazin, *Cahiers* had come under the editorship of Jean-Louis Comolli by the time Metz first published with it in 1965. While later, in tandem with co-editor Jean Narboni, Comolli would steer *Cahiers* on a Marxist course, in the mid-1960s the journal was still very much in keeping with the heritage of the *nouvelle vague* filmmakers it had helped foster in the 1950s (Jacques Rivette had only recently handed over the editor-in-chief position to his younger colleague). With this in mind, Metz's first intervention in *Cahiers* was a curious one: in February 1965, the critic Gérard Guégan had, in a review of Jean-Luc Godard's *Une femme mariée* (1964), accused Metz of ostensibly committing a 'regrettable misconception' in his recently published article 'Le cinéma. Langue ou langage?' by refusing montage and 'assimilating it with the manipulation of the real that Rossellini was so wary of.'[1] Metz hastily issued a corrective: a letter from him, personally addressed to Guégan and published in the journal's April issue, insisted that the critic had misunderstood his text: he had only intended to condemn '*a certain form* of montage (and 'film syntax') which the cinema has, in any case, already left behind," specifying that this "*montage-roi*" consisted of "the abuse of non-diegetic metaphors, superimpositions, rapid editing, etc." While the ideas of Eisenstein, Gance and company are clearly intended as a target (as the 'Langue ou langage' article makes abundantly clear), Metz also asserts that a new form of montage had arisen in the work of Welles, Resnais and Godard, one which was no longer "a caricature of verbal structures." He concludes his missive with the statement that "only a certain form of montage is dead..."[2]

This exchange may not have augured a propitious relationship between Metz and the journal – the theorist bluntly states that he has "very few opinions in common with *Cahiers*."[3] Nonetheless, the next month, the editors of *Cahiers* elected to publish a major article by Metz that would be of considerable importance for Comolli, Narboni and their colleagues, 'À propos de l'impression de la réalité au cinéma'. Borrowing the concept of the 'impression of reality' from Barthes' discussion of photography in his article 'Rhétorique de l'image', Metz argues that cinema has a considerably greater 'projective power' than photography (that is, the spectator has a much greater tendency to project themselves into the world depicted on the screen), owing, above all, to the movement of images, which furnishes 'a higher degree of reality [*un indice de réalité supplémentaire*], and the corporality of the objects," as well as imparting a sense of "being present [*actuel*]" in the events depicted.[4] For Metz, the movement of images is not merely analogous to movement in real life; rather, it actually does provide the spectator with the "real presence of movement" and he defines the "secret" of the cinema as follows: "to inject the reality of motion into the unreality of the image and thus to render the world of the imagination more real than it had ever been."[5]

A year later, Metz would publish a second major article with *Cahiers*, this time on the occasion of a special issue on 'cinema and the novel'. 'Le cinéma moderne et la narrativité' avows the effervescence of cinematic modernism in the 1960s – with the rise of filmmakers such as Resnais, Godard and Antonioni – but seeks to provide a corrective to the overly simplistic oppositions between classical and modern films prevalent in film criticism at the time, none of which truly satisfied the theorist. Rather than a sweeping rejection of narrative, spectacle, or drama, Metz sees the specificity of modern cinema as residing in 'a vast and complex movement of renewal and enrichment' of film syntax, consisting in the abandonment of certain commonplace clichés, the evolution and modification of other figures, and the invention of new, hitherto inexistent syntactic forms.[6] Evoking the classification of his *grande syntagmatique*, then being adumbrated in articles published in other periodicals, Metz confesses that an early sequence in *Pierrot le fou* (1965), in which Anna Karina and Jean-Paul Belmondo flee Paris in their 404 convertible, conforms to none of the syntagmatic categories he had established therein. It is the bold narrative innovation in Godard's films that leads Metz to end his article with a rhetorically florid tribute to the "man with the double-barreled first-name," who is described on the pages of *Cahiers* as "a poet-novelist of unimpeachable narrative inventiveness, a man of a thousand tales in whom the fecundity of fabulation has those natural qualities [...] that belong to the great storytelling temperaments."[7] This dithyrambic conclusion, however, would be substantially tempered when, as with the earlier article on the 'impression of reality', 'Le cinéma moderne et la narrativité' was republished in Metz's *Essais sur la signification au cinéma*.[8]

Much of 'Le cinéma moderne et la narrativité' consisted of a critique of Pier Paolo Pasolini's concept of the 'cinema of poetry', also expounded on the pages of *Cahiers du Cinéma*, which, in Metz's view, unsatisfactorily calques cinematic categories onto those of literary language.[9] In opposition to Pasolini, Metz contends that modern cinema is not to be distinguished from the films of earlier eras by its possession of an inherently 'poetic' quality – if anything, the literary form it most closely resembles (and even here it is a loose approximation) is that of the *novel*. He nonetheless recognizes the Italian filmmaker's analysis as offering "by far the most serious and most penetrating" attempt at defining filmic modernity, and there was much common ground in their parallel attempts to construct a semiology of the cinema. The same year as these articles were published, Pasolini and Metz, alongside Barthes, found themselves attacked by Luc Moullet, a critic for *Cahiers* and filmmaker in his own right, at a roundtable during the Pesaro film festival. In a philippic titled 'De la nocivité du langage cinématographique, de son inutilité, ainsi que des moyens de lutter contre lui', Moullet fulminated, with his typical mordant humor and a taste for *Ubu Roi*-like provocation, against the "congenital artistic mediocrity of cinematic languages past, present and future," and argued that "there is a complete opposition between cinematic language and cinematic art, for cinematic language overwhelms art, invades it, stifles it."[10]

The other panelists at the session were scandalized at this caricature of their project. According to Narboni's account of the proceedings, Barthes accused Moullet of "incessantly confusing language and stereotypes" as well as pandering to "anti-intellectualism" (which Narboni himself took as an accusation of *poujadisme*).[11] Metz would offer a more conciliatory stance, ascribing the difference to that between theorists and artists, and arguing "Our task is not so much to say how films should be made, but to find out how they manage to be understood."[12] Shortly afterwards, Godard would issue a defense of Moullet in his text 'Trois mille heures du cinéma', describing the Pesaro pronunciamento as 'Moullet's sublime missive, Courtelinesque and Brechtian, screaming in the face of the structuralists: language, my good sir, is theft. Moullet is right. We are the children of film language. Our parents are Griffith, Hawks, Dreyer and Bazin, and Langlois, but not you, and in any case, without images and sounds, how can you speak of structures?'[13]

Toward the end of the 1960s, however, *Cahiers* would become much more closely aligned with the structuralist theory denounced by Moullet, a process that occurred in tandem with the journal's political radicalization surrounding the events of May 1968. While this shift meant that Metz would continue to be a valued interlocutor for the journal, the growing influence of Althusserian Marxism and Lacanian psychoanalysis within *Cahiers* saw its writers develop a critique of the analytic method of Metzian semiology. In a roundtable on 'Montage' in March 1969, Narboni would broadly adhere to the argument made by Metz in 'Problèmes de dénotation dans le film de fiction' that a shot in the cinema corresponds to a sentence rather than a word (or, in Metz's famous example, the shot is equivalent to the phrase 'Here is a revolver!' rather than the word 'revolver'), but he would proceed to note that Jean-Daniel Pollet's 1965 film *Méditerranée* strives precisely to transform its constituent shots into lexical units approximating words, by diminishing the oppositions Metz had established and "effecting a perversion [...] of the actualization of the images and of their quality of assertiveness" – a process which is enabled in large part by the 'poetic' commentary to the film provided by *Tel Quel* editor Philippe Sollers.[14] A more strident critique of the analytic method of the semiologists – and proof of *Cahiers*' vexed relationship to it – came later that year. In October 1969, in the same issue in which Narboni and Comolli's landmark editorial text 'Cinéma/Idéologie/Critique' appeared, the journal published Raymond Bellour's painstaking analysis of the Bodega Bay sequence from Hitchcock's *The Birds* (1963). While Bellour himself, at the time closely linked to Metz, took care to avoid a hasty use of semiotic/linguistic concepts in his study, and would admit in the text's preface to the necessarily incomplete nature of any attempt at film analysis, invoking Freud's notion of '*die endliche und unendliche Analyse*' (finite and infinite analysis), Narboni saw fit to append a rejoinder to Bellour's article, which, despite acknowledging its theoretical importance, criticized his "phenomenological attempt to [...] only conceive of the invisible as being temporarily and reducibly dissimulated, or the provisionally masked reverse-side of the visible."[15] To Bellour's close analysis, Narboni preferred the method of symptomatic reading drawn from Althusser's *Reading Capital*, in which "The invisible is not therefore simply what is outside the visible, the outer darkness of exclusion, but also *the inner darkness of exclusion*, inside the visible itself because defined by its structure."[16]

In the ensuing period, the sporadic critiques *Cahiers* would make of Metzian film semiology centered precisely on the question of ideology, or, more precisely, the lack thereof in Metz's theories. In 1971–1972, both Pascal Bonitzer and Jean-Louis Comolli would offer harsh critiques of Jean Mitry – contrasting markedly with Metz's favorable stance toward the theorist's *Esthétique et psychologie du cinéma* – in parallel multi-part studies published over several issues. Bonitzer's 'Réalité de la dénotation', for example, begins with a discussion of the close-up that insists on the ideological nature of the 'technical classification of shot-sizes,' which fundamentally rests, in the *Cahiers* critic's view, on a "metaphysical ordering from the part to the whole."[17] In adopting the system of shot categories established by Mitry, Metz's *grande syntagmatique* thus has an explicitly empiricist foundation, which "reaffirms the illusion of the text's autonomy by privileging linearity, 'lived experience', the 'flow', that is, the diachronic level, where the denotation effects are reinforced."[18] Moreover, his broader distinction between filmic denotation and connotation is similarly critiqued: denotation has the effect of "constraining the film and its reading to a transcendental semantic level that would be 'film language'," at the same time as condemning connotation "to the role of 'artistic' supplement, expressive redundancy."[19] Bonitzer is careful to clarify, however, that he is referring to arguments made in Metz's earlier works, which, he foreshadows, will be addressed in the semiologist's "upcoming book." The "upcoming book" was to be *Langage et cinéma*, published later in the year, and the affinities between Metz's newer thinking and *Cahiers* were highlighted not only in Comolli's more favorable comments toward Metz in the third installment of his 'Technique et idéologie' series,[20] but also in *Cahiers*' willingness to print chapter 6 of Section XI of the book ('Cinéma et idéographie') in their March–April 1971 issue, as well as the essay 'Ponctuations et démarcations dans le film de diégèse' (included in vol. II of *Essais sur la signification au cinéma*) in their December 1971–February 1972 issue.[21]

The Dispute with *Positif*

In the same period, one of the most notorious quarrels in the history of French film criticism broke out when *Positif* published Robert Benayoun's stinging attack on *Cahiers*' new-found Marxist approach to cinema, 'Les enfants du paradigme'. The immediate pretext was *Cahiers*' support for Straub/Huillet's film *Othon*, but the *Positif* writer used the opportunity to launch into a sweeping denunciation of its rival journal, lambasting it for its supposed political tergiversations, theoretical disingenuousness, and general illegibility. In this, Benayoun unequivocally contrasted the output of *Cahiers* with the writing of Metz, who was praised for avoiding the "frivolous, autocratic and threatening attitude" of the journal, and in whose work "the semiological lexicon is natural, restrained, devoid of coquetry and fatuity."[22] Benayoun would even claim that Metz's condemnation of "the fanaticism of the cinema-cinema" and his stated wish for "a junction between thinking on cinema and the general movement of ideas" are tendencies that have always been exemplified by *Positif*, again in contradistinction to the journal founded by Bazin.[23] In their January–February 1971 issue, the *Cahiers* editors responded to Benayoun's charges with vociferous opprobrium, and some degree of haughty disdain: their rejoinder to *Positif*, 'Sur quelques contresens' was presented merely as a corrective to a "calumnious campaign" and was in no way to be considered a response to an ongoing debate: "the true debate," Narboni explained, was taking place "in a field from which, in spite of its parasitic efforts, *Positif* finds itself, owing to its regressive practices, excluded."[24]

Benayoun's broadside nonetheless earned five pages of rebuttal within *Cahiers*, a letter published in his own journal containing vague threats of legal action, and a statement titled 'Cinéma, littérature, politique' co-signed by the editors of *Cahiers*, *Cinéthique* and *Tel Quel* (the latter two journals, while engaged in their own theoretical altercations with *Cahiers*, had also found themselves in Benayon's polemical crosshairs), which accused *Positif* of a "confusionist-reactionary discourse."[25] Additionally, Metz himself sent a missive to *Positif*, rejecting Benayoun's imputation of a fundamental opposition between himself and the journals under attack:

> It happens that I am in relations of work and discussion, more or less close depending on the case, with all those whom your collaborator assails, beginning with *Cahiers du Cinéma*. This is not to say, of course, that I agree with every single one of them on every single sentence they may pronounce. But these people and these groups are carrying out research for which, on the global level, I feel a great deal of esteem, sympathy, and a lively intellectual interest. On the subject of cinema, the most serious effort at theoretical reflection, today, is located in my opinion on the side of those whom your journal attacks. To this extent – and beyond all the complex details one would like – I feel that I am on their side far more than on the side of *Positif*, in spite of the compliments Robert Benayon addresses to me.[26]

Metz, it seems, never had a great tenderness for *Positif*: in a footnote to the version of 'À propos de l'impression de réalité au cinéma' published in *Cahiers*, he accuses the journal of "cheerfully assumed irresponsibility" for publishing a dismissive eight-line review of Mitry's *Esthétique et psychologie* ("one of the most important books on the cinema in existence," according to Metz).[27] Later, in 1976, *Positif* published a harsh rebuke of Metzian film theory by Jean-François Tarnowski, in a text that, ironically, was primarily a defense of Mitry. The article was of such rebarbative vitriol – Tarnowski speaks of the "theoretical quasi-stupidity" of Metz's work, and his "incredibly impotent and strained distortion" of Mitry's ideas[28] – that a petition in defense of the semiologist was launched, signed by Jean Narboni and Pascal Bonitzer among others.[29] This support marked the end of an extensive period during which Metz's work was largely neglected by *Cahiers*: with the journal's adoption of a Maoist political outlook from 1972 onwards, less consideration was given to the purely theoretical questions that preoccupied Metz. It was not until his shift from the semiological method of his earlier work to the psychoanalytic paradigm of *The Imaginary Signifier* that something of a reconciliation with *Cahiers* was effectuated: not only did this new allegiance bring Metz closer to the thinking of *Cahiers* (and particularly the work of writers such as Pascal Bonitzer and Jean-Pierre Oudart), it also came at a moment when *Cahiers* had rejected its earlier political dogmatism and was returning to a spirit of intellectual openness.

Bonitzer's 1977 text 'Voici (La notion de plan et le sujet du cinéma)' draws significantly on Metz in discussing what he dubs the '*effet de voici*': if a close-up of a revolver, to return to Metz's example, conveys the message "here is a revolver," this "here is…" is not only an "actualization effect," as Metz argues, it is also an effect produced by the cinematic gaze, and is thus an "index of fiction" allowing the audience to grasp their own position as spectator of a film.[30] Metz would respond to the renewed interest in his work from *Cahiers* by publishing a segment of his 'Métaphore/Métonymie' chapter from *The Imaginary Signifier* (titled 'L'incandescence et le code') in the journal's following issue (March 1977), despite the rather tenuous connection of the passage's subject matter with film per se.[31]

Cinéthique

While Metz's association with *Cinéthique* was far briefer than his prolonged relationship with *Cahiers*, it was, in many ways, no less determinant for the theoretical outlook of the journal. Founded in 1969 by the filmmaker Marcel Hanoun, *Cinéthique* was quickly taken over by the young critics Gérard Leblanc and Jean-Paul Fargier, who closely allied themselves with *Tel Quel*. In doing so, they also appeared to outflank *Cahiers* to its left, as the more venerable journal was conducting an attempted rapprochement with the French Communist Party at this time. This political radicalism, combined with the nascent apparatus theory developed under the auspices of *Tel Quel* (with interventions by Marcellin Pleynet and Jean-Louis Baudry playing a key role in attuning the *Cinéthique* editors to the literary journal's theoretical optic), led to an almost cinephobic outlook toward filmmaking on the pages of the *Cinéthique*. With the cinematic mechanism understood as being ineluctably imbued with bourgeois ideology, Leblanc and Fargier paid little heed to film history (the work of Dziga Vertov constituting the primary exception to this rule), and their list of films meriting critical approbation was both exiguous and eclectic, with favored titles including *Méditerranée*, *Le Joueur de Quilles* (Jean-Pierre Lajournade, 1969), *Octobre à Madrid* (Marcel Hanoun, 1969) and the post-1968 output of Jean-Luc Godard.

If anything, the theoretical framework developed by *Cinéthique*, while it led to forthright polemics with *Cahiers du Cinéma*, shared with that journal an unabashedly prospective outlook, focused as much on ushering in a new form of cinema divested of 'bourgeois ideology' as it was on evaluating films that had already been made. This, perhaps, formed the key line of demarcation between *Cinéthique* and Metz's semiological project, which, in contrast, was rigorously concentrated on analyzing pre-existing works of cinema, and had an overwhelming focus on narrative films from the classical period. Nevertheless, the interview carried out with Metz in issue no. 6 of *Cinéthique* (dated January–February 1970) – where the semiologist spoke with René Fouque, Éliane Le Grivés and Simon Luciani – was conducted in a fraternal and sympathetic manner. Differences were not disavowed, and Metz would elsewhere express skepticism toward what he dubbed 'cinematic tel-quelism' (see Chapter 4), but points of contact were stressed. Almost inevitably, the discussion turned toward *Méditerranée*, and, more pointedly, the possibility of spectatorial recognition in a film so formally remote from the conventions of narrative cinema. The interview concludes with *Cinéthique* stressing the distinction between "an already-made cinema" and "a cinema to be made," a point to which Metz responds by recalling the modest scope and descriptive purpose of his *grande syntagmatique*. The interview even presents an occasion for Metz to discuss the question of the "ideological apparatus" of the cinema that was of prime importance for *Cinéthique* at the time: here, Metz affirms his agreement with the opposition between "the ideologies that are conveyed by the film and those that the film develops by dint of the very fact that it is a film." He nonetheless confesses to being "less optimistic" than the writers at *Cinéthique*, asserting that, "it seems to me to be more difficult than you believe [...] to draw a distinction between what is ideological, within the very optical possibilities of the camera, or between what is a kind of 'castration' of the possibilities (a factor that certainly intervenes), and what pertains more radically to the camera itself."[32]

In the journal's following issue (no. 7–8, dating from *c.* mid-1970), *Cinéthique* published a lengthy appraisal of Metzian theory by Michel Cegarra, composed in December 1969–January 1970. Although not a regular contributor to *Cinéthique*, Cegarra perhaps best encapsulates the journal's thorny relationship with Metz in the opening lines of his article: "Metz's endeavor appears to be both meandering and precise, hasty and effective, unfortunate and auspicious, uncertain and confident."[33] While appreciating film semiology's gesture of clearing the way for "a radical reading of texts/films," Cegarra warns that it also risks remaining trapped by its own "presuppositions, pre-notions, preconceptions,"[34] and his ensuing study is a patiently elaborated, albeit overly schematic, overview of Metz's key ideas.

In tandem with *Cahiers*, *Cinéthique* underwent a distinct political hardening in the years following these two texts: by 1972, the journal had adopted a more rigidly dogmatic 'Marxist-Leninist' position, which even entailed a spiteful rupture with its erstwhile 'mentors' at *Tel Quel*. Even at its most politically dogmatic, however, *Cinéthique* still felt the need to give a detailed critical response to Metz's *Langage et cinéma* in issue no. 13 of the journal, a book that evinces traces of the impact Metz's interaction with *Cinéthique* and *Cahiers* had on his thinking. This anonymously-authored review (at this point the authorial responsibility for all texts published in *Cinéthique* was collectively assumed by the entire editorial committee) has the merit of soberly elucidating the key differences dividing *Cinéthique* and Metz, while at the same time acknowledging that *Langage et cinéma* 'combats a good number of received ideas, falsehoods [and] spontaneous, naïve notions' that 'block the development of a Marxist-Leninist practice of film and its theory.'[35] The critiques made of Metz are no less fundamental, however. At their core, they again come down to the descriptive/normative opposition. *Cinéthique* censures Metz for disavowing a normative element to his study,[36] and in striving to keep his work strictly descriptive in nature, he ends up reinforcing a "positivist ideology". Metz's concern for scientificity in fact results in an exclusion of the "science of historical materialism" from the terms of his study, and the intended political neutrality of his project is, in reality, an illusion, as it cannot avoid being positioned within "the ideological ensemble of discourses on the cinema."[37] By contrast, *Cinéthique* argues for the possibility of being both "scientific" and normative – it unabashedly, to use Metz's words, "explains to future filmmakers how they should go about making a film," and does so from a self-declared revolutionary perspective. Hence, whereas the question of ideological struggle is central to *Cinéthique*'s theoretical framework, the journal critiques Metz for largely avoiding this matter, and notes that the rare mentions of ideology in Metz's book are generally pejorative in nature, relating to notions such as 'stereotype', 'propaganda', and 'banality'. While Metz is careful to give a clear conceptual definition to terms such as 'film' and 'cinema', he errs, in *Cinéthique*'s view, by blithely rehashing the everyday notion of the term 'ideology' rather than utilizing the concept in the theoretical sense developed by the Marxist tradition, with the result being that "in the place of Marxist concepts, the foreground of semiological theory is massively occupied by vague psychological and sociological notions."[38]

La Nouvelle Critique

Curiously, Metz's appearances in *La Nouvelle Critique* were almost exactly contemporaneous with those in *Cinéthique*: an interview in 1970 foreshadowing some of the main arguments of *Langage et cinéma* was followed by an in-depth review of the work in 1972. While both *Cinéthique* and *La NC* espoused a Marxist perspective on art and ideology, there was little common ground between the two journals. *Cinéthique*'s editors were grounded in *gauchiste* politics, eventually turning to a strain of Maoism that was relentlessly hostile to the French Communist Party (PCF); *La NC*, meanwhile, was one of the PCF's main cultural organs at this time. As a general cultural review, *La NC* concerned itself with literature, art, philosophy and other broader issues, but film criticism played an increasingly prominent role on its pages, particularly due to the contributions of former *Cahiers* writers Jean-André Fieschi, Bernard Eisenschitz, and Eduardo de Gregorio. Having adopted a new format in 1967, *La NC* reflected a period of cultural openness on the part of the PCF following the landmark Argenteuil central committee meeting of March 1966. More cynical minds saw the PCF's new cultural strategy as a way of circumventing the attraction of radical groups to left-leaning intellectuals in the political climate of the late 1960s. Nonetheless, the years 1969–1971 saw productive exchanges take place between *La NC* and journals such as *Cahiers* and *Tel Quel*, and the September 1970 interview with Metz took place in this context. In the 'Battle of *Othon*', for example, *La NC* joined *Cahiers* as virtually the only organs to defend Straub/Huillet's film from the derisive ridicule it received at the hands of the majority of French film critics.

This said, the question of 'ideological struggle' was a much less pressing one – on both the theoretical and political levels – for the *NC* critics than it was for their counterparts at *Cahiers* and *Cinéthique*. It is notable, for instance, that, when interviewing Metz, Fieschi speaks of a "veritable dogmatic, normative peril, conceivable at the level of aesthetic tendencies [...] but unacceptable at the level of a professed scientific analysis."[39] Although this normative tendency is expressly linked to the ideas of Bazin by both Fieschi and Metz, the exchange foreshadows a polemic between *Cahiers*' Jean-Louis Comolli and the PCF critic Jean-Patrick Lebel on the question of cinema and ideology, which would flare up over the course of 1971. Whereas Comolli insisted on the ideological determination of the cinematic apparatus, Lebel viewed the camera as a scientific technology that was, in essence, ideologically neutral, and thus able to be used with equal efficacy by reactionary and revolutionary filmmakers alike. The debate was so acrimonious that it led to a severing of ties between *Cahiers* and *La NC*, and *Cahiers* would soon turn to denouncing the PCF-aligned journal for its ostensible "revisionism" and abandonment of a revolutionary cultural-political perspective.

By the time that Michel Marie reviewed *Langage et cinéma* for *La NC* in February 1972, the 'cinema and ideology' debate was drawing to a close, and the two journals would cease any meaningful dialogue with each other.

Marie – who would later become a key figure in French film studies, and, indeed, an interviewer of Metz for *Iris* in 1989 (see Chapter 10) – is generally laudatory of Metz's book, hailing it as "marking a turning point in reflection on the cinema," but he concludes his piece with two key criticisms of Metz, which are worth outlining in some detail. Firstly, Marie argues that Metz is overly insistent on the notion of cinema as a *'langage d'art'*, and this factor, as well as an overestimation of the role of the individual creator (the auteur director) in the elaboration of film language, leads Metz, in Marie's view, to conflate film language with narrative cinema, thereby neglecting other social uses of the cinema, such as the development of scientific films in the GDR. Although Marie notes that Metz is self-critical of his prior work on this point, he judges that the semiologist has "not completely disembarrassed himself of this 'Bazinian heritage' (*mise en scène* as an activity of arrangement and reorganization proceeding directly from 'reality')."[40] Secondly, and more crucially, Marie takes issue with Metz's definition of film language as "a first, purely denotative level where the code of analogy and recognition intervene + a second level consisting of artistic connotations as a supplement," and he rejects the idea of an "anteriority of the denotative level," even if Metz explicitly declares this anteriority to be a fiction constructed for the sake of analysis.[41] Despite the tense relations between *La NC* and *Cahiers*, to defend his perspective Marie invokes Bonitzer's repudiation of Metz in "Réalité' de la Dénotation", discussed above, and echoes Jean Louis Schefer's warning that the semiological project risks reducing the status of the image to that of a mere text. In the end, however, rather than a clear-cut antithesis, Marie prefers to see the writings of Bonitzer, Oudart, Schefer and Francastel on scenographic representation as providing a complement to the semiology of Metz, Umberto Eco and Emilio Garroni, with the *NC* writer concluding that "all theoretical reflection on the cinema today must interrogate the analogical status of the image and the very notion of representation."[42]

Ça-Cinéma

Our final star in the constellation is a journal of a rather different ilk to *Cahiers, Cinéthique* and *La Nouvelle Critique*. Whereas these three organs were monthly magazines intended, at least in theory, for a wide readership, and blending theoretical texts with reviewing and other critical activities, *Ça-Cinéma* sought to explicitly position itself as being closer to an elite literary review, following the model of publications such as *Tel Quel* or *Les Temps Modernes*, but with a specific focus on film theory. Founded by François Barat and Joël Farges in July 1973 and published by Éditions

Albatros, *Ça-Cinéma* appeared on a quarterly basis, with issues generally containing a small number of long, often theoretically dense articles. A premium was placed on drawing prominent writers: the first issue notably contained texts by Marguérite Duras, Philippe Sollers and Jorge-Luis Borges. The rarefied literary register of the journal, meanwhile, was established by Farges' initial editorial, which stated: 'The anaphoric trajectory (connotation) of the (cleaved) subject is to multiply (by homological locks) the markers of a specific problematic (in the movement of Film practice), to shift across inventories (films, paintings, writing, etc.), the pluralism of systems and, *on the basis of practice*, reveal the constraints that ligate the Film.'[43]

That film semiology would be at the core of *Ça-Cinéma*'s theoretical endeavor was also evinced in the journal's inaugural issue, which published a French translation of Emilio Garroni's article 'Sémiotique des messages artistiques'.[44] It was the May 1975 issue, however, that solidified the journal's link with Metz, with the publication of a 176-page double issue dedicated entirely to the semiologist's work, edited by his pupil Marc Vernet, and featuring, in addition to the interview reprinted in this volume (Chapter 4), texts on Metz by figures such as Roland Barthes, Stephen Heath, Jean Louis Schefer, Felix Guattari, Raymond Bellour, Thierry Kuntzel, and Michel Marie. Vernet described the goal of the dossier as being "to sketch what film semiology is today" at a time when "this domain is in the process of changing orientation, with Metz, alongside other semiologists, departing somewhat from the linguistic approach in order to integrate a psychoanalytic approach into their method."[45] For Vernet, "the current face of semiology is a plural one" and the fact that the discipline was at a methodological crossroads was demonstrated, above all, by the inverse theoretical trajectories of Metz and Guattari: while the former had turned toward psychoanalysis, the latter was "tackling the reading of Hjelmslev proposed in *Langage et cinéma*."[46] The conversation with Metz, meanwhile, was one of the most comprehensive and thoroughgoing interviews he gave during this period (in this its main rival is the dialogue that Metz and Bellour conducted for *Semiotica*, also republished here [Chapter 3]).

Vernet would subsequently become a permanent member of the journal's editorial board, and under his auspices a pair of issues dedicated to psychoanalysis and the cinema were published in 1978–1979: once more, Metz was a privileged interlocutor, with the journal's format again allowing for an in-depth exchange on Metz's theories (see Chapter 6). That *Ça-Cinéma* was experiencing troubles during this time, however, was indicated by the same issue's editorial, in which Vernet lamented the sporadic, ad hoc nature of previous numbers (which made consolidating a regular readership difficult) and announced a restructuring of the quarterly to "allow us to clearly re-situate the journal and the work that it will produce in its field: film analysis."[47] The results of this revamp were mixed, however, and the journal ceased publication in 1980. While *Ça-Cinéma* had a relatively brief, intermittent existence, a number of its editors went on to be involved with the bilingual film theory journal *Iris* in the 1980s, and its texts stand today as valuable documents of an incomparably fertile, albeit turbulent, period for reflection on the cinema in France. To a significant degree, such a state of affairs was a legacy of the groundbreaking theoretical work carried out by Christian Metz during this time.

Notes

1. Gérard Guégan, 'Décollages', *Cahiers du Cinéma* 163 (February 1965), pp. 81–82.
2. Christian Metz, 'Godard et le montage', *Cahiers du Cinéma* 165 (April 1965), p. 5.
3. *Ibid.*
4. Metz, 'À propos de l'impression de la réalité au cinéma', *Cahiers du Cinéma* 166–167 (May–June 1965), pp. 76, 79. Translated as 'On the Impression of Reality in the Cinema' in *idem*, *Film Language: A Semiotics of the Cinema* (Chicago, IL: University of Chicago Press, 1991), pp. 7–8.
5. *Ibid.*, p. 82 (p 15).
6. Metz, 'Le cinéma moderne et la narrativité', *Cahiers du Cinéma* 185 (December 1966), pp. 43–68.
7. *Ibid.*, p. 68.
8. See Metz, 'Le cinéma moderne et la narrativité', in *Essais sur la signification au cinéma* (Paris: Klincksieck, 2013 [1968]), pp. 177–211. Translated as 'The Modern Cinema and Narrativity', in *Film Language: A Semiotics of the Cinema* (Chicago, IL: University of Chicago Press, 1991), pp. 185–227.
9. See Pier Paolo Pasolini, 'Le cinéma de poésie', *Cahiers du Cinéma* 171 (October 1965), pp. 55–64, translated as 'The Cinema of Poetry' in *Cahiers du Cinéma in English* 6 (December 1966), 34–43; and 'Le scénario comme structure tendant vers une autre structure', *Cahiers du Cinéma* 185 (December 1966), pp. 77–82.
10. Luc Moullet, 'De la nocivité du langage cinématographique, ainsi que des moyens de lutter contre lui', in Moullet, *Piges choisies* (*de Griffith à Ellroy*) (Paris: Capricci, 2009), pp. 235, 236–237. Long a mythical text, known only from second-hand accounts, 'De la nocivité' found its first publication in 2009 in an anthology of Moullet's critical writings. The same collection gave Moullet's more recent views on theoretical activity: "I wrote a few theoretical texts. Not too many. It's dangerous. Metz, Deleuze, Benjamin and

Debord all committed suicide. Maybe they discovered that theory gets you nowhere, and the shock was too much (not to mention Althusser)." *Ibid.*, p. 234.

11. Jean Narboni 'Notre alpin quotidien', *Cahiers du Cinéma* 180, pp. 58–60, here p. 60.
12. *Ibid.* For more on the Pesaro dispute, see Marc Cerisuelo, 'Tu n'as rien vu (à Pesaro)', *CinémAction* 52 (June 1989), pp. 192–198.
13. Jean-Luc Godard, 'Trois mille heures du cinéma', *Cahiers du Cinéma* 184 (November 1966), p. 48. Translated as 'Three Thousand Hours of Cinema' in *Cahiers du Cinéma in English*, 10 (May 1967).
14. Jean Narboni, Sylvie Pierre and Jacques Rivette, 'Montage', *Cahiers du Cinéma* 210 (March 1969), p. 24. Translated as 'Montage', in Nick Browne (ed.), *Cahiers du Cinéma, volume 3: 1969–1972 The Politics of Representation* (London: BFI, 1990), pp. 28.
15. Narboni, 'À-propos', *Cahiers du Cinéma*, 216 (October 1969), p. 39.
16. Louis Althusser *et al.*, *Lire le capital* (Paris: PUF, 1996 [1965]), pp. 20–21. Translated as *Reading Capital* (London: Verso, 2009), p. 27. Cited in Narboni, 'À-propos', p. 39.
17. Pascal Bonitzer, 'Réalité de la dénotation', *Cahiers du Cinéma*, 229 (May 1971), p. 39. Translated as 'Reality of Denotation', in Browne (ed.), *Cahiers du Cinéma, volume 3: 1969–1972 The Politics of Representation* (London: BFI, 1990), pp. 248–253.
18. *Ibid.*, p. 40.
19. *Ibid.*
20. Jean-Louis Comolli, 'Technique et idéologie (4). Caméra, perspective, profondeur de champ', *Cahiers du Cinéma* 233 (November 1971), p. 40. For an English version of this text, see Jean-Louis Comolli, *Cinema against Spectacle: Technique and Ideology Revisited*, trans. Daniel Fairfax (Amsterdam: Amsterdam University Press, 2015), pp. 210-211. In this passage, Comolli foreshadows a planned, deeper analysis of Metz's ideas in a later installment of 'Technique et idéologie', but this never materialized.
21. Metz, 'Cinéma et idéographie', *Cahiers du Cinéma* 228 (March–April 1971), pp. 6–11; and 'Ponctuations et démarcations dans le film de diégèse', *Cahiers du Cinéma* 234–235 (December 1971, January–February 1972), pp. 63–78.
22. Robert Benayoun, 'Les enfants du paradigme', *Positif* 122 (December 1970), p. 11.
23. *Ibid.* The quotes are taken from Metz's interview with *La Nouvelle Critique* in September 1970, see Chapter 2 below.
24. Narboni, 'Sur quelques contresens', *Cahiers du Cinéma* 226–227 (January–February 1971), p. 116.
25. 'Cinéma, littérature, politique', *Cahiers du Cinéma* 226–227, p. 115. Signed Jean-Louis Comolli, Jean-Paul Fargier, Gérard Leblanc, Jean Narboni, Marcelin Pleynet and Philippe Sollers (Paris, 21 December, 1970). Translated as '*Cahiers du Cinéma*: Cinema, Literature, Politics' in Browne (ed.), *Cahiers du Cinéma, volume 3: 1969–1972 The Politics of Representation* (London: BFI, 1990), p. 187.

26. 'Une lettre de Christian Metz' (9 January 1971), *Cahiers du Cinéma* 226–227 (January–February 1971), p. 121.
27. Metz, 'À propos de l'impression de la réalité au cinéma', p. 82. The footnote does not appear in the version of the text published in *Essais sur la signification du cinéma*, or in the existing English translation.
28. Jean-François Tarnowski, 'De quelques points de théorie du cinéma (à propos d'une lettre de Jean Mitry)', *Positif* 188 (December 1978), p. 48.
29. For details of the affair seen from a point of view sympathetic to Tarnowski, see Nicolas Bonci, 'Jean-François Tarnowksi. La théorie des dominants', http://louvreuse.net/dossier/jean-francois-tarnowski.html [accessed 27 June 2017].
30. Bonitzer, 'Voici (La notion de plan et le sujet du cinéma)', *Cahiers du Cinéma* 273 (January–February 1977), p. 18. Translated as "Here: The Notion of the Shot and the Subject of Cinema" in *Film Reader 4* (Evanston, IL: Northwestern University, 1979), p. 119.
31. Metz, 'L'incandescence et le code', *Cahiers du Cinéma* 274 (March 1977), pp. 5–22.
32. See Chapter 1 below.
33. Michel Cegarra, 'Cinéma et sémiologie', *Cinéthique* 7–8 (undated, *c.* mid-1970), p. 26. Translated as 'Cinema and Semiology' in *Screen* 14:1–2 (1973), p. 130.
34. *Ibid.*
35. Anon., 'Sur 'Langage et cinéma'', *Cinéthique* no. 13 (2nd trimester, 1972), p. 27. Translated as '*Cinéthique* on *Langage et cinéma*' in *Screen* 14:1–2 (1973), p. 189.
36. Metz does this explicitly on pp. 65–66 of *Langage et cinéma* (Paris: Larousse, 1971), where he states: "Film semiology has sometimes been accused of wishing to establish normative rules, destined to explain to future film-makers how they should go about making a film! Let us simply recall that the most fundamental method of semiological analysis is situated precisely to the contrary of such an intention."
37. Anon., 'Sur 'langage et cinéma'', p. 28.
38. *Ibid.*, p. 36.
39. See Chapter 2 below.
40. Michel Marie, 'Langage et cinéma. Sur un ouvrage de Christian Metz', *La Nouvelle Critique* 50 (February 1972), p. 81
41. *Ibid.*, pp. 82–83.
42. *Ibid.*, p. 84.
43. Joël Farges, 'Éditorial', *Ça-Cinéma* 1 (July 1973), p. 1.
44. Emilio Garroni, 'Sémiotique des messages artistiques', *Ça-Cinéma* 1 (July 1973), pp. 54–62.
45. Marc Vernet, 'Introduction', *Ça-Cinéma* 7–8 (May 1975), p. 3.
46. *Ibid.*
47. Vernet, 'Éditorial', *Ça-Cinéma* 16 (undated, *c.* 1979), p. 2.

Interviews

Works of Christian Metz frequently cited in the interviews

Essais sur la signification au cinéma, tome 1 et 2 (Paris: Klincksieck 1968; 1972); volume 1 translated as *Film Language: A Semiotics of the Cinema*, trans. by Michael Taylor (New York: Oxford University Press, 1974). This book consists of the following sections and chapters:

I. Phenomenological Approaches to Film
1. On the Impression of Reality in the Cinema
2. Notes Toward a Phenomenology of the Narrative

II. Problems of Film Semiotics
3. The Cinema: Language or Language System?
4. Some Points in the Semiotics of the Cinema
5. Problems of Denotation in the Fiction Film

III. Syntagmatic Analysis of the Image Track
6. Outline of the Autonomous Segments in Jacques Rozier's film *Adieu Philippine*
7. Syntagmatic Study of Jacques Rozier's Film *Adieu Philippine*

IV. The 'Modern' Cinema: Some Theoretical Problems
8. The Modern Cinema and Narrativity
9. Mirror Construction in Fellini's *8 1/2*
10. The *Saying* and the *Said*: Toward the Decline of Plausibility in the Cinema?

'Propositions méthodologiques pour l'analyse des films', in *Social Science Information/Information sur les sciences sociales* 7 (4) (1968), pp. 107–119. Translated as 'Methodological Propositions for the Analysis of Film' in *Screen* 14 (1–2) (1973), pp. 89–101.

Langage et Cinéma (Paris: Librairie Larousse 1971); *Language and Cinema*, trans. by Donna Jean Umiker-Sebeok (The Hague/Paris: Mouton, 1974).

'Le perçu et le nommé', in *Vers une esthétique sans entrave. Mélanges offerts à Mikel Dufrenne* (Paris: Union générale d'éditions 1975), pp. 345–377.

Translated as 'The Perceived and the Named' in *Studies in Visual Communication* 6, 3 (1980), pp. 56–68.

Le signifiant imaginaire. Psychanalyse et cinéma (Paris: Union générale d'éditions 1977). Translated as *Psychoanalysis and Cinema: The Imaginary Signifier*, trans. by Celia Britton, Annwyl Williams, Ben Brewster, and Alfred Guzzetti (London: Macmillan 1982); also published as *The Imaginary Signifier: Psychoanalysis and Cinema* (Bloomington, IN: Indiana University Press, 1982). This book contains four essays:

'The Imaginary Signifier'
'Story/Discourse (A Note on Two Types of Voyeurism)'
'The Fiction Film and Its Spectator'
'Metaphor/Metonymy, or the Imaginary Referent'.

L'enonciation impersonnelle ou le site du film (Paris: Méridiens Klincksieck 1991); Translated as *Impersonal Enunciation or the Place of Film*, trans. by Cormac Deane (New York: Columbia University Press, 2016).

A detailed bibliography of Christian Metz's work from 1964 to 2009, compiled by Hans J. Wulff and Ludger Kaczmarek, is available from the following website at the University of Hamburg: http://berichte.derwulff.de/0100_09.pdf

1. Semiology, Linguistics, Cinema: Interview with Christian Metz

René Fouque, Eliane Le Grivés, and Simon Luciani

Buckland, Warren and Daniel Fairfax (eds), *Conversations with Christian Metz: Selected Interviews on Film Theory (1970–1991)*. Amsterdam: Amsterdam University Press, 2017.

DOI: 10.5117/9789089648259/CH1

Abstract
In this interview, conducted in 1970 for the journal *Cinéthique*, Christian Metz discusses his film semiology from the 1960s (including his *grande syntagmatique*), as well as the work of Sergei Eisenstein, *cinéma-vérité,* the concept of verisimilitude, and the film *Méditerranée* (Jean-Daniel Pollet, Volker Schlöndorff, 1963).

Keywords: Christian Metz, film theory, film semiology, Sergei Eisenstein, *cinéma-vérité, Méditerranée* (1963)

'Sémiologie, linguistique, cinéma. entretien avec Christian Metz'. René Fouqué, Éliane Le Grivès, et Simon Luciani. Published in *Cinéthique* 6 (January–February) 1970, pp. 21–26. Translated by Daniel Fairfax.

Cinéthique: Can you situate your work on the *grande syntagmatique* and its history within your general semiological project?

Christian Metz: Insofar as my general project is indeed a contribution to a semiology of the cinema, a contribution to overcoming the state of most writing on film (which is, for the most part, journalistic in nature), in favor of a more theoretical approach, which, for me, is a semiological approach, I have encountered a code operative within each film – that is, one code among many others. It is this code that I dubbed, at the time, the *grande syntagmatique of narrative film.* I conceive this *grande syntagmatique* as something partial: firstly, because it can only be applied to a certain historical phase in the development of the cinema. It is applicable, let us say, to classical narrative cinema, from roughly 1935 onwards (that is, with the stabilization of sound film), up until around 1955, with the appearance of the tendencies known as 'modern cinema' or 'new cinema'. Thus, I believe that the code of the *grande syntagmatique* is *diachronically* partial. It is also partial in a second way, because, even in films from the period in question, it was not the only code. It is a code that simply offers a breakdown of the major units of filmic narration, and that puts to one side the organization of all the other motifs and themes in a film. I already believed at the time that this attempt was doubly partial, but I believe this even more today. Simply put, it seems to me that we must have a point of attack in order to study the problems of film. The problems of the *grande syntagmatique* and of film narrativity were particularly ripe at this point in time (it was three years ago now). Perhaps this is why I chose to attack it from this angle. Today, what I find more striking is the multiplicity of codes at work in a film, of which only some – for example, the *grande syntagmatique* – are specifically cinematic, while others appear inside the film in much the same way that they appear outside of the film. In other words, they are not specifically cinematic – which does not prevent them from being filmic.

Cinéthique: Could you try to define the different codes operative within a film, and, more particularly, those that are specific to the cinema?

Metz: It seems to me that research has not reached the point where it could give an exact enumeration of specific codes – or of any other codes, by the way. But initially, one can think that the specifically cinematic codes consist of all those codes that relate to the work of the *moving photographic image organized sequentially*, and of *sound*, of their reciprocal relations, as well as of the relations between the image, the sound and the spoken word.

Aside from this, there are codes that are not specifically cinematic. For example, in certain cases (though not always), the social systems that organize the content of film are not systems proper to the cinema. I find it more and more striking to see that the content of films – or what we call the content of films, because there is a real problem with this notion – is organized by systems, by codes that are, I would say, ideological; that is to say, they are susceptible to appearing in the cinema, but without a major change in their structure, for they can appear just as well in languages other than the language of film: in a novel, for example, or on a poster, or on TV, etc. Another example of a non-specific code that nonetheless plays a very important role in the cinema is, quite simply, the language code [*langue*] that the film uses: there are films that speak English, German, etc. Now, this code, obviously, is not cinematic, and yet this does not prevent the *use* of this language (which must be distinguished from the language itself), once it is in the film, from being susceptible to becoming specifically cinematic.

I am not saying that it is always cinematic, but it is susceptible to becoming so. At the time of the *Manifesto for Orchestral Counterpoint* [*A Statement on Sound*], there were many things that were very advanced in what the three signatories, Eisenstein, Pudovkin, and Alexandrov stated. They said, for example, that intertitles may be used, that is, that written language (but this is also transposable to spoken language) may be used in a specifically filmic manner, a manner that would be different from the code of ordinary writing, different from *written language outside of the cinema*. And they had in view specific kinds of systems concerning what we could call a *typography of the intertitle* (titles increasing in size, for instance). Moreover, they actually used these techniques in their films. I was sensitive to the fact that Solanas, in *Hour of the Furnaces* [1968], totally resurrects this kind of approach. In this film, there is an absolutely (or at least proximally) Eisensteinian usage of the intertitle, which plays around with the size of the writing. By contrast, the language code [*langue*] – the language-system itself, the language-system of Saussure, the phonological system for instance – is reiterated as such by films.

Cinéthique: Is it possible to think of the ideology of film practice and to define the code of this ideology?

Metz: In your journal, I have noticed that you make a distinction, with which I am fundamentally in agreement – between those ideologies that are conveyed by the film and those that the film develops by dint of the fact that it is a film. I have also noticed that among this latter category of ideologies, you accord the greatest importance to the impression of reality. I do too, by the way; but I am not sure if we are in agreement on its definition. Nonetheless, there is a point of contact between us here.

One thing first: you often insist, in various articles in your journal, on the fact that the camera is *regulated* [*réglée*]: initially on the level of its construction, and then on the level of its operational settings in the strict sense of the term (its buttons, and so on), since, even with the instruments manufactured today, there are still regulatory forms that are not used. So, on this double level, the instrument is regulated in order to reconstitute a monocular perspective, which is, roughly speaking, the non-disorienting perspective of the Quattrocento. This is also how I see things. This properly optical 'castration' of the camera is something that had already been studied, in particular (and in spite of major divergences between you and him) by Jean Mitry, who showed that, by constructing camera instruments differently, by regulating them differently, and so on, one could obtain very surprising perspectives, and that these were expressly refused due to the desire to attain the impression of reality. There is indeed a kind of underemployment of the optical possibilities of the camera, because one sought, in general, to use it to attain the perspectival space of the Renaissance, by wagering on the possibilities offered by the monocular factors of the impression of three-dimensionality.

But I am less optimistic than you. It seems to me to be more difficult than you believe (I even ask myself whether it is at all possible, in the current historical situation to which we are ourselves limited) to draw a distinction between what is ideological, within the very optical possibilities of the camera, or between what is a kind of 'castration' of these possibilities (a factor that certainly intervenes), and what pertains more radically to the camera itself, which has limitations that are, I would say, not simply technical, but scientific in nature. It is an apparatus that, like any other, is not quite capable of doing anything and everything. I have written a study, 'On the Impression of Reality in the Cinema', in which, by the way, I make no mention of this aspect you are so insistent about (that is: the properly ideological limitation of the possibilities of the camera), and where I put greater emphasis on the limitations that I considered to be inherent to its nature. I am a little less certain of this today. I must revisit the text from this perspective. On the other hand, I have the impression that your journal has just reactivated a debate that had been, in a way, *terminated* before your intervention. I am thinking of the quarrel that took place in Bazin's day between his ideology of the sequence-shot, of 'non-montage', etc., and the theories of the likes of Eisenstein, Kuleshov, and Vertov – who offered rather extremist theories of montage. Even after your intervention, this debate does not appear completely clear to me, and it seems to me that there is ideology on both sides.

In certain passages in Bazin's writings, there is indisputably something like a shift to metaphysics (a metaphysics which, in this case, is called phenomenology), a sort of cosmophanic myth according to which the function of the cinema would be to render the real more eloquent than it is – it is, as it were, as if the real itself spoke through the means of the cinema. We can also, by the way, find this mythology in certain attempts at *cinéma-vérité*, which proceed from a truly magic belief in the innate purity [*adamisme*] of the image, with the idea that everything that is uttered [*énoncé*] by words is guilty, loaded with heavy connotations, and that suddenly, through the passage of the word to the image, we could accede to an absolutely innocent rendering of the real. I am thinking, for example, of dialogues that are deliberately garbled in order to 'seem real' – or rather, to create reality-effects, as Barthes puts it. I can clearly see where the part of ideology is situated in Bazin's thinking (and it is a considerable part): it lies in the idea that the world is unveiled, in all its innocence, by the image, whereas what is actually revealed is only ever the real as seen by someone in particular.

Robbe-Grillet and others have insisted on the fact that the image is never innocent, even if this is only due to the necessary choice of camera angles, that is, to the most immediate constraint of a filmmaker's work. God does not take the photograph; the camera angle cannot be the doing of God, or of nature (which amounts to the same thing in this ideology). Rather, it has been chosen by a filmmaker who had his reasons, whether conscious or unconscious. Robbe-Grillet, at the time of his 'turning-point' – that is, when he himself reinterpreted objectivity [*l'objectal*] in a more subjectivist sense – insisted on this point in a text called, if I remember correctly, 'Note on the Localization and Displacement of the Viewpoint of the Camera in Novelistic Description'.

In contrast, however, I find that the montage theories developed in the 1920s among the great classics of the Soviet school are themselves not exactly bereft of ideology.

Firstly, in his theoretical writings (but much less so in his films), Eisenstein willingly assumes the mantle of what I would call the 'artistic type'. He speaks about montage in an ambiguous fashion: at times, he claims that it must be at the service of the ideological point of view of the working class, but at other moments he states that it should be at the service of film art, or a sort of genesis in the mind of the spectator (reproducing what has gone through the mind of the filmmaker). He does so with a very forceful insistence on things in which we believe less and less today – such as expression, creation, etc. In short, with Eisenstein we find an entire romantic ideology of pure creation, in such a way that he often mingles problems of montage with his claims to being a creative artist (which are fatally overdetermined and opaque to themselves). There is another problem, that you also present in your journal, when you say that the *work of the film* (the economic conditions of its production on the one hand, and on the other hand the directorial [*cinéastique*] texture in the midst of being made) must be legible in the film itself. Now, Eisenstein, in his theories on montage, at certain moments, almost arrives at the same conclusions that you do. At times, he seems to say that rapid editing is necessary so that *it becomes visible*, whereas at other times he presents montage as a kind of *agogia*, a technique for training, or even conditioning, the spectator – this is montage as an effect that, he states, mobilizes people, in a sense of the term that is occasionally close to deception. It almost amounts to forcing people, without them realizing it, to adopt the same point of view as the creative filmmaker. Conversely, in his texts on *The Best Years of Our Lives* [William Wyler, 1946], and the films of Welles and Renoir (*La Règle du jeu* [*The Rules of the Game* (Renoir, 1939)] for example), Bazin affirms that 'non-montage' leaves the spectator with the freedom to choose, to create his own montage within a complete action, through the use of extended takes in deep-focus long-shot. The only problem with this is that 'non-montage' does not exist. That said, however, I am not so sure that there is not an element of truth in this aspect of Bazin's thinking. This is why I would say that, fundamentally, nothing is very clear in this polemic.

Cinéthique: In a way, montage can lead Eisenstein to speak of mobilizing the people, intending to partly deceive them, or using his mobilizing effects to create rupture effects with respect to an expected model. In fact, if you take a commercial film, which is made for a particular public, you are certain of the model that will be supplied, in terms both of its content and of its editing principles. It nonetheless remains to be known whether there are not codes which have dual effects, which at a certain moment, within apparently traditional forms of editing, create rupture effects. Likewise, Sade's writing, for example, which very often obeys the model of the eighteenth-century novel, with an entire tradition born of the Gothic novel, creates a rupture effect, precisely at the level of what we currently call the 'reality effect'. But what, precisely, is this reality effect, and how is it constituted at the level of editing? Can we see it on the level of the constitution of a model that would be an ideological vehicle, not on the level of the content, but on the level of the filmic work in the strict sense of the term?

Metz: I can perceive what I call a 'reality effect' more on the side of 'non-edited' films, those *cinéma-vérité* films that I spoke of earlier. Films that, through the absence of montage, shooting in continuity, or through *deliberately disordered montage*, seek to 'appear real'. To simplify matters, I see it more on the side of films in the Bazinian tendency.

Cinéthique: In effect, *cinéma-vérité* does indeed make ample use of non-montage, with garbled discussions, shaky close-ups, bad framing, etc. And yet, these do not belong to the order of the real, but to that of the camera. And through their very means of expression, there is an effort to create a truth effect rather than a reality effect. The reality effect is more due to the complete synthesis of something that has been broken into pieces, presented as a single tableau. In *cinéma-vérité*, there is an emphasis on surface appearance that seeks to confer truth on every element it represents, but which does not actually yield a reality effect on the broader level.

Metz: Perhaps there is a difference between us in vocabulary. I tend to call 'truth' something constructed and quite theoretical, and I consider the reality effect to be a sort of pretense that protects itself from 'raw material'. *Cinéma-vérité* strives to give us an impression of the real captured unawares; or, alternatively (and here you are correct), it introduces, through specifically filmic means, a type of disorder in the traditional ordering of the narrative. Something that struck me in *cinéma-vérité* films is that, for example, one can take a social situation (I am thinking of films that are more or less based on the techniques of the psychological drama) and disrupt it in some way, and we are supposed to believe that one has raised by this disruption some kind of hidden content, when in fact nothing comes out but pure and simple artifacts.

Cinéthique: Exactly. In *cinéma-vérité* films there is no reality effect at the level of the image, because all the images that are shown to us are shown through a gaze that seeks to be true, that does not seek to determine a real, but a series of true points: the camera suddenly captures an awkward facial expression, or a meaningful look, or a hand trembling, etc. That is to say, it tries to create what is held to be, not so much a psychoanalysis, but a psychomorphology, or the psychoanalysis of gestures. The reality effect would be something much more elaborate, but in a contrary sense, in order to constitute a recognition model for the individual who is looking at it. In all films, there are attempts at reality effects: people recognize themselves, and it is possibly here that we should look for rupture effects. We should find out where, precisely – when one shows people things in which they could recognize themselves – is the moment that they no longer recognize themselves.

Metz: All this returns us to a problem that greatly interests me, and on which I have written: namely, the problem of verisimilitude. It seems to me that the cinema, perhaps even more than other modes of expression (due, I suppose, to the fact that, through the sheer magnitude of the material means it requires, it is more closely controlled), is pervaded by verisimilitude. And this takes place insofar as, I would not even say in a film, but, in general, in a tiny fragment of a film, a rupture is produced, where something unexpected happens, and where, for a single moment, on a single point, filmic verisimilitude gives way. This is a dialectical problem because, in the history of the cinema, it often happens that these moments of 'true truth' themselves become the basis for a new verisimilitude, which feeds off them. This is typically what has happened to what we could call the Czech New Wave, the school of intimist cinema derived from Forman, Passer and their ilk, which has very quickly become a type of system, in the bad sense of the term, a new verisimilitude, a verisimilitude such as Aristotle defined it, as that which conforms to common opinion or to the rules of a genre.

Cinéthique: But how has it come about that people recognize themselves in an episode of *Knowledge of the World* on Palmyra, for example, but that they no longer recognize themselves in *Méditerranée* [Jean-Daniel Pollet, Volker Schlöndorff, 1963], which shows an entire series of images of Palmyra? All the same (it would be necessary to see what cultural and social level one is placed on), in *Méditerranée* there is a whole series of cultural commonplaces that can be found in any documentary on the same geographic area. Here, it would perhaps be necessary to interrogate the film's technique, its use of the camera, editing, etc.

Metz: People no longer recognize themselves in *Méditerranée* because the cinema is not only the image, it is also the work done on the image, and in *Méditerranée* this work is evidently very different from what it is in a classical documentary. In this way, we could equally return to the problem of the *iconic analogy* between the moving photographic image and that of which it is the effigy. Personally, I think that analogy itself is already coded: under the cover of this analogy, the different social codes that function in the deciphering of reality are intended to function to the film's benefit, in the deciphering of photographic spectacles. I no longer have the same ideas as five years ago when I wrote 'Cinema: Language or Language System?' In this text, my point of departure was the word 'analogy', taken in opposition to the *arbitrary* (in the Saussurian sense). From the fact of this point of departure, I was led to posit antagonistic relations between analogy and codification. And yet analogy can very much be coded without, however, ceasing to function for the user on a psychological level, as analogy. The basis of the problem is possibly that this resemblance is not so much between the photograph and its model, as it is between the structuring activities of the viewer [*récepteur*] placed respectively before these two instances.

Cinéthique: So, in *Méditerranée*, where we see the sea, and in a documentary where we also see the sea, people should be equally capable of recognizing themselves, in the sense that, as you say, it is no longer the model and its effigy that are placed face to face, but the effigy and a viewer [*récepteur*] who carries out work, which he likely would have done if he had been on the beach in the position of the camera. It is through the intervention of the camera that people cease to recognize themselves.

Metz: In the case of *Méditerranée*, I don't think so. I feel that if it happens to the spectators that they cease to recognize themselves, when confronted, for example, with the image of the sea, this is not due to the image itself, but to the ordering of images. In other words, there has been a disruption to spectatorial habits on the level of editing to such an extent that the spectator becomes inhibited, in his decoding activity, on the level of the image itself.

Cinéthique: I even think that there has been a disruption on the level of the camera, because, in the documentary, the camera is seen as an archetypal spectator – that is, the spectator is the deferred camera and the camera is the deferred spectator, whereas in *Méditerranée* there is a specific role for the camera, which is precisely not this role of *différance*, to subsequently provide the spectator with something to see. There is another function of the camera, with, as you said earlier, in spite of everything, a series of implications that we cannot overcome.

Metz: Yes, but what I find striking is that, all the same, there are images in *Méditerranée* that, if you took them one by one, if the film was left unedited, would allow the spectator to recognize himself. In other words, I wonder if it is not the work of montage that prevents spectatorial recognition in these images.

Cinéthique: Exactly. I wanted to ask you about knowing how we can define those units that are not as great as those defined by the *grande syntagmatique*, and how far we can go with this. Because, obviously, if you extracted static images from *Méditerranée*, and if you chose well, everybody would be able to recognize themselves in them. But as soon as there is not simply a static image, but a series of images in motion, at a given speed, forming lexical units of varying size, then perhaps people will recognize themselves, but it is far from certain. There is, perhaps, work to be done on this matter. If people recognize themselves, then this may be because the film has not gone far enough, has not sufficiently broken with norms.

Metz: I am not so sure, because we could admit (and, roughly speaking, this is my opinion), that the conscious or unconscious purpose of *Méditerranée* was to carry out a deconstructive activity on the assemblage of images, and not at the level of the image itself. There is the problem of the relative autonomy of each level: the *image* and the *succession of images*.

Cinéthique: This remains to be proven. Take certain shots from *Méditerranée* where the camera moves in a lateral tracking shot on a background that remains monocular, on a completely flat perspective. We see row upon row of columns, and I am practically certain that the images, taken one by one, are all identical, which would, perhaps, deconstruct the very notion of images which are generally supposed to reproduce movement. Here, unlike, for example, an image of a man walking, they do not reproduce a segment of motion.

Metz: Yes, if you like, but I retain the impression that the essence of the film's deconstructive purpose is at the level of editing. Nonetheless, this does not exclude there also existing a deconstruction at the level of a given image.

There is something else that complicates the problems we have spoken about, and this is the notion of *cinematic specificity*. Personally, I think that there is a cinematic specificity, which I would define as a set of codes that appear nowhere else but in the cinema. In your journal, I have noticed that you believe that the principal object of a theoretical practice, when it is concerned with the cinema, is to focus on what is specifically cinematic and not, for example, to use film to disseminate the results of a theoretical praxis of a more general, non-cinematic nature.

Cinéthique: Yes, in order to pass to another level, we must first resolve the problem of the specificity of the cinema.

Metz: Well, it may be that we do not exactly understand the same thing by this term. But in the end, there remains the fact that we believe in it. Now, in 1968, in Italy, a book by a Marxist semiologist called Emilio Garroni was published with the title *Semiotica ed estetica*. Garroni completely refuses the notion of cinematic specificity. He considers it to be a sort of confusionist myth, and he critiques me, among others, for having spoken about it. He relies on texts by Eisenstein (which does not make our conversation any simpler) in order to insist precisely on the fact that Eisenstein always conceived of the notion of montage as not being particular to the cinema, and that it can be found everywhere. Garroni thinks that a language [*langage*], like cinematic language for example, is only specific by the combination of codes it uses, but that there are no codes that are specific to a language. I wrote a response to his book, in which I said that, in my opinion, certain codes are specific to the cinema. But, even though I disagree with him, I do not think that his idea is entirely false. According to Garroni, we must make a careful distinction between language and code. He operates a complete break [*coupure*] between this material of expression and its form (in the sense in which Hjelmslev uses these terms). In other words, the technico-material or technico-sensorial specificity of the cinema absolutely does not lead, for him, to even a mere probability that there are specific codes. I agree with him on one point: namely, when you have the technico-sensorial specificity of the cinema, you do not yet have its structural specificity.

Cinéthique: Yes, but you can push this technico-sensorial specificity further. I do not understand why we should stop there. Montage, such as it is practiced in the cinema, is fundamentally specific to the cinema, and the same thing is not done in literature or painting. And, beyond montage, we should see how far we can push this specificity. Perhaps Garroni has not done this work, but if it is done, we would perhaps perceive that, simply at the technico-sensorial level, specificity goes very far indeed.

Metz: Yes, that is your opinion, and to a large degree it is also my own. But the crux of the problem is that Garroni rejects the fact that montage is specific to the cinema, because it is also manifest elsewhere. In contrast, I have personally been puzzled by the inexact notion of 'pre-cinema' (configurations pre-existing the cinema that anticipate cinematic procedures). In general, you can look very far back indeed, and see tracking shots in Livy, or shot/reverse shots in Tacitus...

Cinéthique: Barthes has done so, but not to show that there is a 'pre-cinema'. Rather, it was simply to show that, in history, we proceed as we do in the cinema, because we have the means to do so, by, for example, depicting an overarching tableau of a battle, then focusing suddenly on a detail of the general commanding his troops, then a detail of the battalion attacking, etc. Of course, this is true, but in history it only serves to write history, while in the cinema, it only serves to make a film. So there is still, at least, a specificity of the final product.

Metz: I agree with your conclusion, but you should not be so dismissive of Garroni's objections. I think that the specific codes of the cinema could appear, once they have been established (which would be the most urgent thing to do), as not being radically specific *from within*, in the same way that an analogy can be coded without ceasing to be an analogy. The units figuring in the *grande syntagmatique* owe a lot to a rhetorical culture. Figures such as alternating montage or parallel montage are only possible in a civilization profoundly impregnated by forms such as antithesis or parallelism. My current work, and, for example, the book that I am presently writing [*Language and Cinema*], corresponds to a double movement. I would be inclined to express the first movement as a distinction between the *filmic* and the *cinematic*, by baptizing the filmic as everything that appears in the film (a nomination that appears quite logical to me), and cinematic as being only a part of the filmic, that which is linked to the film itself. The second movement would involve showing that, within these properly cinematic constructions, there is a kernel of non-specificity. In sum, it is something of a self-critical movement.

Cinéthique: Do you not have the impression that Garroni may be speaking of a cinema already made and a cinema to be made? That is to say, at bottom everything we say about cinematic codes relates to a cinema already made, and what Garroni says relates to films to be made – that is, a cinema that would once again examine what it believes to be specific to its own function. The *syntagmatique*, which is close to rhetoric, undeniably exists, but maybe it needs to be interrogated in order to see how it conveys an entire series of ideologies (not only in the film, but on the film and on the cinema in general), and to know if it ought to continue to exist. What Garroni says seems interesting to me at the predictive level: namely, can we make films without utilizing what we believe is a code specific to the cinema? If there are no specific codes, then all codes are generalized. It remains to be seen if there is not some kind of barrier that ensures that we continue to consider montage in the way it is currently practiced as being indispensable to making a film.

Metz: I do not agree with your interpretation of Garroni. I believe that he places himself in, let's say, a traditional conception (which is also mine) of semiology as non-interventionist, analyzing films already made. Consequently, he does not pose the problem of films to be made, which is one of the differences with your journal, for example, since you resolutely place yourselves within an interventionist perspective.

Cinéthique: Yes, of course, Garroni should not explicitly come out and say: this is what is done, and this is what should be done. But it seems to me that, from the semiological study of what is made, we should draw out what is not acceptable at a certain level – above all at the level of the product. Perhaps the element of confusion in this conversation is the role played by semiology. Semiology makes no illusions about its role in a comprehensive theory of the cinema, that is, a complete reading of films, which would not only be semiological in nature, but which could also incorporate politics, economics and psychoanalysis.

Metz: I would respond to you that this depends on the semiologists. My conception of semiology is relatively modest, in the sense that, for example, I do not think that, in the present state of things, semiology can seriously claim that it will decode a film in its entirety. That said, however, I am obliged to mention a historical fact, which is that, quite often, semiology implicitly presents itself as a total science, as a type of general science of culture which, ideally, could subsume psychology, sociology, etc. In a way, this is a dream that we already find in C.S. Peirce, which personally I do not adhere to, but which I do not completely reject, at the level of ambition. To a certain extent, semiology can be a kind of epistemology of the social sciences. But I think that, as long as we do not possess the sufficient scientific tools for realizing such a program, arrogant declarations of exclusivism and totality do a great disservice to semiology.

It simply seems to me that semiology can provide a contribution that, on its own level, is rigorous. This is what I consider my *profession* to be: undertaking this contribution inspired by linguistic methodologies (whether generative or structuralist). From that point on, people should do with it what they want! By the way, even if this contribution is rigorous (given that semiological work, like every activity, is susceptible to being poorly done), I do not believe that absolutely anything can be done with it. But I believe semiology *qua* semiology must make an extremely precise analysis of codes, and demonstrate these codes – and that is all. As a result, I have never been bothered about being in a rather partial position; that is, lending my semiological contribution to enterprises that could well be, in their center of gravity, very out of step with respect to my own project. I am referring to encounters such as our own one today, but also to encounters between semiologists and psychologists, pedagogues, etc., where the ultimate endpoints are very different. If a semiological contribution is rigorous on its own level, it represents progress in our knowledge of the cinema, and a more general theory, of whatever kind, can then utilize or criticize this contribution.

2. On 'Specificity': Interview with Christian Metz

Jean-André Fieschi

Buckland, Warren and Daniel Fairfax (eds), *Conversations with Christian Metz: Selected Interviews on Film Theory (1970–1991)*. Amsterdam: Amsterdam University Press, 2017.

DOI: 10.5117/9789089648259/CH2

Abstract
In this interview for the journal *La Nouvelle Critique* in 1970, Christian Metz discusses the semiological concept of 'film language' and the concept of 'specificity'. He defines specificity in terms of underlying abstract structures and codes rather than the surface qualities of film. He also makes the distinction between the 'filmic' and the 'cinematic', and aligns the 'cinematic' with 'specificity'.

Keywords: Christian Metz, film theory, film semiology, specificity

'Cinéma et Sémiologie: Sur la "Specificité". Entretien avec Christian Metz.' Jean-André Fieschi. *La Nouvelle Critique*, 36 (September, 1970), pp. 48-53. Translated by Daniel Fairfax.

This interview with Christian Metz conducted by our regular contributor Jean-André Fieschi aims to illuminate the current theoretical debate – both here and abroad – on the cinema: the contribution of semiology to this debate is designated as one of the possible (and desirable) components of a general theory of the cinema.

In order to deepen the following reflections, we refer the reader to the author's other works, notably *Essais sur la Signification au Cinéma* (published by Klincksieck), and, taking stock of the current state of this important research, to recent interventions published in a number of journals: 'Propositions méthodologiques pour l'analyse des films' (in *Information sur les sciences sociales*), 'Spécificité des codes et spécificité des langages' (in *Semiotica* vol. 1 no. 4 [1969], pp. 370-96), and 'Au delà de l'analogie, l'image' (in *Communications* no. 15, an issue entirely dedicated to the 'analysis of images', and including, alongside several enlightening texts – Eco, Schefer – a bibliographic guide for a semiology of the image).

Jean-André Fieschi: To help situate historically the current stakes of the theoretical debate concerning the cinema, would you mind looking back, even schematically, on the evolution, since the silent era, of the various conceptions related to the infamous problem of 'specificity'?

Christian Metz: Well, it seems to me that there was an initial period in thinking on the cinema in which the dominant idea, the dominant drive, among all the film critics and theorists, as well as among those filmmakers with a theoretical pretension, was a certain conception of filmic specificity. This notion recurs today, but it does so in a much more detailed manner.

At bottom, this idea of specificity was, in this initial period, a largely normative idea. There was also a demand for cultural legitimacy: there was always, in the background, sometimes even in the foreground, the idea of demonstrating that film is as noble as the novel, for example, or as the theatrical play, and that it is also a language [*langage*] – this is the expression most frequently used at the time – or a form of writing (to tell the truth, a distinction was barely made between the two), a specific form of writing, in the same way that literature or painting are specific forms of writing.

It seems to me that this is the central idea, or in any case the central motivation, for a whole period of thinking on the cinema.

Very well. It is in this period, notably, that what I would call the ideology of montage was developed, which I have spoken about in certain of my articles, because montage was seen as a convenient argument for demonstrating the specificity of the cinema in a manner that saw itself as peremptory. The cinema is specific, it is a language, it is not merely a recording medium, *because* there is montage. This is both correct and false at the same time. It is true that there is montage but, first of all, there can very well be montage without editing [*collures*] – montage within a sequence shot, for example; and, moreover, if there is cinematic specificity, it is not reducible to montage alone, it also entails the composition of the image and a host of other factors.

Subsequently, it seems to me that there was a second period dominated, let us say, to simplify matters somewhat, by Bazin, with the various theories of non-montage, of shooting in continuity, of shooting with wide-angle lenses (*La Règle du Jeu* [*The Rules of the Game* (Renoir, 1939)]) or in depth of field (Orson Welles). There was an entire second period which was a reaction against the theories of montage, and which at the same time was an effort to account for the advent of sound cinema. This effort at accounting for the sound cinema is, in fact, much rarer than one may believe. Even today, many people continue to reason as if the cinema were still silent.

In this second period, therefore, the belief in cinematic specificity becomes less arrogant, less importunate, and tends to assume subtler forms. I am referring to Bazin's studies, in which he shows that, for example, the profound cinematicity of a film like *Les Parents Terribles* [1948] by Cocteau consists in exacerbating its theatricality by means of a properly cinematic procedure.

Thus, in sum, I believe we pass from an unsophisticated demand for specificity to one that is subtler, more at ease, that is less prone to insecurity, and hence goes more on the attack.

Very well. It seems to me that we are presently in a third period of thinking on the cinema, a period where we have returned, in a way, to the reflections on the great era of montage, and where the problem of the specificity of film is once again posed in a quite radical fashion, much as it was posed in the first period, but in a wider cultural horizon. That is to say, at bottom, that what is beginning to be done (and which, by the way, has, in my opinion, not yet been carried out as much as one could wish), and what has, in the end, never been done until now, is the creation of a junction between thinking on cinema and the general movement of ideas. The fact is that film and thinking on film are progressively leaving behind the provincial status in which they had hitherto always been confined, are leaving behind the status of cultural isolation, that the fanaticism of what I would call the cinema-cinema tends to be dissolved, and that thinking on film becomes less and less separate from more general thinking on the text, on writing, on the relationship with linguistics, Marxism, analysis, etc.

Fieschi: In the 1920s (a moment of intense theoretical research, and of formal experimentation with rich repercussions), specificity was the node for thinking on the cinema, among film theorists (Balázs, Arnheim) and among theorist-filmmakers (Epstein and his friends in France; Kuleshov, Vertov, and Eisenstein in the USSR). But this word often encompassed notions that, from one school to another, from one thinker to another, were very contradictory. Thus Vertov, on the basis of certain Proletkult temptations, postulated a kind of *tabula rasa*, a radical virginity of the cinema with respect to cultural heritage, whereas others sought its specificity, as a function of the naturally composite character of this new art, on the side of polyphony, or 'synthesis', to adopt a word that was widely used at the time.

Has this quarrel, after a long detour and multiple contributions, been, in a certain manner, reactivated and resituated today?

Metz: Indeed, I believe that during the great period of, let's say, naïve thinking on the cinema (without intending anything pejorative by this at all, certain of these thinkers were exceptionally brilliant), during the period of naïve thinking on specificity, one of the two currents – and here I am fully in agreement with you – tended to recuperate the cinema as a synthesis of the arts, and this is the period where it was said that the cinema had, for example, realized the Wagnerian dream of the total work of art, or Diderot's dream of a spectacle for the masses that would appeal to all the senses at once, that would mobilize all of them, etc.

Fine. But where do matters lie today?

Well, let's say that we are at the stage, it seems to me, where these conceptions can be resumed – I am not saying they *have* been resumed, but that they *can* be resumed. The general cultural state makes this possible, but not necessary, nor ineluctable. ... It becomes possible to resume these reflections on a more precise basis.

To put it simply: personally, and from my point of view as a semiologist (a point of view, let me clarify, that can only be partial, a partial contribution to a general theory of cinema), what strikes me the most is that the specificity of the cinema cannot be defined in terms of its "material of expression" – I am taking the word in the sense in which Hjelmslev uses it – *that is to say, in terms of the physical or technico-sensorial definition of the signifier.*

In particular, I am thinking of these extremely widespread definitions – to which we cannot even give a name, since they belong to a common vernacular – according to which we are told that the cinema is movement, or that the cinema is the image, for example. These two themes are particularly impoverished and foolish, but they circulate furiously in certain publications.

Now, this genre of definition consists in defining cinematic specificity in terms that Hjelmslev would have called the material of expression, that is, I repeat, the material definition of the signifier.

It is indeed true that film language (if we take film language in its widest sense, that is, as the set of messages that society calls a film) can effectively be defined with technico-sensorial, physical criteria. It is a fact that society bestows the word film on any message whose physical definition is pretty much the following. A film is composed of five materials of expression (here I am speaking of sound films), namely, moving photographic images placed in sequences. I am obliged to clarify all these adjectives in order to differentiate, on the level of the material of expression, cinema from painting, or from the comic book, etc. So: the moving photographic image placed in sequences, that makes one. Secondly, there is phonetic sound – I am still at the level of the material of expression, so I will not say spoken words [*paroles*], but phonetic sound in talking films, then there is musical sound in films with music, and what we call real noises, which is in fact another system of signification, or another set of systems of signification, and finally the graphic trace of written texts. Once again, I will not even say 'written texts', because I am at the level of material, but 'the graphic trace of written texts', that is to say, the title sequence, intertitles, and even written texts figuring in the image itself, for example in the films of Godard, or many others.

So, from this point of view, we can evidently envisage a definition of film language that would be purely technico-sensorial. I hereby understand technique to be on the side of the emission, and sensorial on the side of the reception. In simple terms, such a definition does not seem interesting to me, or even operative, and offers nothing different to what is already implicitly contained in common sense notions of the cinema.

There is another possible notion of film language – this is what I am reflecting on and working on at the moment – which would be formulated in codic terms, that is, not in terms of the material of expression, but in terms of the forms of expression, and the form of the content, in other words, in terms of structures and codes.

In the traditional conception, let us say that there exists a certain number of 'languages' [*langages*] – and I am placing the word between a lot of quotation marks – that are aligned alongside each other, following each other, and uniformly enjoying relationships of exteriority with each other, in the sense in which the logicians use this term, that is, absent of any common zone, as if, for example, it were not possible for a code to be common to several languages. And we imagine, albeit confusedly, that there is a pictorial language, musical language, verbal language, etc., with each one being a homogenous set without any fissures.

On the contrary, it seems to me that one could give the name film language, and this time in terms of codes, to the set of codes that are specific to the cinema and that are not the only ones to appear in films. We would thus be led, in my opinion, towards a new formulation of the difference between the cinematic and the filmic, if we considered that the filmic is the entirety of what appears in films, the set of signifying configurations appearing in films (and many of them are not specific to films, as they equally appear in all sorts of other cultural manifestations, and not only in the novel, the theater, etc., which have always been spoken of in connection with the cinema, but also everyday life, social rhythms, and, in the end, anything you wish; but, from the moment when such structures actually appear in a film, they are filmic, and they can be subject to a coefficient of remodeling which, for its part, is specifically filmic, and which does not prevent the code itself being filmic from the very beginning). Alongside this we can also find other filmic codes, filmic because they appear in films, but that one can, in addition, call cinematic (this is why I speak of a new distinction between cinema and film) in the sense that they are linked to the preferential adoption of the cinema as a vehicle rather than of any other vehicle.

So, there are specific and non-specific codes. Both are filmic, because they can be located in films, but only certain among them are cinematic. Thus, the cinematic is a subset of the filmic.

Among those codes that I would now call cinematic (and not merely filmic), there is the set of structures and configurations that concern the specific arrangements of moving images and large segments of speech (I specifically refer to large segments of speech because the study of smaller segments of speech cannot be carried out by a theory proper to the cinema; the study of speech in its smallest segments, such as phonemes, morphemes, etc., is quite obviously the domain of linguistics, which is another discipline; and from this point of view, at the level of the smaller segments, a film spoken in Italian, for example, is purely and simply content with borrowing a code, another code, which has absolutely nothing cinematic about it, i.e., the Italian language [*langue*]; here we have a good example, particularly crude perhaps, but striking all the same, of a non-cinematic filmic code: in a film in which Italian is spoken one of the codes mobilized is the Italian language, which is in no way cinematic). By contrast, the relationship of the large segments of Italian utterances with the image or with the music of this same film obeys constructions that, for their part, are properly cinematic.

We can thus make a distinction between film and cinema, with the idea that the cinema is only a part of the film, and with the idea which, at bottom, seems to me to be more and more central in contemporary thinking, of a necessary pluralism of codes; the idea, in sum, that we will never get to the bottom of all the semiological material locatable in any film whatsoever, including even the weakest, most common of them all, with the aid of single code.

In other terms, we must carefully distinguish between language [*langage*] and code, we must carefully distinguish between the sets that are given, and that correspond to social perception and the usual social classification such as cinema, painting, theater, etc., and the sets constructed by the analyst.

In yet other terms, we would need to distinguish, it seems to me, between two sorts of homogeneity: the observed homogeneity, which is that of the language [*langage*], and constructed homogeneity, which is of a codic nature, the physical, technico-sensorial units on the one hand, and the purely logical (or codic) units on the other hand, which simply correspond to sets within which one can substitute [*commuter*] codes, but whose boundaries one may not cross.

This is what is known as a code, a field of differentiality, under the influence, among others, of Garroni's book, which has had a major influence on me of late. (Emilio Garroni is an Italian semiologist and aesthetician who is professor of aesthetics at Rome, and who published a book called *Semiotica ed estetica* – that is, *Semiotics and Aesthetics* – in 1968. Although its title does not point this out, Garroni's book is entirely dedicated to the cinema, and its point of departure is the principle of a distinction between code and language [*langage*].)

Fieschi: What you say here seems to imply a certain evolution with respect to your earlier works. On what precise points would you now refute yourself?

Metz: In order to study the cinema, we must abandon any idea that there should be a cinematic code. In this sense, in any case, I was right, in my 1964 article "The Cinema: Language or Language System?," when I said: there is no language system [*langue*] in the cinema. It is quite true that there is not a code in the cinema. But I also believe that I was wrong to have looked for it; obviously, I did not find it, I found its absence, but finding its absence means looking for it in the first place.

There is obviously nothing in the cinema that corresponds to a language system, this goes without saying. But there is, by contrast, within a film, a set of specifically cinematic codes, which are to the cinema, to the cinema as a totality, what the language system is to language, language as a totality.

Saussure had already remarked that the language system is not the entirety of language, that the language system is one of the codes of language. In the same way, I believe, the set of specifically cinematic codes are only one of the sets of codes among those which appear in a film, and which, with respect to the film, play the same role that the language system plays with respect to language.

So I would be, let us say, half self-critical with respect to my work in the years 1963-1964, and even in the two years following, in the sense that – how can I put it? – as much as it is true that from the point of view of internal description, we do not find in the cinema any code that might have the characteristics of a linguistic code, with articulations, etc. (from this point of view, I believe that what I said at the time remains true), and as much as it is true, therefore, that from the point of view of internal description we will find nothing in the cinema that could correspond to a language system. By contrast, from an external point of view, that is, from the point of view of the relationship of codes with each other, we do indeed find an instance which, in the cinema, plays the same role with respect to the other codes that the language system plays with respect to language in general.

From this point of view, therefore, my current position is a little self-critical with respect to the position I held several years ago.

As for the question you put to me regarding the conception of cinema as a synthesis of the arts, from this point of view I think that the cinema actually does offer us the synthesis of several codes, which is what I was just speaking about. It is the synthesis of several *codes*, but this does not at all mean the same thing as the synthesis of several arts, because the *arts*, or what we have traditionally called the arts, the various art forms, each one of them would merit, in my opinion, that we say of them what I have said of the cinema, because each one of them is also a set of codes.

There is a widespread tendency to confuse two matters. From the fact that the cinema is materially composite, because certain of its signifiers are visual, while others are auditory, and so on. In other words, due to the fact that the cinema already includes several languages [*langages*], there is a tendency to conclude that it should, in the end, be more pluri-codic than the other arts. And yet, I believe that we must not confuse material homogeneity, which is specific only to certain means of expression, like the cinema (certain signifiers are physically visual, others are physically auditory, etc., it is a composite on the physico-sensorial level…), that is, we must not confuse this material composite, which characterizes certain art forms and not others, with a much more general and much more essential phenomenon, which is pluri-codicity, and which can very well manifest itself within an art or within a means of expression that is not composite, that is to say, *of which all the signifiers are materially of the same nature*. It is quite evident that in a painting, for example, as someone like Jean-Louis Schefer has ably demonstrated, in spite of the homogeneity of the material of the signifier, which consists uniformly in a series of lines and colors, etc., there are a large number of codes.

Thus, the widespread idea that insists on saying: the cinema is at one and the same time music, because there is a music track, as well as being similar to the dialogues of a novel, because there are speeches, and it is also a painting in motion, because there are images. This idea in fact confounds the physico-sensorial composite with codic pluricity, which is a much more important and much more substantial phenomenon; all the more so because nothing tells us that the different codes within a film coincide with the different sensorial spheres. And here, on this point, I believe that the work of Eisenstein was extremely advanced when he showed, apropos of *Alexander Nevsky* [1938] for example, that the same structures in a given passage in the film (the same structures, that is to say, in my vocabulary: the same code, if we remain at the level of form), or the same code, can apply to the image track and to the music track.

In other words, if there are several codes in the film, this does not mean that the distribution, the division of these codes coincides with the distribution of the sensorial spheres of the film.

Codes are not sensorial spheres, they are sets reconstructed by the analyst, they are fields of commutability, they are fields of differentiality, inside of which the units acquire meaning in relation to one another.

Hence, for this problem of synthesis, I believe the following: every film actually does operate a sort of synthesis, if you will, between several codes, but this synthesis does not seem to me to define the art of cinema in general. I believe that we are concerned, here, with a combination of several codes, and that this combination is different in each film. Consequently, the instance that operates this synthesis is not the cinema, as the old aestheticians said, but rather, the instance that operates this synthesis is the film, that is, the *text* (the word synthesis, by the way, is not to my liking, and not only due to the rather antiquated air the word has to it).

At present, therefore, I would be tempted to distinguish between, let's say, two types of systems: the codic systems, that is, the systems that are codes, or codes *tout court*, whose specific quality is to be applied to several texts without concern for any of them individually, on the one hand, and, on the other hand, textual systems, that is to say systems linked to a text, to a single text in particular. Obviously, I have taken the word 'text' in a sense in which each film is itself a text. Here, the combination of different codes is operative, and not at the level of some kind of cinema in a metaphysical realm, but in *every* film, inasmuch as it is a textual unfolding [*déroulement*], and inasmuch as this textual unfolding is itself constructed and can itself be taken as a corpus by the analyst. Here there is a textual system that combines several codes, a textual system constructed from several codes, and not from a single code – on this matter, too, I have changed my mind – and above all a textual system that is constructed against these codes just as much as it is constructed with them. I would say that it is constructed on the basis of them – with 'on the basis of them' meaning on, with and against them. It is constructed on the basis of them; that is to say that, on the one hand, each film takes different structures that were either in earlier films, or elsewhere, that were wandering around somewhere within the culture; or, on the other hand, it is the specific nature of every film, insofar as it is declared to be a stable unfolding text, to actively add value [*projeter dans les redevances*] to the codes on which it is constructed. It is the text's specific nature to declare that the only relevant system is at the level of the combination and displacement of these codes, and not at the level of these codes themselves.

Fieschi: From this perspective, how would you define the current tasks of film analysis?

Metz: At present, I find that there are two tasks for film analysts (by this I mean those film analysts who place themselves in a semiological perspective, because there are plenty of other types as well...). These two tasks are related but distinct, and the principles of pertinence they obey are twofold: firstly, there is the study of codes, and more particularly the specific codes of the cinema, and secondly there is the study of filmic textual systems, which is what is currently called the study of films. I would immediately add, by the way, that the denomination 'study of films' appears absurd to me, because whoever studies a cinematic code also studies films.

If you consider that studying films means that the given object on which the analysis is developed is the film, then in this case it remains true that whoever studies a cinematic code has, as their point of departure, the film, and whoever studies a filmic textual system, that is, the system of a filmic text, also has, as their point of departure, a film. The only difference is that the analysis of a textual system has, as its point of departure, a single film and studies all of its codes, as well as, perhaps even more so, the manner in which these codes displace each other, combine with each other and form what we earlier called a synthesis. (But, in my opinion, it is more a general movement of displacement, which is at the same time a form of placement [*mise en place*], so it would be a displacement-placement, that is to say that there is a general displacement of the codes that influence each other, and at the end of which each one of the codes finds its place in the very unfolding of the filmic text...). Nevertheless, the study of a filmic textual system has *a* film as its point of departure, whereas the study of cinematic codes has *film* as its point of departure. In the study of a cinematic code, we do not have, as the point of departure, a film in its entirety, but partial segments of several films, a cinematic code concerning several films – either all films if it is a cinematic code, or (which equally occurs) an entire class of films if it is a cinematic sub-code: the code of the Western, things like that. Hence, in any case, whoever studies a cinematic code or sub-code has film as their point of departure. They simply have a great number of films – as opposed to the analysis of the textual system – and none of the films are studied in their entirety; for if one studies a cinematic code, let's say the code of the usage of the paradigm of the dissolve in the films of a given era, a given nation and a given genre (here is a good example of the study of a cinematic sub-code), at this point it would be necessary to have, as material, all the films of this era, of this genre, of this nation, but it is not necessary to study them in their totality. At no moment would any of these films be studied as a singular totality, whereas this is precisely the goal of textual analysis, which takes a single film only, but takes it as a singular totality.

The analyst of cinematic codes – or sub-codes, it is the same thing – will always, it seems to me, consider more than a film and less than a film: more than a film because a code, by definition, is an anonymous structure that concerns several messages without specifically concerning any one of them (as there will be several films in the corpus); and less than a film because if I study, for example, the code of the dissolve, I am only authorized, methodologically speaking, to investigate in my group of films those isolated passages where there are dissolves, unless there is a need for catalysis (in Hjelmslev's sense of the term, that is, unless there is a need for taking into account the elements that necessarily enter into relations with the dissolve, then we are obliged to bring catalysis into operation). Catalysis minimally re-establishes, that is, takes into account, elements other than those fixed by the principle of pertinence, but only by mobilizing the minimum number of them. Hjelmslev called catalysis the fact that, for example, if you want to study the subject-predicate structure in a given language, and if the utterance that has been recorded on tape and that has been provided by the informant only bears the subject, then one can re-establish the predicate, but it alone, if it is the subject-predicate structure that one is studying. Thus, catalysis is the minimum addition to the methodologically indispensable corpus that facilitates research in relation to the principle of pertinence that has been adopted.

I said that there is currently, in relation to the cinema, two major types of study inspired by semiology, which involves either pursuing a code across several texts (the study of codes), or studying all the codes in a text (textual analysis, the analysis of a filmic textual system). The only difference is that what we see when we are the spectator of a film is the unfolding of the text, and the textual system is the intelligibility of this same unfolding such as it can be established by the analyst, or if needs be by the creator himself, insofar as he undertakes the deconstruction of his work, self-explanation, etc.

Fieschi: In certain periods of critical thinking (and this danger is still far from being averted), people – Bazin for example – have often fallen into a type of essentialism, pure and simple. Certain cinematic figures have thus been adorned with intrinsic qualities (cf. "The Life and Death of Superimposition" by Bazin[1]) and, at the same time, have been either valorized or prohibited. Here there is a veritable dogmatic, normative peril, conceivable at the level of aesthetic tendencies (for such perils have often led to progress in research), but unacceptable at the level of so-called scientific analysis.

Metz: This normative peril, which until now has only very rarely been avoided, was itself linked to what you call, quite correctly, essentialism – that is, the idea of values, in which each cinematic procedure, each cinematic figure, has a certain value. In sum, each cinematic procedure possesses a meaning, or even three or four easily catalogued meanings, like a polysemic word in language systems, it is basically the same... This essentialist idea inevitably resulted in normative conceptions because one was either for this value, or one was against it, and one either had to say that dissolves must be used, or that dissolve must not be used, or superimpositions, and so on.

To my mind, the problem can now be posed in an entirely different way. I believe that a great number of cinematic figures are – at the level of the most general cinematic codes – *signifiers without a signified*, that is, there is a certain number of figures of which one can say that they are cinematic because their realization (even in the most literal form) requires cinematic equipment. The signifier appears on the level of general cinematic codes; the signified, meanwhile, appears either in the cinematic sub-codes, or in the filmic textual systems – the dissolve has a given value in a given film – or, if needs be, in both. In other words, it assumes an initial meaning that is still rather general at the level of the sub-code; and then it subsequently receives additional meaning through its place – that is, its displacement and its placement – in the textual system of a particular film.

Note

1. [English translation published in *Film-Philosophy* Vol. 6 No. 1 (January 2002): http://www.film-philosophy.com/index.php/f-p/article/view/665/578]

3. Interview on Film Semiology

Raymond Bellour and Christian Metz

Buckland, Warren and Daniel Fairfax (eds), *Conversations with Christian Metz: Selected Interviews on Film Theory (1970–1991)*. Amsterdam: Amsterdam University Press, 2017.

DOI: 10.5117/9789089648259/CH3

Abstract
In this wide-ranging interview, carried out by Raymond Bellour for the journal *Semiotica* in 1971, Christian Metz outlines the progression of his film semiology from his earliest essays in 1964 to his book *Langage et cinéma* (1971). He discusses his *grande syntagmatique*, the notion of code, and introduces the distinction between 'film analysis' and 'film semiology'.

Keywords: Christian Metz, film theory, film semiology, film analysis

'Entretien sur la Sémiologie du Cinéma,' Raymond Bellour et Christian Metz. *Semiotica*, 4, 1 (1971), pp. 1-30. Reprinted by permission of Walter De Gruyter Publishers. Translated by Daniel Fairfax.

Raymond Bellour: Can we consider your *Essais sur la Signification au Cinéma* (Paris, Klincksieck 1968) as the first book of film semiology?

Christian Metz: On a level that I would call 'official', we could indeed, and it has been done. Nonetheless, in my opinion, this is not the first book where we can find reflections of this nature. We must not forget the various contributions of the Russian formalists, in particular the collective anthology *Poetika Kino* (*Film Poetics*), on which Shklovsky, Tynianov and Eichenbaum collaborated. Additionally, in a more diffuse, scattered manner, there are certain passages in the writings of the best film critics and/or theorists: Eisenstein, obviously, but also Arnheim, Balázs, Bazin, Laffay, Mitry; and, in another perspective, Cohen-Séat and Morin. These authors (and others I have not thought of at present) posed with a reasonable degree of precision various problems of *signification* – it would thus be absurd to flatly ignore them under the pretext that they did not officially brandish the 'semiological' label.

What we can say, simply, is that my 1968 book is the first work on film that explicitly and systematically draws on the concepts and methods of modern linguistic theory.

In sum, I wanted to *get to the bottom of the 'film language' metaphor*, to try to see what it hid, and in view of this goal to mobilize in a sustained yet 'compact' manner the experience of those who have best studied language – that is, linguists.

Bellour: The text introducing the second section of your book, its true core, expresses this very precisely. (Let us recall that these *Essais*, various contributions that perfectly complement one another, are ordered in four sections:
1. "Phenomenological Approaches to the Cinema"
2. "Problems of Film Semiology"
3. "The Syntagmatic Analysis of the Image Track"
4. "The 'Modern' Cinema: Some Theoretical Problems.")
This decisive, relatively polemical text poses by its very title ("The Cinema: Language or Language System?") the question that is of necessity located at the origin of the semiological project.

Metz: In effect, Lévi-Strauss says in *Structural Anthropology*, with regards to rites and different ethnological systems, that we can and must pose, for every system of signification (I won't say 'system of signs', because the notion of the sign, narrower than that of signification, is much less central to semiology today than it was in the past), a fundamental question which is something like this: to what extent is it actually a language [*langage*]? The only system that is thoroughly made to signify is language in the strict sense of the term (= phonic, or 'articulated' language). As for all the others (those that semiology studies), there intervenes a prejudicial question that is well formulated by Lévi-Strauss. This question is both prejudicial and contradictory, because in order to respond to it we must, in a sense, have already covered the fields of knowledge that it allows us to define: we must have already *saturated* what it *opens*.

Bellour: How did this question come to be uttered in the cinematic field?

Metz: Its formulation is based on an astonishment, which explains why the 1964 text ("Cinema: Language or Language System?") can appear so polemical. My astonishment was at seeing numerous works dedicated to 'film language' that totally dispensed with the findings of linguistic research, but that nonetheless insistently affirmed the idea that the cinema is a language, or a language system. What's more, it has often occurred (even in Eisenstein) that these last two terms are employed as if they were synonymous.

I wanted to uncouple these two terms, as is apparent in the very title of the 1964 article. My starting point here was the Saussurian notion of *language system* (which would no longer be the case today, at least not in the same manner), or more precisely the Saussurian trichotomy 'language system/speech/language', which defines language as a vast ensemble of phenomena in which are grouped the language system (a very well-organized system) on the one hand, and various speech acts on the other hand. It seemed to me that the cinema could be compared to a language, but not to a language system: one does not find, in the cinema, a highly integrated set of fixed structures, which defines a language system, but one does find recurrent assemblages, more or less codified schemas, 'patterns' of all kinds, which evoke the phenomena of partial codification proper to 'speech', or rather to what we now call discourse, in the sense that Benveniste, for example, understands this term. (I have become, in the meantime, quite skeptical about the notion of 'speech', at least once it is conceived as a sort of unorganized residue; 'speech', in reality, is a set of sub-codes.)

In traditional literature on film, one of the most widespread ideas is that the cinema is a language because images are organized within the sequence like words are organized within a sentence. Now, not only are these two modes of assemblage entirely different (as both structural linguistics and transformational generative linguistics show), but furthermore the shot is in no way assimilable to a word, and nor is the sequence assimilable to a sentence. If you must seek out assimilations, it would be less false to liken the shot itself with, if not the sentence, then at least a discursive segment on the level of the *utterance* [*énoncé*].

This allows, I feel, for a sort of morality: very often, excessive linguistic assimilations do not involve *too much* dependency on linguistics, but *too little*.

A little linguistics leaves one disoriented, but a little more leaves one enlightened. There are two sides to this remark. It is polemical, because among the reproaches of unwarranted linguisticity that have been made against me (as is the case with many semiologists), there are some that I categorically deny. But it is also self-critical: my own reflections on the relations between linguistics and film analysis (and notably in the article we are speaking about) had not been sufficiently thought through. Since then, I have been hard at work, and there still remains much work to do.

Nonetheless, I persist in believing that the majority of traditional considerations on film language rested on a type of widespread misunderstanding of logical successivity. In the first stage the cinema is declared to be a language. In the second stage it is studied like a language system. In the third stage (if I can put it like that), linguistics is ignored, even though it is the study of language systems and their relationship to language.

The semiological enterprise, at the beginning, appeared to me to have two sides. The first, the negative side, involves clarifying what the cinema is not (we thereby proceed by difference with what we know about language systems, which have the advantage of being better known). The second, positive side, theoretically following on from the first (even if, in the mind of the researcher, they ceaselessly depend on each other in a bidirectional dynamic), must study what the cinema is. Linguistics, then, remains useful for its methods, to the extent that it transcends itself in moving towards a general semiology. It thus serves a twofold function in the study of the cinema, but not in the same way, and it is not exactly the same linguistics.

Bellour: This negative, critical phase indeed appears totally decisive, and I believe that the weight of the equivocations linked to the history of film art and film theory largely explains the acute terminological rigor of your book. You bring to an end a movement whose two extremes are simultaneously incomparable and comparable: one, that of Dziga Vertov and Eisenstein, where the excessive reference to language is inscribed in the purely creative, futurist perspective of the cinema as the language of revolution, an admirable utopia with scientific lyricism destined to interpret reality through the methodological prism of historical materialism; the other, that of all those film 'grammars', which are essentially reductive and passé, insofar as, operating *a posteriori* a wild assimilation with the structures of phonic language and, through them, the expressivity of literary forms, it denies the art of cinema any specificity. (Let us note that while the former programmatically target the being of the cinema, in reality they instruct us about the structures and the genesis of their own films; the latter meanwhile, speaking naïvely in the name of all films, are logically led back to only ever being able to utter erroneous propositions on any given film.)

I think it is particularly important that the terms that until now have been almost taboo – *shot* and *sequence* – appear, at the conclusion of this negative operation, to lose value, any stable reference, whether this be an extrinsic one, with respect to the language system, or an intrinsic one, insofar as the raising of any trace of phonic language breaks them up and redistributes them according to a specific code, analogically determined by the linguistic model, and whose positioning [*mise en place*] constitutes the truly positive aspect of your work.

In all this, it seems to me that film semiology has only been able to provoke a series of oppositions, to the extent that it also confronts head-on an idealist tradition that, far from wishing to recognize a language system [*langue*] in the cinema, denies it even the possibility of being considered a language [*langage*].

Metz: It does indeed challenge the validity of a dual trend: on the one hand, a metaphysics of the *visible*, which constitutes the cinema, on the basis of its photographic precision, as an authentic double of reality, maintaining it in some way *beneath* language; on the other hand, a confused and spontaneous ideology of pure creativity, which initially propels cinema *beyond* language.

For me, film semiology seems to offer, among other things, the possibility of overcoming this double pitfall, by considering, on the one hand, that the film assembles various spectacles in a different way to what they were or would be in a-filmic perception (known as 'reality') – and that it is thus an act of language, and on the other hand, that filmic productivity is only intelligible on the basis of a set of pre-existing codes, even if their combination (or, sometimes, their destruction) remains a fully 'creative' act.

I would add that the resistance of the resolute defenders of the citadel of iconicity (and visuality) – those who accuse semiology of utilizing linguistic notions to tackle a non-linguistic object (this last point, by the way, is not even true since the advent of talking cinema) – finds its analogue in the resistance of linguistic purism, which aims to critique all exportation of linguistic notions outside its own field. These two forms of resistance, which come from entirely different horizons, nonetheless manifest a kind of objective complicity, because they both communally rest on the idea of 'undue extrapolation', thus risking an abandonment of the study of cinema in favor of the generalizations of the worst of traditional aesthetics.

Personally, I find that there is a lot to say on the very notion of 'undue extrapolation'. Linguistics offers us two distinct types of concepts that the semiologist must untangle from each other. It is evident that a notion such as that of the *phoneme*, for instance, does not concern all signifying systems; nor is the question of claiming to locate phonemes within the film image (here I am thinking of certain reproaches that [Pierre] Francastel has addressed to semiology, and which seem to me to be ill-founded – all the more so given that his own work, in my opinion, is authentically semiological in nature, setting aside all debates on labels). In no case is it a matter of exporting to semiology those linguistic concepts that are linked to language [*langue*] alone. But in the work of linguists, we also find a series of notions that are of great interest to general semiology.

Bellour: In the sense that, for Saussure, linguistics was only a privileged sector of general semiology.

Metz: Exactly. And this according to two different modalities (but which both lead to the same result): either, in certain cases, linguists, when defining a term, situate it initially in the explicit perspective of general semiology, thus forbidding the very idea of a '*borrowing* from linguistics' (see the 'sign' in Saussure, 'form/substance/ matter' and 'content/expression' in Hjelmslev, etc.); or, alternatively, such and such a notion was posed by linguists who did not especially think of semiology, but was defined in a movement and an acceptance which were sufficiently ample that they enabled the notion to be rightfully applied to codes other than phonic language systems. 'Paradigm' and 'syntagm', such as they have been defined by Martinet, are legitimately exportable concepts, because the fact that units may be co-present in a text, or that, inversely (if we can put it like that), they may be 'co-absent' – a unit of the text being commutable with another one which is not in the text – is in no way linked to the specificity of language systems. The syntagmatic fact and the paradigmatic fact do not number among those that separate language systems from other codes, but which connect them. There is therefore no unjustified borrowing (and, at bottom, no borrowing at all): we simply draw from general semiology's arsenal of notions, which happens to have been constituted, to a significant extent, by linguists, but which has been equally elaborated by logicians, psychoanalysts, specialists in informatics, etc.

Nevertheless, there remains, among many people, a kind of reflex, a genuine blockage. If a notion has been emphasized by a writer who was a linguist by occupation, it is once and for all 'purely linguistic', prohibited from being exported. The only thing that counts is the profession of the father.

Bellour: How, in your view, has semiological description in the strict sense, on the basis of this prior operation of destruction-definition, been concretized?

Metz: I chose to study closely a cinematic code, which I called the code of the *grande syntagmatique*. It is one cinematic code among many others. Today,

I am fully aware of this – but when I was carrying out this research things were much less clear in my mind: I was studying *one* code of the cinema, but without brushing aside from the margins of my consciousness the vague impression that it was possibly *the* code of the cinema (the vacillation is noticeable in my book).

In any case, my starting point was the notion of the 'sequence', which is endowed with a strong degree of sociological existence, as much in the practice of filmmakers as it is in the perception of spectators. It seemed to me that this vague term 'sequence' in fact covered several distinct modes of combining images, that these different modes entered into opposition with each other, were organized in a code, and that they were finite in number in a given synchronic state of film language (even if a later evolution of the language-object can modify this code, just like any other code). I have clarified the very notion of the sequence with the linguistic concept of the *syntagma*, because a sequence, by definition, is an alignment of several successive images co-present in the text (= the film). As for the differences separating the various types of sequence from each other, I gave them the name *paradigms*. By substituting them for each other, I strove to take stock of the various types of sequence that are distinguishable in the image-track of narrative films from the classical era (= three limitations, therefore, in order to reach an object that could even come close to being mastered). I thus arrived at a paradigm with eight types, or rather twelve types, as the first type contains five sub-types.

This is the example of a code which is at once, and indistinctly, 'grammatical' and 'rhetorical'. Grammatical, because it assures the most literal intelligibility of the visual narrative (it is a code of denotation, although, on top of this, it strongly connotes). Rhetorical, because it concerns syntagmatic elements of major dimensions (= 'sequences', precisely), and because it is thus tied to the composition of the film and its narrative organization (it is a code of *dispositio*, in the technical sense that this word had in classical rhetoric). Of course, there are other codes that organize, in the film, the play of elements of a smaller syntagmatic dimension (the relation of motifs within a single shot, etc.); but as we advance towards the 'smaller' elements, we encounter a problem that, for me (even today) remains open: among the codes intervening on this level, which ones are specifically cinematic, and which ones are integrated into the filmed spectacle? In the latter case, we are dealing with what is commonly called, in discussions of cinema, 'reality', that is to say, in fact, a set of perceptive, iconographic and symbolic structures which pre-exist the intervention of the camera, which is content to *relay*, under the cover of analogical recording (the notions of 'representation' and 'iconicity' used by the American semioticians, or Charles Sanders Peirce's 'likeness') – something which does not preclude superimposing its specific codes on them.

To return to the larger segments (sequential types), I was struck by the lack of distinction, in the domain of film studies, between grammar and rhetoric. Under various forms, this idea was also expressed by others (recently, for example, by Pasolini and Mitry). Connotation can be extracted from the very form of denotation; by choosing between several denotative structures, a connotative signifier can also be established. Maybe the language system (the phonic language system) is the only code in which we can isolate a 'pure' grammar logically separable (even by abstraction) from all rhetoric, even if this is only because of the existence of *several* idioms? Obviously we should leave aside, in this discussion, those codes which, at least ideally, have no connotation whatsoever (mathematical languages, logical languages, etc.). But it is too early to draw conclusions on such a vast and complex problem.

Bellour: Can you briefly recall the eight types of this '*grande syntagmatique*'?

Metz: I initially make a distinction between the *autonomous shot* (type no. 1) and the seven other types. The autonomous shot is a single shot equivalent to a 'sequence' (= an entire episode of the film treated in a single shot); the seven other types (including types 2 and 8) are sequences in the proper sense of the word: each one has several shots and thus rests on 'film editing' in the narrower sense of the term (splicing shots together [*collure*]).

The autonomous shot includes, on the one hand, the 'sequence-shot', well known by film analysts and frequently studied since Bazin, and on the other hand what I have called 'inserts': single shots which owe their autonomy to their status of syntagmatic *interpolation* in the filmic chain, and which are not on the same level of reality as contiguous images (a typical example: the non-diegetic metaphor, which presents an object external to the action of the film and only having a 'comparative' value). I have distinguished four kinds of inserts, the definitions of which would take us too long to recall here.

Within the 'autonomous syntagmas' (= 2 to 8), the a-chronological syntagmas (2 and 3) are opposed to the chronological syntagmas (4 to 8). In the a-chronological syntagmas, the filmic discourse deliberately abstains from clarifying what, in the storyline, is the chronological relationship between the different images of the same 'sequence' (= a momentary, voluntary defection of the signified from temporal denotation). Here we find the *parallel syntagma* (type no. 2), better known under the name of 'parallel montage': several recurrent motifs are interwoven together, to directly symbolic ends, without any knowledge of their temporal relation in the action of the film. There is also the *bracket syntagma* (type no. 3): a succession of brief evocations that the film does not 'date' with respect to one another, but which it gives as samples of an identical order of realities (by way of example: the initial erotic evocations in Jean-Luc Godard's *Une femme mariée* [1964]).

In the chronological syntagmas (4 to 8), the film explains the literal temporality – and not only the symbolic or 'profound' temporality – that links the images of a sequence to each other. The *descriptive syntagma* (type no. 4) represents the only case where this temporality consists exclusively in simultaneities. (It is a matter here, of course, of the temporality of the signified; on the level of the signifier, every 'sequence', whatever it is, consists of the unfolding of a succession of events.)

Opposed to the descriptive syntagma are the various narrative syntagmas (5 to 8), in which the temporal relations between shots – which are still relations of the signified – can be categorized as consecutive. When a single 'sequence' presents, in alternation, several (most frequently, two) distinct events consecutively, we are dealing with the *alternate syntagma* (type no. 5), often called 'cross-cutting' [*montage alterné*]. For example, a shot of the pursuers, then a shot of the pursued, then a shot of the pursuers, etc. Between the different images of each series of events, the relation is consecutive. Between the two series taken *en bloc*, the relation is simultaneous.

Distinguished from the alternate syntagma are linear narrative syntagmas (6 to 8), 'sequences' dedicated to a single consecutive action. In the case of the *scene properly speaking* (type no. 6), the chronological limits of the single consecutiveness of the signifier (= what unfolds on the screen) and the single consecutiveness of the signified (= the temporality of the fiction) coincide: the scene 'lasts in real time', even though it results from the editing of several separate shots (= there can be spatial hiatuses, but not temporal hiatuses).

On the contrary, these temporal hiatuses – moments that 'jump', and that can be perceived to do so – characterize the sequences properly speaking (types 7 and 8): single but discontinuous consecutive actions (it is in this sense that, among the eight types, only they truly merit the name of sequence). In the *episodic sequence* (type no. 7), discontinuity is erected into a principle of construction and intelligibility, the segment is built around its ellipses: each image resumes a 'phase' or a 'stage' of a long, monodirectional evolution, and is separated from the preceding and following images by a major gap. For example, the famous sequence from *Citizen Kane* (Orson

Welles, 1941) where we see, in a sort of short-cut, the affectionate relations of the hero and his first wife progressively deteriorate before our eyes. On the contrary, the *ordinary sequence* (type no. 8), which is very frequently employed in films, is content to dispose of its ellipses in a dispersed order, in order to 'skip' those moments that it intends to skip, and thus without conferring a short-cut value to the others.

There you have it. I have tried to summarize, in order to respond to your question, the general tableau of my '*grande syntagmatique*', such as I conceived of it in 1968 (see text no. 5 of my *Essais sur la signification au cinema* [chapter 5 of *Film Language*]). But I fear that I have been both too brief and too long-winded...

Bellour: What is the domain of applicability for this code, to the extent that you have us understand that it responds to a given synchronic state of film language, which you designate, in this case, by the term 'classical narrative cinema'?

Metz: It seems to me that the *grande syntagmatique* translates the effort the cinema has made to return to the classical 19th century novel. The eight types of sequences are charged with expressing different kinds of spatio-temporal relations between successive images within an episode, so that the film can have a clear and univocal storyline, and the spectator can always tell if image no. 3, on the level of the diegesis (the signified) 'takes place' before image no. 2, or after it, or at the same time, etc. Historically, the validity of this code overlaps with what I would call the 'classical' cinema: since the stabilization of the sound film (in the early 1930s), up to the first manifestations of what is known as 'modern' cinema, which can be approximately situated, in France, to around 1955 (= the first short films of the *nouvelle vague*). Obviously, many films made after 1955 have remained very classical in the way they are made and do not witness any effort at innovation, at least on the level of what is considered here; to this extent, the grid that I have just summarized can be applied to them.

There are also *generic* limitations. This code only applies to narrative cinema (= fiction films), and so it excludes – unless the grid is specifically rearranged on the basis of a new *corpus* – pedagogical cinema and a certain category of documentary films.

As for 'modern' films, their goal, and/or their effect, is precisely to enrich, modify, loosen and diversify (and sometimes even to destroy or corrupt) this *grande syntagmatique*. This amounts to saying that the structures are situated in history, and that in the cinema (as elsewhere) there is diachrony.

It is not an essential aspect of the cinema to have eight types of sequences (supposing that there even are eight of them, that is, supposing that I have not committed an error of formalization). This character is attached to given films in a given period.

Bellour: I suppose that the establishment of this code is the result of an inquiry that is all the more empirical given that you are the first to have considered the cinema entirely from this angle.

Metz: Certainly. We cannot even conceive that an empirical inquiry, even if it is restrained to a defined period and genre (which would already comprise thousands of films), manages to unconditionally establish that there are not, in such and such a film, sequences unable to be categorized in one of the eight types. We cannot view every film sequence by sequence. The table of the *grande syntagmatique* has been obtained, inevitably, in a rather intuitive manner: successively viewing numerous films of this genre and this period led me to progressively add more types of sequences until the moment when, having arrived at eight of them, I could not find a ninth. In semiology, this is what is known as the saturation of the corpus, when examining the text no longer reveals a new structural figure, but only new occurrences of figures already located.

Here we touch on the problem known as *discovery procedures*. In linguistics itself, the most recent theories judge that they do not exist. This is *a fortiori* the case in semiology, where we are groping around much more.

Bellour: It seems that the constitution of the *grande syntagmatique* comes up against an obstacle that you underline in a long footnote, which applies to the very high degree of complication that the first type in your table offers. You reach a point where you express the idea that it might be necessary to create *two* syntagmatic tables of the image-track. What do you mean by this?

Metz: There is indeed a complication in the autonomous shot, and above all in the 'sequence-shot' which is one of its sub-types (I will not mention the other sub-types, such as inserts). The era that my *grande syntagmatique* covers is principally characterized by what Bazin called 'classical *découpage*': an analytic *découpage* which, in order to apprehend a complex segment of the action, prefers to fragment it into several successive shots rather than film it in continuity. We then find ourselves, by definition, in one of the seven other types of my classification (= autonomous segments formed of several shots). But before and after this classical period, filmmakers have been more willing, in their practice, to allow the inclusion of much longer and more complex elements of the storyline in a single shot. This often happened in Feuillade's films, for example, and it often happens, to varying degrees, in 'modern' cinema, which Bazin correctly defined, in a rather symbolic manner, by the appearance of the sequence-shot. But these periodizations overlap each other – and are intertwined with one another – in such a way that the films I have dealt with offered me both sequence-shots (type no. 1) and syntagmas (types 2 to 8). This coexistence is particularly striking in the work of Orson Welles, for example.

The sequence shot, a particularly long and complex variety of the autonomous shot, gives rise to an internal construction ('internal montage', as it is sometimes called), which plays on the duration of the continuous take (see the famous gluttony episode in Welles' *Magnificent Ambersons* [1942]), the axial staging of the motifs (= the problem of depth of field; see the episode of the pianist in *The Best Years of Our Lives* [1946] by William Wyler), their lateral staging (= the width of the field; see the crossed paths of the characters in *La Règle du Jeu* [1939] by Renoir), characters entering and leaving the frame, etc. In short, it plays on a whole range of spatio-temporal relations, but which the filmic discourse operates inside a single shot, without recourse to cutting [*collure*].

What also strikes me is that in the sequence shot we can find, at least up to a certain point, various spatio-temporal schemas that equally appear in the types that I have numbered 2 to 8. A given logical connection which, in these latter cases, is operated by montage in the narrow sense can also be achieved within a sequence shot, by means of camera movements. Here we have an idea that was clearly formulated by Jean Mitry: montage in the broader sense (= the general activity of syntagmatic assemblage) is a more expansive notion than mere 'editing' [*collage*]. It can be a *description*, in a film. So it can be carried out in several shots (shot 1: the stream; shot 2: an adjacent tree; etc.) – in which case it is a 'descriptive syntagma' (type no. 4). But it can also be brought about in a single shot – the passage of visual details being here the result of a pan. Now, the logical schema is the same in both cases: the consecutiveness of signifying elements = a simultaneity of corresponding signifieds (this is the very definition of the term 'description').

In this sense, the methodological task would consist in pinpointing which of my syntagmas (of types 2 to 8) are susceptible to having equivalents within the sequence shot. Not all of them are. It is obvious, for example, that the bracket syntagma or the episodic sequence could not be realized in a single shot.

We thus arrive at a second table in the *grande syntagmatique*, which would more specifically concern 'internal' montage. In comparison to the syntagmatic table, its homology would be partial and lacunary in nature. As for the *grande syntagmatique* itself, it finds itself split into two, in a way. Our present type no. 1 would no longer be placed on the same axis as the seven other types.

Nonetheless, I left it in there – for the meantime. Why? Because the sequence shot (as its name indicates, by the way) is commutable with a true sequence, and represents, in comparison with the entire film, a subdivision of the same rank. Certain linguists estimate that, in order to get to the bottom of the phonological system of a particular language system [*langue*], it is more economical to establish two distinct sub-systems, one for vowels and one for consonants. All the same, in language systems such as French, a consonant can commute with a vowel, and this substitution may suffice to differentiate two morphemes whose phonematic tenor is otherwise identical. These problems, as you can see, only have a methodological resemblance with my own. But this counts, and it has helped me to glimpse – but only glimpse, at least at the present moment – the possibility of dividing my typology of 'classical' sequences into two.

Bellour: It is certain that the mere constitution of a second table allows us to incorporate, without an excessive degree of schematism, a film like *Rope* [1948] for example, which Hitchcock, as if he were intentionally laying a trap for the semiologist, insisted on filming in a single shot (or in eight shots, if you want to take account of the pans to black determined by the length of film contained in the camera's magazines) but where we can find, within this codic displacement, all the laws of assemblage specific to his other films, which are constructed on an extreme fragmentation of the shot. (Hitchcock rightly states: "The camera movements and the movements of the actors exactly reconstituted my usual way of cutting, that is to say, I maintained the principle of the proportion of images with respect to the emotional importance of a given moment.")

It seems to me that this double table also presents the advantage of being able to alleviate a certain arbitrary periodization. I was actually quite struck by the fact that, by approximately delineating the classical cinema to the years between around 1933 (the stabilization of sound film) and 1955 (the appearance of 'modern' cinema), you naturally cited the most remarkable examples of sequence shots in films like *The Magnificent Ambersons* and *Rules of the Game*, which date from the 1940s. It is as if the classical cinema lost its unified nature as soon as it had found it, and as if your diversified code was capable of marking, more than the overly simplistic division between periods, the levels that make them intermesh with one another, hence allowing us to re-establish, with the rigor of formalization, the concrete motion and pluralism of a historical process.

Metz: Your second hypothesis corresponds to the attitude I have adopted towards my own work. In the book we are speaking about [*Essais sur la Signification au Cinema/Film Language*], a large number of copious footnotes demonstrate my dissatisfactions and the problems that remain unresolved (= the notions of 'alternating syntagma', 'frequentative variant of a syntagma', etc.). I think there remains much work to be done.

Conversely, I criticize my classification, in its current state, for placing on the same level types that I would call *hard* and other types that seem *soft* to my mind. Hence, the bracket syntagma or the non-diegetic insert are very distinct, particular configurations that can be easily recognized without error. At the opposite end of the spectrum, the ordinary sequence or scene has rather indistinct contours. Sometimes it is difficult to distinguish them from a shapeless mass, isolate them from the general filmic flux.

In my opinion, there is no need to hide the fact that film semiology as a discipline is still in its infancy (this does not, however, prevent it from having made considerable progress in comparison to traditional reflections on film language). We are starting off from zero (or almost zero). This is why I feel – including in the affectivity of my work – a considerable disproportion between the breadth of my efforts and the degree of certainty for the results attained up to now. This is a result of the *situation* – in both scientific and historical terms. I think we have to accept this, and keep going forward nonetheless.

Bellour: You said you were tempted, when you started your research, to consider the *grande syntagmatique* of the image-track as *the* code of the cinema, whereas it appears to you now as merely one code among others. This pluralization of codes presents a field of essential questions that you have not truly addressed in your book.

Metz: In fact, this problem of the plurality of codes was not ripe in my mind at the moment when I wrote this book. It happens that the first code I studied is that to which I gave the name *grande syntagmatique* (it is also the only one which, for the moment, I have studied in a truly detailed fashion). This is the source of a certain wavering that is inscribed in the book itself: in some passages, I explicitly state that it is one code among others, but elsewhere I let it be understood that, even if it is not exactly the cinema's only code, it could at least be its most important code.

Today, the pluralist hypothesis strikes me as the only one that gives us a chance of mastering a film's semiological material. At the beginnings of semiological research, it is difficult to escape a sort of common representation that seeks to recognize *a language code* – aligning languages such as 'film language', 'musical language', verbal language', etc. with each other in a relationship of uniform exteriority (in the logical sense of the term). In fact, this is to confuse language with code.

The same year as my *Essais*, Emilio Garroni published a book on film semiology, *Semiotica ed Estetica* (Bari, Laterza 1968), which helped me a lot to reflect on this point in a self-critical perspective. This book established, with great clarity, the distinction between 'language' and 'code', which is not very well formulated in my *Essais*, but occupies a central place in my current thinking, and notably in the book that I am in the process of completing [*Language and Cinema*]. It seems to me that we can give the name 'language' to a unity that defines itself in terms of its *material of expression* (a Hjelmslevian notion), or the 'typical sign' as Barthes puts it in *Elements of Semiology*. Literary language is the set of messages whose material of expression is writing (primarily physical writing); film language is the set of messages that are identical in their material of expression, which is fivefold: moving photographic images, recorded phonetic sound, recorded noises, recorded musical sound, and writing (intertitles, credit sequences, etc.). Hence 'language' is a technico-sensorial unity, immediately discernible in perceptive experience, and consequently in the usual social classifications: 'cinema', 'painting', 'gesture', etc.

Conversely, a code is a purely logical and relational set that only the analyst may construct, and which is not based on material but on *form*, in the sense understood by Hjelmselv (= form of content + form of expression). A code is a field of commutability, signifying differences. Thus, there can be several codes in a single language, and inversely a single code can manifest itself in several different languages (see Garroni's book).

Garroni, by the way, goes further than me in this line of thinking. He adjudges that only languages are specific, and that codes are not: what is specific to the cinema is the combination of several codes, and this alone. And so each one of the codes can be found in other languages, and does not have specific links to the cinema.

I do not think it is necessary to go this far: I explained my views on this matter in an article ('Spécificité des codes et spécificité des langages,' *Semiotica* 1: 4 [1969], 370-396), which constitutes something of a reply to

Garroni, and which will be further developed in my next book *Langage et cinéma* (Larousse, 1971). Certainly, it is clear that many codes *that appear in films* are not *specifically cinematographic codes*: a film carries along with it collective representations, ideologies, forms borrowed from other arts, cultural symbolisms of all kinds. But the cinema equally forges its own codes, for the cinema is an apparatus (a machine), and it is also a technique (the way the machine is used). There exist many figures – which are made of forms, and not pure matter – that the cinema alone is capable of realizing: dissolves, panning shots etc. (this list is longer and more complex than this).

Bellour: In this way, you have strictly redefined the ambiguous notion of cinematic specificity, by establishing a theoretical split between the material basis of the film and the codes that nonetheless structure it, as if to mark that this codification is, more than the effect of an ontological pre-determination, the fruit of a historical process and a cultural logic which lead to the film – as a means of mechanical reproduction – being the site *par excellence* of a fictive language.

In this sense, the specific object of film semiology would be – by means of a second, much more radical split between the codes themselves – the logical description of the set of codes that you recognize as being specifically cinematic.

Metz: This is indeed the object of *film semiology*. But it is not the object of the *structural analysis of films*. The latter is the singular structure of each film taken as a totality: we must therefore take into account all the codes that appear in the film under study, whether or not they are specific to the cinema. There are, it seems to me, two fundamental approaches, which are related, complementary, but nonetheless distinct, as they do not obey the same principle of pertinence. You can follow a single code across several texts, or you can analyze a single text in all its codes. The first approach is the study of codes (a code always appears in several texts), while the second is the study of texts (a text always includes several codes).

If I study the *grande syntagmatique* of which we have just spoken, I learn nothing concerning any of the particular films in which it nonetheless imprints its form – this is a study of the code. Inversely, those who analyze a given film must locate all the codes active in it, without the proper object of their efforts being any one of these codes, but only their unique combination in a *textual system*. This combination is the very movement of the text (its advancement, its concrete displacement), which is constructed on the basis of these codes, but equally against these codes. For it is a property of the textual system – inasmuch as it affirms itself through the text as the sole pertinent system – to actively push back into irrelevance the different codes on which (= against which) it constructs its development.

Bellour: Do you think, even if the proposition can appear a little utopian, that semiology, to the extent that it seeks to be descriptive, can and must proceed to an exhaustive inventory of those codes that are specifically cinematic?

Metz: We can already carry out a similar project: highlighting specific elements, linking them with one another, beginning to organize them in codes and sub-codes (for example: depending on the period, individual film and genre, there are different systems of opposition between the fade-to-black and the dissolve). Certain figures seem to me to be incontestably specific, as they are linked *as forms* to the material of expression by which the cinema is defined.

Nonetheless, I do not believe that film semiology, even if it were more advanced, could establish a closed and exhaustive list of specifically cinematic codes. There is, in fact, a fundamental to-and-fro movement between the code and the text: the text is constructed on pre-existing codes, but it still leaves behind the elements of new codes or new sub-codes. The list of codes could therefore only be exhaustive if films were no longer being made.

Bellour: I understand your reservation inasmuch as semiology always intervenes after the creator, the code after the text. But is it not contradictory if you take a distinct historical field as your object? Must we invoke, in this case, the impossibility of an experimental verification of the corpus, always susceptible to offering new elements to the activity of codification, or is it more the case that exhaustiveness cannot, in and of itself, enter into the program of semiology?

Metz: We can always – we must always – strive to be exhaustive with respect to the partial task that we fix for ourselves at each stage of our work. But absolute exhaustiveness (and here, I willingly adopt your own terms) does not, I feel, enter into the program of semiology. It cannot, and it must not. For, even if films were no longer made (and even if the semiologist was thus presented with a closed text), nothing could *achieve closure* – which is, by the way, real on a smaller scale (when, for instance, the complete output of a dead filmmaker is studied). When applied more generally to the historical evolution of film, which is the history of analysts just as much as it is the history of 'creators', the principle of infinity is not only on the side of new modes of writing [*écritures*], but also on the side of new modes of reading [*lectures*]. Film semiology would evolve even if the cinema stopped evolving.

Bellour: I would now like to ask you a few rather discontinuous questions, which are implied, in my opinion, by this series of statements on the status of the *grande syntagmatique*, the plurality of cinematic codes, the relations of structural analysis and semiological description. Can you, first of all, pinpoint some of the other codes which seem to support the very notion of cinematic specificity?

Metz: There is, for example, the code which is traditionally designated by the name 'filmic punctuation' (fades, wipes, irises, swish-pans, etc.), with its different sub-codes corresponding mainly to particular periods. From one sub-code to the other, the total list of optical effects used varies considerably, and the system according to which they are opposed to each other varies even more dramatically.

There are camera movements: tracking shots, pans, crane movements, handheld cameras (in 'direct' cinema, for example), optical tracking shots (the zoom, the Pan Cinor). Here again, the code overlaps with numerous sub-codes: the forward tracking shot on the face of the hero thus functions, at a certain point in time (cf. *Brief Encounter* [1945] by David Lean) as the signal for an imminent passage to 'interiority': it was used to introduce so-called 'subjective' flashbacks, in which the evocation of the past is not directly assumed by the subject of the filmic enunciation, but ascribed to a character remembering the events.

There is also a code (or set of codes) that is particularly important for organizing the relations of speech and what can be seen on the screen. This is an enormous problem, which goes well beyond the famous discussions in the 1930s on the 'off-screen voice' and 'a-synchronism' (Pudovkin, Balázs, Arnheim, René Clair, etc.). I am thinking of the *large segments* of filmic speech: sentences, sentence fragments, sometimes just words – and of the manner in which they are articulated with the image-track. For in its smallest segments (phonemes), speech – even filmic speech – has nothing cinematic about it: it simply refers to the language system in question.

Moreover, there are all the editing codes (or at least those editing codes which are truly specific to the cinema), all the types of relations between music and images (the experiments by Eisenstein and Prokofiev), etc.

Bellour: Thus when you say, with respect to the descriptive filmic segments, that two distinct shots or one single shot including a pan are strictly equivalent as far as the act of description is concerned, I suppose that – independently of any stylistic connotation – the difference between the two constructions must be marked semiologically by the mediation of a second code: the code pertaining to camera movements.

Metz: Yes, absolutely. Here there is an interference between two codes, that of the *grande syntagmatique* and that of camera movements.

Bellour: On the issue of description, let us return to one matter in particular. The fourth syntagma that you have identified is the 'descriptive syntagma', opposed to the category of 'narrative syntagmas' (divided into 'alternating syntagma' and 'linear syntagmas') within the category of 'chronological syntagmas'. Let us take an extremely frequent example, particularly striking illustrations of which can be seen in the Western. A man on horseback moves forward and discovers, at a bend in the road, a ranch that the Indians have ravaged and set ablaze. He approaches, framed initially in front of the incinerated house with his back to the camera, then frontally, alone, in a mid-shot. There then follow three shots: the first, static, shows a smashed fence, the second, equally static, a broken window, and then, in the courtyard, a tracking shot progressively reveals a body with an arrow poking out of it. Finally, to cap off this 'moment' (what immediate perception calls a sequence), a forward camera movement with a slight pan frames the departure of the horseman.

These three central shots cannot truly said to be 'subjective', since nothing explicitly denotes (for example, through an alternation between seeing subject/seen object) that these are the visions of the character, but everything lets us understand that this is the case, through the ambiguity that the cinema shows so often in the interplay of looks.

These three shots, therefore, in your codification, would be noted as a descriptive syntagma, as opposed to the narrative syntagma, which is represented by the first and last shots of the horseman. Is there not something contradictory here, inasmuch as the very discovery (successive, syntagmatic) of the different shots must – as much as it can be seen as a description in the strict sense operated by the filmmaker (although even this notion should itself be interrogated) – be understood as the progressive discovery of the character (even if, I repeat, it is not directly subjective), and in this sense, as rightfully inscribing itself in the narrative process?

Metz: My attempt at a *grande syntagmatique* was carried out on a very *narrow* principle of pertinence, which deliberately leaves many things to one side. This is where your objection is right. I have exclusively taken account of the diegesis, and not the *points of view* from which it is apprehended. In the case you cite, I would indeed code it as a 'descriptive syntagma'. And yet, it is true, as you say, that this description is in a sense a narration, the narration of the perceptions of the character. But on the level of diegesis, it is impossible to say that the body is 'after' or 'before' the window; rather, it is *to one side*. In this respect, the difference between narration and description remains total, depending on whether the elements that are successive in the signifying chain are equally successive in the chain of signifieds (= narration), or whether, on the contrary, they are simultaneous and spatially coexistent (= description).

Your objection still stands. But what exactly is its status? It seems to me that its aptness does not authorize saying that my descriptive syntagma would, at the same time, be a narrative syntagma – or at least, that the classificatory axis on which it is descriptive should not be confused with the axis on which it is narrative. The point of view is temporalized, but the diegesis is not. I believe that we have two distinct codes here: the *grande syntagmatique* on the one hand, and on the other hand the code of the points of view and looks, which you yourself have superbly analyzed (I am thinking of your study of Melanie's looks in 84 shots of *The Birds* by Hitchcock[1]).

Bellour: How do you envisage, on an entirely different level, the possibility of a codification of the soundtrack? In this respect I was struck by a seminar that attempted to describe Jacques Rozier's short film *Blue Jeans* [1958]: this presentation had the courageous, but somewhat imprudent, goal of applying your typology not only to the image, but also to the entirety of the narrative process, thus tearing apart both the autonomy and the intertwining of the different levels, as well as the particular difficulty of logically analyzing sound elements.

Metz: These are very complex problems indeed, but we should have a stab at them. Simply put, I do not believe that we can use my classification to do so, since it is entirely conceived for the image track. Analyzing the soundtrack is a different task, and should be conducted as such (of course, although this is only a minor point, we can ask ourselves which of my image assemblages have sonic equivalents, and which ones do not).

In any case, it does not seem to me that the filmic chain divides into two (a visual chain and an audio chain). Rather, it divides into four: images, speech, music, noise (in addition to which there are, intermittently, written texts). Either we study each of these four series separately, or we try to apprehend filmic discourse as a whole, that is, we try to directly locate the mixed assemblages (image-speech, speech-music, etc.). The notion of the 'soundtrack', which covers three of the four series, is particularly uncomfortable and problematic in the current state of research. It is already a composite ensemble, while still being partial.

Bellour: The very notion of sub-code, to which you often make reference, seems on the one hand to respond to a historical breakdown, at the same time as sanctioning other limits, whether in terms of genres (in the strict sense, like the Western, for example, or the musical comedy) or in terms of nations, schools or tendencies. Does this not, in your opinion, imply the idea of a partial overlapping, at the two extremes, between semiological description and structural analysis, with the former becoming more restricted to delimiting the circumscribed forms of language, and the latter widening its field, from single films to broader cultural combinations?

Metz: Yes and no. Yes, for the reasons you have mentioned. No, because the overlapping you talk about only concerns the dimensions and the surface of the corpus (the respective principles of pertinence continuing to remain distinct). It is true that we can study a given sub-code specific to the classical Western, and that we can also study the classical Western as a vast continuous text, going beyond inter-filmic boundaries. In both cases, the corpus would be the same: the sum total of classical Westerns (or at least a representative sample of this genre). But the study would not be the same. In the first case, each of the films of the 'group' would be examined separately, and we would only retain from it the traits that are realized by the sub-code under study: through the very proposition of the research, the group would see its unity shattered, in twofold fashion: firstly, by the fundamentally *enumerative* approach presiding over the grouping process (an approach implying that the films of the group only form a group from a very particular point of view, and for the mere sake of a very small number of their traits), and subsequently because *each of the films* of the group which, in the same movement, sees its unity dismantled (the codically pertinent traits being taken into consideration, by abstracting them from the rest of the film). In sum, studying a sub-code still means studying a code, even if it does not relate to the entirety of the cinema. Inversely, a textual study, even if the text is longer than a single film, remains pluri-codic and retains the pertinence of the concern for a singular totality (= combination of codes in a 'textual system'). Anyone who undertakes the structural analysis of the classical Western will be interested just as much in its non-cinematic codes (the concept of honour, the theme of the horse, etc.) as in its cinematic codes (long shots, treatment of wide open spaces, slow pans, etc.), and even more so in the manner in which the two are articulated with each other. Anyone who studies the cinematic sub-codes specific to the classical Western can only ever study them one by one, and by definition they will neglect the non-specific sub-codes. For both these reasons, they will never (in spite of what the exterior contours of their corpus might suggest) deal with the classical Western as such, in its entirety, but only with a certain number of rather precise schemata, about which they will observe, in each case, that they are not at work outside of the limits of the classical Western.

When structural analysis involves more than one film, it apprehends a *group of films*. When the study of a code becomes the study of a sub-code, it apprehends a *class of films*. On the one hand, we have a single and total, albeit pluri-filmic, text. On the other hand, we have a set of manifestations of an abstract, partial matrix.

Bellour: Do you find that semiology can reach, by pinpointing codes, what film analysis can only encounter in its general undertaking to read an imaginary object: that which formally marks the place of the enunciating subject, and thus refers back to a symbolic order which can only, in the last instance, be articulated in the field of psychoanalysis?

Metz: There certainly exists, in films, codes that relate to the enunciating subject – or more precisely to its mode of presence in the filmic discourse (for it is evidently not the person of the 'author' that is important *per se*). Like you, I think that Freudian psychoanalysis is the only possible basis for a serious study of codes of this order. But I am not sure that these codes (*all* of them) are specifically cinematic. To a large extent, the configurations explored by psychoanalysis are located, more or less unchanged, outside of the cinema, and invest the most diverse cultural objects.

In this aspect, I am not opposed to the terms of your question, but to a widely held opinion according to which the *film-object* retains in its own right a relation with the mechanisms of the unconscious (and in particular with the primary processes) that is more intimate and radical than other forms of expression, such as the book. We are often told that a film is like a dream, and that a dream is like a film. We emphasize the *visual* nature of the film. This idea has had a number of advocates in France during the time of the 'avant-garde film' and surrealist cinema. Right now, it is seeing a revival (Lyotard, Green, Chasseguet-Smirguel), which assumes much more subtle and nuanced guises. Nonetheless, I remain somewhat perplexed as to the connection suggested between the visual nature of a film and a type of specific and supplementary coefficient of 'psychoanalycity', which would distinguish cinema from other languages.

I have found all the 'dream sequences' that I have seen in films to be fanciful and not overly true to life. Ordinary sequences, meanwhile, although they may be composed of images, seem to me to have no relation with the phantasmatic flux (I would, however, make an exception for certain passages in Buñuel, Fellini and a few others). Inversely, we can only be struck by the importance of the analytic level in written texts, musical works, etc. We could thus think that, to the extent that the analysis is structural in nature, it does not acquire a special force by the singular virtue of its material of expression (= visuality and motion).

I still do take into account that it would be absurd to deny the privileged relations uniting the image and the dream. However, I presently know of no text – at least in the domain of film theory – that comments on these relations even in a somewhat convincing fashion.

Bellour: I wonder if, in spite of the reserves that any overly simplistic assimilation between film and dream, or between the mechanisms of the unconscious and the process of filmic discourse, can incite, the cinematic phenomenon is not susceptible – on the level of a specificity linked more to the material of expression than to the nature of its codes – to being marked more directly on the side of certain structural categories in psychoanalysis: in particular, narcissism (through the implications specific to the moving image, as a mirror and a site of the visual reduplication of, and the fascination for, the body), and hallucination, doubly visual and auditory, and strengthened through this very relationship. But my excessively elliptical question in fact targeted something else.

I wanted to return to the cinematic problem of *point of view* in order to know if, beneath every systematization of a psychoanalytic nature (founded, for example, on the system of identifications, as we can see very explicitly in the work of Hitchcock), you think that the interplay of looks can make the object of a specific code susceptible to, on the one hand, permitting a certain codification of the performance of the actors, and on the other hand, determining the syntagmatic links that mark the place of the enunciating subject in the image, in the same way that the linguistic paradigm does for grammatical 'persons'.

Metz: Maybe not *like* the persons of a verb do in language systems. But in another manner, yes, absolutely. You have studied these problems very precisely in analyses of filmic sequences in far greater detail than I myself have done. But quite so, your analyses are foremost among those that have me think that 'point of view', in the cinema, gives rise to extremely elaborate and largely specific constructions, of which we should formally take stock.

Bellour: In order to illustrate your *grande syntagmatique*, you have carried out an exhaustive inventory of the autonomous segments in Jacques Rozier's feature film *Adieu, Philippine* [1962], which comprises the third section of your book. In this sense, you have preferred to follow a code throughout a single film rather than spread your description across several films. Do you think it is possible and instructive to attempt – from within a strictly semiological perspective – this descriptive operation in order to somehow reduce the filmic material, by articulating, in a single film, *all* the codes recognized as specifically cinematic?

Metz: It would be really desirable, but I do not think it is currently possible. For, to do this, it would be necessary: 1) to possess at least a rough list of the specific codes; 2) for each of these codes, to possess a 'model' of functioning which, even on a hypothetical level, would be sufficiently precise to be either confirmed or repudiated by the analysis of a film.

These two tasks are logically primary. If we do not have a preconceived idea of what we are looking for in a film, we can 'view' it without seeing anything at all.

In contrast, each time a hypothesis reaches a certain degree of precision – even if relates to a single code – it is preferable to submit it, without delay, to the test of an *entire film*, or several films.

Bellour: I would like, in conclusion, to return to the relationship that unites and divides film analysis and film semiology, which you distinguish in your upcoming book by the object that they determine: in the case of the former, *film writing*, in the latter, *film language*.

In a sense, everything, ideally, brings them together. We can indeed think of them as strictly intertwined with one another: with analysis resting on the acquisitions of semiological description, in order to recognize, in any textual system, the proper function of cinematic codes determined by the articulation of all the system's codes – thereby returning to semiology a positive image, permanently enriched by its codes, in a flawless logical reciprocity.

Alternatively, however, I wonder if the movement of analysis, and its own exigencies, do not fatally contradict this harmony: think of codic plurality (which you have correctly insisted on), which necessarily inscribes the analysis of the field of human sciences, thus posing at each moment the prejudicial question of a unification of the epistemological field, primarily between linguistics, historical materialism and psychoanalysis. Or we can think, more modestly, of one of the immediate effects of this state of affairs, which leads the analyst, for the sake of the relations of desire implied by all analysis, to break up [*découper*] its own units rather than adopt those of semiology, even if it recognizes their rich, precise nature. In short, I wonder if, in spite of the essential and multiple areas of overlap that prohibit us from choosing one of the two movements without finding ourselves immediately thrust towards the other, there does not remain a distance (presently almost irreducible) between them, which is marked both in the strict distinction maintained by you, as well as in the playfully transgressive indecision which enables Barthes to keep the wager of *S/Z* (Paris, Seuil, 1970).[2]

Metz: It is difficult for me to respond to your question, for it has the fullness of an answer, and it is impossible for me to answer your answer, since I find myself in total agreement with what you say.

In other words: we cannot accept that the law is perpetually aligned with the fact, but nor is it desirable to always (and at all costs) forcibly align the fact with the law.

As long as the study of codes and the study of texts have not accomplished a real convergence, the former will retain a rather skeletal, emaciated allure, while the latter will continue (in spite of everything, including its considerable internal progress) the old tradition of the *explication de texte*. This is why this convergence, to my mind, constitutes a (distant) objective of critical importance, the principles of which should now be posited as a major goal for future research.

But, in order for this convergence to be realized, both approaches must affirm themselves, develop themselves and *live*. And for this, we must let them live. Research is not developed by applying programs, it needs to breathe.

You speak of the desire of those who study texts. We could speak just as much about the desire of those who study codes. Here there is much more than (and something other than) a sort of division of labour within a harmoniously organized 'scientific collective': this rationality itself – which is nowhere to be found – is a phantasm, the phantasm of the scientist.

Researchers have a kind of official morality, which is an *ethics of knowledge*. And yet, it is clear that the real motivations of scientific work, like any other activity, are akin to drives, because researchers are people. This presence of the affective at the root of intellectual discourse is not something to be deplored: without it, nobody would have written anything.

Every researcher, at every moment, can only speak usefully about what matters to him as a subject (in all the senses of the word). One of the consequences, among many others, is what we have just discussed: the study of codes and the study of texts have difficulty in truly being articulated with one another.

But it seems to me to be indispensable to equally maintain, in principle, the demands of rigor and communicability – for they too can respond to personal investments that give them the opportunity to be realized in one form or another.

In sum, we must be capable of a certain kind of empathy. At one and the same time, we must make the effort to forge a path straight ahead, and accept that we must occasionally make a sideways turn.

Notes

1. [Raymond Bellour, "System of a Fragment (on *The Birds*)," in *The Analysis of Film*, ed. Constance Penley, trans. by Ben Brewster (Bloomington: Indiana University Press, 2000), pp. 28-67.]
2. [Roland Barthes, *S/Z*, trans. by Richard Miller (Hill and Wang, 1974).]

4. Interview with Christian Metz

Daniel Percheron and Marc Vernet

Buckland, Warren and Daniel Fairfax (eds), *Conversations with Christian Metz: Selected Interviews on Film Theory (1970–1991)*. Amsterdam: Amsterdam University Press, 2017.

DOI: 10.5117/9789089648259/CH4

Abstract
In this wide-ranging interview, carried out for the journal *Ça-Cinéma* in 1975, Christian Metz reflects on the nature of theoretical research and on the problematic issues involved with teaching. He also discusses the problems with a purely semiological study of film (especially those articulated in his book *Langage et cinéma* (1971)) and introduces his shift from film semiology to a semiological-psychoanalytic study, a shift evident in his essay 'The Imaginary Signifier' (1975).

Keywords: Christian Metz, film theory, film semiology, psychoanalysis and cinema

"Entretien avec Christian Metz," by Daniel Percheron and Marc Vernet. *Ça-Cinéma* 7/8 (1975), pp. 18-51. Reprinted with the permission of Daniel Percheron and Marc Vernet. Translated by Meryl Suissa.

I – The Fiction-Effect

On the notion of 'general issues'

Question: It seems to me that amongst your works on cinema, what primarily catches your attention is the fiction film. Not a specific film or a specific type of fiction but the 'fiction-effect' in general.

Metz: There are two things. First of all, I like the idea of general issues. I intrinsically enjoy them, for they become my object (and an object is constantly linked to desire). Moreover (and this might be the consequence of the first point), I do not see them as general. If I call them that, it is because I am following the current trend. But in my opinion, they are immediately broken down into a set of specific issues. Speaking of camera movements rather than editing is exactly the same thing as speaking about one film rather than another. I think we all have our own 'concrete' topics of interest: a certain field that is real. Anyhow, my intellectual affectivity should not entail the notion of the 'general'. They are issues that I experience in a very precise and focused way.

Q: Do you prefer to tackle those so-called general issues because you are able to control them better, or is it a question of an unfounded drive?

Metz: It has become the unwavering direction my work follows, because with time you are more likely to accept your own working methods and their limitations. In the world of research, I think that we always have to play a (partly real and partly mythical) role regarding other research projects and in relation to other colleagues. But it seems that at the very beginning, ten years ago, my work was not so unwavering. This direction at the very core of research came from an urge, a drive and it remains that way. This drive is the relationship between the object and its theory.

The specificity of theory, of course, is that it aims at enlightening 'concrete' and directly observable phenomena. But this is linked to the real. In the realm of the imaginary, it is possible to like theory in itself, otherwise there would not be such people as 'theoreticians'. And it does not mean that their theories will be 'groundless'. It simply means that at the root of theory lies a great interest in theory.

Q: You mentioned camera movements and editing. These specific findings are constantly related to narration, which is another topic that interests you.

Metz: Let's just say that 'general issues' regarding the fiction film are my objects of interest (or have been of interest; in my latest work entitled "The Imaginary Signifier," I have tried to look at both fiction and nonfiction films as part of an institutional apparatus [*dispositif*]). But in so far as I focus, it is true, on the fiction film (to 'critique' its objective and subjective conditions of possibility), I find myself dealing with two different levels. In terms of the general strategies of research, it seems impossible to say that film semiology should only focus on fiction films; that is why I have never said it. Semiology should also deal with non-fiction films. On the other hand, for my personal research projects, I have often chosen (and it may very well last; frankly, I can't really predict it, I don't know), I have very often chosen the fiction film. It is because I do not feel obliged to personally cover, with research projects signed 'Christian Metz', the entire field of film semiology. I do not feel obliged to personally complete the totality of the program I have been drafting in *Language and Cinema* for example. Fortunately, there are other researchers who can tackle these issues for me.

The main reason for this choice lies in my age and my generation. When I became involved with film studies (it was during the Liberation), the findings at the time around the deconstruction of the fictional text, on the questioning of representation and other similar issues, did not exist: none of us had any idea they existed. The general cultural climate around cinema was that we all agreed that cinema and fiction films were synonymous (this confusion can be read in my first articles). Loving cinema meant loving fiction films. I actually really like the fiction film, it is the one form that is biographically rooted within me (in my adolescent memories, which are irreplaceable) and I found a theory for this deep interest – everybody works that way but no one dares to say it – this liking came back to itself (or against itself) and was transformed into a theoretical choice: to study a certain type of cinema, a certain object.

And without any disapproval coming from my part (and I would like to clarify a frequent misunderstanding) towards those who chose to study another type of cinema. There is something very important in the world of research (something that is often forgotten): one should study what he wants to study. As a start, I apply this principle to my own work.

The importance of fiction, the challenge of deconstruction

Q: Don't you think there is an issue with the method? If done in haste, the deconstructive process is incomplete, and it may very well leave space for the repressed to return in the classical narrative structure.

Metz: I do indeed believe that a real critical study of fictional cinema can progressively help lead to the creation of non-fictional cinema (it is a vexed area of expertise that cannot resolve itself with voluntary manifestos). I actually believe that non-fictional cinema does not exist. The 'non-fictional' films that I have watched, and I do not want to generalize, either bored me (= a raw emotional reaction), or incorporated some fictional aspects (of course, to various degrees).

Q: Don't you think that these two things come from cultural training? 1. You cannot enjoy a film outside the realm of fiction. 2. You have the tendency to systematically find fiction where there is none.

Metz: Yes, I am definitely inclined to do so. But in this case, I do not think it is a personal trait. One of the main objective issues with non-fiction cinema is that it is immediately 'reclaimed' by the fictional, because fiction is historically dominant. If I study fiction and the fiction-effect, it is mostly because of the dominant role it plays. In as much as they can be objectified, my motivations are markedly sociological: a majority of films made nowadays are fiction films. I am not an historian per se, for I do not research the historical facts concerning the films that interest me, but I am very interested in the place of cinema in history. I essentially work with 'longer' historical periods.

When you look at it from this angle, one can only be amazed by the dominant and impressive presence of fiction in cinema. This observation needs to be clarified, irrespective of certain examples of fiction films (there are so many that the very phenomenon can overwhelm us: the audience likes the fictional formula because it responds to dominant forces). This fact also asks to be explained irrespective of films that escape certain aspects of this formula – they constitute another historical force, currently in the minority, which would have no effect on the first one during that period. And, moreover, one should research this phenomenon regardless of the naïve attempts that significantly underestimate their adversary and who believed they have 'revolutionized cinema'. (In Paris, such films are screened every week.) Traditional cinema is an institution: it will change, but not in that way. The very concept of a 'cinematic institution' seems increasingly important for a materialistic study of cinema; it is progressively becoming the centre of my work.

There is also another factor that brings me back to what you mentioned before. The objective situation of cinema is not comparable to literature – which we often forget is far more 'advanced'. This aspect of the issue was truly striking to me in a time when people tried to constitute a cinematic 'Tel-quelisme'. There is a big difference between this movement and *Tel Quel*, one of which is that behind *Tel Quel* there is not another *Tel Quel* trying to imitate it. The literary tradition has been here for a thousand years, it is highly 'cultivated', it has acquired (but not in 80 years!) real metalinguistic tools, abilities to turn back and question its own processes. The question of deconstruction is deeply rooted. Moreover, there is the material of expression: the signifier [of film and literature] is not the same; this changes things a lot.

The fiction film as mechanism of pleasure. The difficulty of displacing pleasure

Q: There was a time when, following a rather critical movement, a series of political and ideological deconstructive films entered the film market. These films are often rather boring. Don't you think that this is partly due to criticism's – politically or ideologically founded – failure to take into account the spectator's pleasure in watching fiction?

Metz: I think you are right – even if the term 'deconstruction' (or rather its referent) risks swaying our conversation. It is a very precise notion, with a very specific meaning in Julia Kristeva's theory. Well, the films that are currently on our minds, in the vast majority of cases, are creations of filmmakers who hardly know or have no idea about this philosophical movement, and these films act on the desire (in a very romantic way) to 'renew', to create a 'different' cinema. We should then agree to use term 'deconstruction' in its loose and wider sense: this meaning really fits into what we are speaking about.

Coming back to your question, it brings me to my core idea on the metapsychology of the fiction film. This type of film has historical, ideological and psychoanalytic (= metapsychological) mechanisms to awaken the spectator's pleasure. Like any other mechanism, it does not always work, but it can objectively trigger some pleasure, due to its mix of similarities and differences to dreams and fantasies.

In my opinion, the problem with non-fiction films in the world of cinema was often raised in a superficial manner, by an enthusiastic spirit of will and an avant-garde approach (aesthetic or political depending on the case), all wrapped up in the ambiance of the superego. One wonders if it was the 'right way' to make it work. But in order for a specific type of cinema to survive, there needs to be a fair number of spectators, not too small, to make it live, and consequently, to enjoy it. And not only meta-spectators, for the filmmakers' close friends should also find pleasure in comparing the film's achievements in relation to similar films. Of course, there can also be completely different audiences, civilizations, for whom the concept of pleasure does not make any sense to us. In the state of our society and many other societies that we know, the mechanism of a non-fictional cinema would assume that the spectator renounces a significant amount of his pleasure, or displaces it onto something else.

This displacement is an important process, and is very often underrated and inconspicuous, especially if it relates only to thousands of spectators, rather than all of them (here again, cinema is not literature: the link to distribution is not external to an art, but enters into its definition).

Moreover, we often speak of the 'rejection of the fiction film' with a force that always amazes me; people speak under the pretext that some traits of the narrative formula that have been put into question can be rather dubious. For example, a film is said to be deconstructive because its chronological order is more scrambled than usual, another because the 'real' and the 'imaginary' are tightly interwoven, a third one because the fiction is criticized while it is shown on the screen etc... But one should really see what an entirely non-fictional film would be (and you realize that it is hard to imagine what it actually is, that it is almost an impossibility): this film should not present any recognizable object (not even a landscape, not even a piece of the sky...), this film should not have any characters (whether fictional or not), and no actors (the actor remains a powerful imaginary signifier, before 'enacting' any characters). No more 'non-actors' (unqualified actors etc... another rip off of our times: they become actors by leaving their traces on the spectacular device which is the cinema screen). No logical relations of time, space, causality; they should be removed, leaving nothing except the signifier in its materiality. In other words, no element should ever 'create a diegesis' etc.

Finally, without really going into details, non-fiction films assume that, while consuming the film (which would not be the case anymore), the spectator takes real pleasure in knowing the mechanisms of its deconstruction. The spectator should be able to transfer his libido, a sort of metapsychological conversion, from the cinematic pleasure as it always existed to a sheer sadistic pleasure of knowing, dismantling and controlling what is on screen. The pleasure of having a toy would be to eventually break it, and it seems rather unlikely to me right now [in regards to cinema]. Paradoxically, this very same operation is constitutive of its science, of the theory of cinema, and in this form it can function perfectly. This is actually well known. But the theory of cinema and cinema going are, and remain in our current culture, two different things. It is undoubtedly why the best deconstructive films are those that keep the diegesis and play with it, or destroy it 'from the inside' (Eisenstein was in favour of this technique). They keep one foot in the pleasure of the tale and take advantage to rally us against it. This clever approach seems far more interesting to me than the direct attempts of destruction and tabula rasa. It is more interesting and more adapted to objective conditions and, in this sense, is more political.

Q: The sadism of the person who studies the film can only kick in at the second viewing. It is very rare that it starts straight away, at the first viewing.

Metz: Yes, I agree. It is because, in that specific case, there is a phenomenon of 'the entanglement of the drives', where sadism is closely linked to another pleasure which is on the side of the libido, a pleasure of bonding, of company: to become familiar with a film, to stay a long time with the same object, and 'court' it (and yet, it is true, to dissect the machine). The two opposite impulses work together, and the pleasure is doubled, whereas in the real non-fictional film, the all-knowing sadism should take charge of the metapsychological cinematic viewing regime. And that, it seems to me, is where the real difficulty lies...

II – Resistance towards the film as an object

The split between cinephilia / linguistic training

Q: You have never carried out any film analysis until now. Why is that?

Metz: There has always been something rather problematic in my relationship with my work. A sort of division – rooted in my work as a cinema semiologist – comes from two deeply engrained origins that are rather easy to articulate in terms of theory, but more difficult to unify on an emotional level. On the one hand, since my film buff teenage years, I have always loved films, I loved going to the cinema, I supported the 'ciné-club' movement during the Liberation and, on the other hand, I chose to study linguistics. The idea of film semiology came with the encounter between these two sources. In principle, the operation is simple: it is true that, in order to establish film semiology, one should know films and therefore go to the cinema rather frequently. Moreover, one should also be acquainted with linguistics. The fact remains that in my life, my memories, my schedules, my personal phases, the two sources are clearly distinctive. When you bury yourself in tough and 'technical' books, like linguistics books, you should love them for what they are, otherwise it is impossible to continue. By doing so, you gain many things that will help you to study the language of films, but it takes days and days of work in which you are immersed in another universe, phenomenologically remote from the world of cinema, a universe with its own logic, which is self-sufficient. In the way I imagine my work, there are two 'series', and I currently struggle (maybe I will always struggle) to join these two in my daily desire, and that is why I think that until now I have never carried out any film analyses.

This can seem strange since my work consists in joining the two strands together on a conceptual level. I do not think it is contradictory either. I even suppose that they should go together, at least when one chooses an object that is already dialectical and complicated, that is not the direct and 'forthright' outcome of enthusiasm. Don't forget that I have chosen my current job quite late, in my thirties. Before, I was a High School teacher and I did not do any research. I did not find any path that suited me, so I waited and hesitated.

Desires and fears of textual analyses

Q: Are you reluctant to carry out a textual analysis?

Metz: In all honesty, I think I am. I think I am resistant, which I would actually like to overcome. In order to do so, I intend to analyze a short film. First, because it is less daunting (= it is probably a mythical protection, but it matters to me, as they are often the most efficient) and also because I would like to look at the concrete issues that emerge in the analysis of the 'textual system' of a whole film, like the ones I mentioned in *Language and Cinema*. I am hoping (or I am probably deluded) that with a short film I can manage, in terms of the quantity of elements and their relations to one another, to get a quick and more comprehensive grasp of its textual system. After that, I would like to analyze some of the films I loved in my youth such as *Citizen Kane* [1941] by Orson Welles; I would like to analyze it scene by scene; it would certainly make a book and not an article.

I have remained on the theoretical level mainly for two reasons. The first one is that there are in the field of film semiology, amongst my friends and students, a number of people who analyze films, who enjoy doing it and are good at it, whereas there are far less people (the difference is striking) who are tempted to look into theory 'head on'. Of course, what I am saying is a rationalization, an excuse in the face of my own difficulties. But in terms of the distribution of tasks, this remains a real fact. In fact, fantasmatic distributions are in a way the most rational as everyone does what he likes.

And I also feel a real resistance towards the film as an object; it is as if I was standing in front of a threshold that I was afraid to cross. It is probably due to the fact that I previously loved film so much. The criticisms I have made against cinephilia and that are everywhere in my writing can only emphasize an old argument I had with myself. When I think about it, these may be the only aggressive and polemic passages in my books. Nowadays, cinephilia is an attitude that I have left behind, that makes me laugh, but I must not have completely left it behind since I have to admit that I still hold a grudge against it.

In fact, in my current study, "The Imaginary Signifier," I touch upon this problem from a psychoanalytic perspective, by showing that the cinematic institution rests on a dual relation between the cinema-goers and the cinema as a 'good object'. I think that it is that very same issue that explains my reluctance to analyze films. If I were to try it, I would take on the role (at least partly) of the cinephile, stick to a specific film, and continue to use a theoretical discourse (for I would like, of course, my analysis to be really semiological). I have never taken these two positions *at the same time*. The difficulty is not in the intellectual synthesis of these two positions: a lot of people write these syntheses (or analogous ones), it is not beyond human abilities. The difficulty lies in finding the right balance in relation to desire, when I have been involved for years with so-called 'pure' theory.

At the moment, I would like to carry out a textual analysis. But I want to do it because I do not really want to do it, because I want to dialectize this resistance, to make it useful, to understand it, to come to terms with it (not necessarily by succeeding but by acknowledging the effort I have put into it). I truly believe in the importance of textual analysis, and even if I realize that it is a work I am not very talented at (here, once again, I have to try), I will continue to believe in it. Textual analysis, as I said in *Language and Cinema*, represents a good half of the work in film semiology.

Q: Have you chosen to analyze a short film for fear of losing yourself in a long film, in a forest of codes? It seems that the reason explaining people's caution towards *Language and Cinema* stems from the fact that, if you take the codes apart, it is very easy to lose yourself.

Metz: No, I think that choosing a short film, as I mentioned before, is a magical protection against my resistance (also magical) towards textual analysis. It is not the length of the decoding work that scares me. My books, in another way, have required long and painstaking scholarship. The forest of codes does not scare me either, for that is the smooth and loveable part of the text. I do not feel any anxiety for completeness, the desire to unravel all the film's codes; this comprehensiveness seems unnecessary, it is not part of a semiological program, it would contradict its spirit. No, my resistance comes from the text itself.

Cinema-'object', cinema-'corpus'

And I have the impression that, compared to most people who study film, close friends of mine included, my perspective is slightly different. I talk to researchers everyday and what they tell me makes me feel that their subject is truly cinema. For me, cinema is more of a corpus. Who says corpus says fetish. Cinema is my fetish, it is what establishes within me the power of my work, my drive to work. It is my reservoir of examples; it is what makes me speak about the things close to my heart. In summary, cinema is my 'subject' [*thème*] rather than my predicate.

It does not make a big difference in practice, but it sometimes introduces a slight difference to the discussions I take part in.

For example, something strikes me: when I studied cinema from a linguistic perspective, the linguistic mechanism was the object of my intellectual passion. And now that I am more oriented towards a historical psychoanalysis of cinema as an institution, it is the Freudian adventure, psychoanalysis, that fascinates me. In a way, cinema has never really been my subject per se, but rather something I often talked about.

If we think about the objective results of this attitude, if we wonder how my cinematic interests may affect my other interests (and theory in general), then I think that my *oblique relation to the object* shows a specific mix of pros and cons. The cons are obvious: my work is quite often too 'abstract', not close enough to cinema, or at least to what I call in my own language the 'cinema-cinema'. There are a few issues, not all without intrinsic interest, of which I am not personally interested in and that I am unable to write about. These are points in which colleagues cannot expect anything from me. They reproach me for being abstract, of being 'stratospheric', and I reject this statement, sometimes rather dismissively, especially when it comes from a very low level such as film criticism (the journalistic film criticism) and I believe I am right to do so when the place of enunciation makes sense. But it happens that the same reproach (and it is not quite the same) can be made by people who work with me and that I value, people who are far from this anti-theoretical Poujadisme (or in Italian, *qualinquisme*). In that case, I accept it without feeling bitter because it is true, that is my limit, I do not have the brains for images, I prefer conceptual thinking.

The advantage of my position of desire, which is slightly skewed in relation to cinema, is topographic: I am in a good *position* to notice things that others have not noticed, or at least I am more sensitive to them. I am a little outside the cinema world and I am intensely involved in the intellectual world. I can see the object from another angle and I find it easier to *turn it around* (that is, to turn filmic voyeurism back onto the institution itself). I hardly get attached to films, even those I love. In my opinion, looking at cinema as a social event like any other, with as much relevance as any other, using the same general methods of analysis, is a painless operation that does not involve overcoming internal barriers.

For an 'a posteriori' allocation of work

Finally, I am deeply convinced that each of us has only one thing to say. If you have one thing to say, it is quite a lot already, as many have nothing to say. What I mean by 'a thing to say' is – the way I expressed it is not the right one – rather a single path to follow, a single set of interests to follow. The path may be winding, it can change every three years, and yet in another way it is the same path. If you do not take it, nothing changes.

I have an amazing example (if you can say that) with issues regarding Ph.D. theses. Institutionally, I have to 'direct' or supervise theses ('direct' is such an absurd term; it is a matter of discussing with the Ph.D. students, giving them bibliographical references and above all 'transferring' to them enough (goodwill, benevolence) to sustain – without too much personal damage (to me) – the mythological exploitation, i.e., projection – another transfer – they make towards me). In this activity (or passivity) that I actually enjoy a lot, I often see that students, especially at the beginning of their doctorates, choose a topic that does not interest them, that they are not really involved in. (It would be useless and even detrimental to tell them at once.) The student chooses a topic for its objective importance (as if this actually existed! It is just for the title), or for its genuinely semiological matter (as if a good non-semiological work was preferred to a bad semiological work), in any way that engages a scientific superego rather than a desire or drive. The student cannot write his thesis. What generally follows is that the student, when starting his first real work, takes some perspective in regard to his superego (and stops projecting it on to me, which is rather nice) or manages to make it pleasurable, to determine it himself: he changes the subject, the new topic appeals to him and the thesis can progress.

In the end, I only believe in assigning work-related tasks after the work is done (or not, which proves that it was not possible to achieve, at least not by the person who was doing it). Post-assignment of tasks can seem absurd, even contradictory, but I really cannot see how you can achieve scientific work with a predetermined program in association with someone else. A few practical requirements obviously necessitate meeting with others, but the less the better. And yet, I do not feel like an anarchist at all; I do believe that tasks should be assigned, for they are useful: I call 'objective' those tasks that are created by oneself and that are imposed upon oneself (not by *conscious intention*, delusion, or bad faith). What I mean is that after a few years, sometimes months, one notices that for a certain type of work there are such and such persons who have the right dispositions and taste. These are people who know how to deal with the work, and that is when it is time to talk to them. The best service each of us can give to the 'scientific community', if it exists, is to find our own path (our own voice). The assignment of tasks is done only when the tasks are done. From this standpoint, I am in complete disagreement with a certain mentality in the world of research. We spend hours reformulating research when the principal point in common is that no common point exists. And at the same time, you realize that each researcher has succeeded in completing some work, or has written something that he has not mentioned during meetings, yet he really wanted to conduct it and it was worth it. During meetings, he was absent, he left the role to his superego, or his respect for the Institution, or his desire to not appear condescending to his colleagues, to be kind to them and show his good will.

Scientific work is very demanding, it tires us in the deepest places of our being, it takes a lot of energy (part of which can be found in the libido we experience for the object). It is schizophrenic work that you have to maintain *against* your everyday life (with which it is incompatible, even if you schedule your time, or become less obsessed with the tasks): it is not something you do out of good will; instead, you need to have a long lasting, strong and real desire. To speak here of pleasure and desire is not a luxury stemming from individualism, but is an objective condition without which research cannot take place, it cannot happen.

When I say 'post-assignment of tasks', I think about all this. And in my case, as someone who remained until the age of thirty in a rather unhappy and tortured relationship with my work, I was unable to do anything. I now have to be honest (and with a tinge of 'fatalism', I have to admit) that there are things that I will be happy to do and others, even within my own field, that I will not do. When colleagues tell me that these things are quite important, I do not deny it, but the subject no longer interests me, even more if I know that I will not be able to do it. I always feel like telling them, especially when they insist: 'Do it yourself then!' I have often given this answer. The fact that it is even been felt as aggressive rather than a natural statement says a lot about the alienating *pathos* going on in the world of research.

III – The driving force of work

A desire to clear a space, to cover the territory

Q: It seems that there is in your work a quasi-obsessive determination to exhaust your field of study, to analyze its every corner. ...

Metz: I do enjoy a certain type of work that also feels essential. In this regard, I am rather amazed to see that, in my current psychoanalytic research, I reproduce the same steps from the beginnings of my linguistic project in 1962-1964. It is a certain 'working method', in which the driving force is a desire to *overcome* something (a problem, an inner question). It generates pleasure, or at least the feeling of achieving something; the feeling that a task, a period or a train of thought is 'completed'. There are certainly feelings of control (and maybe a tinge of quiet, unyielding sadism), an obsessive fantasm for accuracy, of filling field X, a field that I would rather be small but very 'busy'. At the moment I have two contradictory feelings, or at least they seem contradictory to me, but deep down they are not: the first one is that you have to stop being obsessive regarding the *completion* of your work, for if it is filled with too many doubts or compulsive revisions, it then becomes a burden. Yet, simultaneously, scientific work is at its roots obsessive: a stubborn perseverance, a meticulousness without which we would not have the courage to finish what we started. And then there are the distractions of our daily responsibilities, the less sublime pleasures and constant storm of professional emergencies that present themselves to us.

What I like to do is to proceed slowly, to make steady progress and to place each development in its own separate section, which prevents me from making general, banal statements that are 'almost right' or only 'partly accurate'. It is important to clear a space and attain something new for this discipline. This desire was already at the root of my rather long first article entitled "The Cinema: Language or Language System?" I wanted to go beyond the *linguistic metaphor* (but, at that time its form was not very clear to me, and Roland Barthes told me that this expression is not mentioned in my article). Yet, it is correct – linguistic metaphors exist in cinema (which is to say that cinema is a language etc...), it does not come from me, nor my fellow linguists, but belongs originally to film aesthetics, and I really wanted to see what this metaphor held once we had taken seriously (like linguists do) the concepts of '*langue*' and '*langage*'. I wanted to rip open this metaphor and look at it from the inside, and I'm not saying that in the sense developed by Melanie Klein, but rather to better understand certain things (epistemophilia, voyeurism, and sadism, in their persecutory as well as their depressive aspects).

And now, if I think about one of my most recent articles (on the spectator's metapsychology in relation to the fiction film ["The Fiction Film and its Spectator: A Metapsychological Study"]), I find the same dynamics in my work: to tackle a commonplace idea, but one that in my opinion had never been fully stated: that cinematic fiction is related to the spectator's fantasy, that it is like a dream, that the spectator sees the film as his object etc. ... We have observed hundreds of times that the 'filmic state' resembles sleep but, exactly like the linguistic metaphor, we have not taken seriously this notion of sleep. Yet, sleep is a very specific state of psychic economy that has often been at the centre of Freud's attention. I therefore wanted to look closer. What really makes me work is always the same thing: the drive to develop a scientific perspective on things that everyone thinks they know but in fact they do not, to *unravel* 'ordinary' social phenomena that are frequently hidden behind banalities. I am fascinated by the ordinary (far more than rarity, in fact), I find it extraordinary. I feel an urgent call to decipher and explore it.

The unsolved residue

Q: But it seems to me that the idea of finishing is tied to the impossibility of finishing, for you always return to and re-examine what you have already researched. For example, in your book *Language and Cinema* (in which you 'return' to your previous research three times!) or in two books where you question again the concept of connotation, or more recently the impression of reality.

Metz: I believe that these two seemingly contradictory operations (to finish and the impossibility to do so, to return often) come from the same insatiable drive. I would like to 'be over and done with it', but I never wish to end it. Each time I finish a work, this drive is rarely satisfied. Like any desire, it is reborn from its ashes and begins again. Six months or three years later, I still feel dissatisfied with my former research and I work on it again...

Q: What motivates you to do it again? From where to do you start? Your former research?

Metz: The trigger of this dissatisfaction is variable: it can come from criticism that was made and I found interesting, from reading colleagues' works etc.

... But the real impulse is the constant dissatisfaction, the rereading of my former articles, this inner desire to understand.

Q: Aren't we coming back to Freud's text on knowledge, where he says that for each step we climb, there is an 'unsolved residue'?

Metz: Certainly. We always advance on many fronts. On the one hand, we progress, which means that we have acquired enough objective information and subjective desire to be able to move forward. And on the other hand, in the phase where issues are in principle resolved, there remains uncertainties, outstanding issues. Staying with Freudian metaphors, when most of the army is moving forward, at the back small detachments are busy getting rid of the remaining enemy forces. When I had just started my work with psychoanalytic influences, I was also interested in the relationships between perception and linguistic naming, and the study that came out of it ("The Perceived and the Named") returns to classical semiology, which is not Freudian but returns to the notions of language and metalanguage. This was a small digression, and I wrote this article with great pleasure.

Long term commitment, or working in long phases

I also have to admit that I work in long phases (except for the overlaps that I mentioned a minute ago), phases that, if I can extrapolate from the past to the future, seems to last ten years each. These are periods in which I am particularly interested in something and then I move on to something else. What I call a 'thing' that serves as my 'object' is generally a method, or at least a mix of the two: a process, a new 'approach' (as we say) to cinema.

Q: Are there within those long phases any sub-phases?

Metz: Yes. I will spare you the smallest ones, which would lead us to the anecdotal, but I sense a spontaneous, volatile organization, divided into two relatively important sub-phases. First, there is an initial sub-phase which is very intense, in which I am completely invested in my work that involves a great amount of reading, and that is when the joy of learning emerges (and the fascination of hearing the thought of others; when you write, you forget the other, even if you quote him; and you continue reading important texts. There are obviously very few of them, and yet there seems to be quite a few of them. You rediscover this strange thing: the existence of others, his existence, and the fact that he can bring you something).

The second sub-phase is exploitation in its most industrial sense, for you have to make a profit from what you have found (time flies very swiftly, things that we really know are very small, and the moments where you can intervene are few and far between). But there is more than that, there is more than this reluctance to feed the influx of scholarly Parisian papers. Other desires return, the desire to teach, to be an Other who people will learn from, the desire to write (following the drive to read – it does not have to be chronological, it is a deeper 'post' reading), the desire to undertake new problems, to come back to the pure theory of cinema.

In the second phase, I can feel that the passionate beginning has diminished slightly. Exhausted by the intense activity of the first phase, I often have the tendency to get tired from an excessive interest in this work. What follows is calmer, involving a process of clarification, based on an impetus that is probably residual and that goes on and on. It can last a long time – many years, which is enough for me to want to continue; it has a very specific affect, 'to continue', very different from initiating the work, but also very different from the desire to do nothing.

In my 'linguistic period' (a rather pompous name!), the only article that corresponds to the first sub-phase, created in a great burst of enthusiasm, is "The Cinema: Language or Language System?" The rest has been carried out under calmer conditions (with various degrees depending on the articles), which attempt to take this linguistic approach to its conclusion. Of course, I cannot unravel all the consequences of this hypothesis (my entire life would not be long enough, and other people have decided to do it), but there are many things *I* could say about it, based on my interest in this topic, until my desire wears out (except it will 'return' and be developed, as we mentioned earlier).

Disciplinary frameworks that enable one to work

Q: It seems to me that one could say that your thought on cinema is always linked to a kind of disciplinary framework rooted in fundamental and transferable concepts.

Metz. Indeed, the disciplinary framework matters a lot in my choice of work. The only insights that interest me (that motivate me – those that are discovering the similarities between linguistics and psychoanalysis) are well-established and incorporate a set of conceptual tools. Or, more simply, 'real' disciplines (there are very few of them) that produce real concepts and do not just prolong common sense understanding (that is to say, ideology).

These disciplines have their own *domain* (not a 'field'), a domain in which you must enter and where everything is logical. Hard disciplines, with strong hypotheses, that create their 'own universe', metalinguistic disciplines that give you at once a completely different perspective. These are the slightly 'technical' disciplines, as we sometimes call them, but I think the word is not right, because the empirically-based American psycho-sociology, for example, which is a typical soft discipline, involves a lot of technical statistical work, and yet at its core it contains 'common sense' notions that do not work.

I enjoy working with these disciplines that break from current mainstream views, that provoke a different way of thinking, that show the object in a different light. I find great pleasure in successively making them function around my body of work on cinema. Deep down, what annoys me (in its strongest term, it is most repellent), is all this omnipresent discourse surrounding cinema, a discourse that is reduced to such statements as: 'Cinema is a very important social event. ... Nowadays, in the 20th century, there isn't just verbal and oral language. ... It's not just an industry but also an art and if we think about it, as enriching as the other media. ... And also, it is a new language that does not only reflect society but also the creative individual. ... The form is as important as the content, in fact they are inseparable, etc. ...' I do not want to be mean but there a lot of books on cinema (not only newspaper article but books) that do not say more than that. As with other authors, there is in my work certain negative motivations (= aversions); for me, it is the desire to get away as far as possible from this literature.

It makes me think about Barthes' observation on Michelet. He said that something is all the more interesting once it is far from our expectations (for Michelet, we expected him to write a historical and political book, but instead he wrote a psychoanalytic book). It is an informative criterion (= contrary to expectations), a maximum distancing criterion, a criterion of improbability. Such processes are very appealing to me. Talking about double articulation and morphemes in relation to cinema was, in 1964, unheard of. On the one hand, it is actually common: in principle, we write to deal with new things and not to repeat what everybody knows already. But there is something more specific, more 'subjective' (to speak simply), something directly linked to the desire to work. It is a certain attraction to a method, this conviction that the object seen through it will reveal something new. Of course, there is a risk of being disappointed, for the method can be less helpful than expected. But we are sure of not seeing anything without the method.

The linguistic transformation → psychoanalysis. Return to the object

Q: Could you talk to us about your new direction, your decision to let go of linguistics and to embrace psychoanalysis? Was your change of direction due to the fact that your linguistic energy was exhausted, or simply because you desire to try out a new approach? Do you feel that you needed to get out of a coded or textual semiology that puts your object between parentheses (your object-spectator, if we remain in the field of cinema)?

Metz: At the moment, my work evolves and for two reasons. In terms of theory, I've always had the impression, even in the 'linguistic' work, that a real theory of cinema comprise three components: a linguistic component, classical semiology, inasmuch as the film contains evidence of linguistic phenomenon, discourses, stories etc. …; a psychoanalytic component of vital importance, linking cinema to topics such as identification, voyeurism, the fetishistic splitting of belief (= disavowal), the apparatus [*dispositif*] of the cinema room itself (material topography with its mental disposition); and a social-historical component, for cinema is in certain ways a socio-economic institution (= huge funding and the necessity to attract large numbers of spectators), with ensuing ideological consequences (ideology also lies in the first two aspects, it is not reduced to the content of films). In the article I'm working on at the moment, I actually try to explain further how the interlocking of these three perspectives work. It also seems that the psychoanalytical input could join semiology, for there is a true *psychoanalysis of codes*; and on the other hand, this linguistic-analytic study of a certain type of symbolism is directly linked to a socio-historical enterprise for the signifier is an institution.

I notice that choosing between these three perspectives is becoming less difficult. The more I think about it the more I realize that, at a certain level, you can see them linked – and even intertwined – with one another. Until we reach that stage, it is the linguistic perspective that most interests me. And then there was some kind of driving force towards the intrinsic nature of cinema, and I found myself rushing to the second perspective. I like to turn the object by changing the method, and I have also felt that the object was turning in my hands by its force of rotation.

The second reason is more personal. I am persuaded that a certain domain of research can be momentarily exhausted (especially if this individual has spent a long time on it) without being exhausted from its scientific and collective perspective. In our work, objective importance and everyday life events, like the desire to change or weariness, often get mixed up. I keep on encouraging good work on classical semiology, defend it in front of juries and even try to publish it. A lot has to be done in this direction. But, for me, I would like to do something slightly different at the moment. *Slightly different*: in spite of appearances – we always overestimate changes, it is a Parisian habit (it is also the structural principle of fashion). There are changes, but they are more connected than they seem; obviously not at the most visible level (what strikes me the most is the change of vocabulary and bibliographic references etc. ...); it connects somewhere else: in what I have to say on cinema.

Q: Did you feel that you could no longer leave Freud in the cupboard anymore? You felt there was a lack somewhere. ...

Metz: As I just told you, I *thought* about it but I did not really sense it. In reality, my encounter with psychoanalysis was made outside, not directly (or not firstly) in my work. At the start, I was pushed into analysis for personal reasons. My 'scientific' and epistemological interest in psychoanalysis (or, my intrinsic interest in its method) came later, a few years later. At the beginning, the 'patient' that I was worried little about film theory. There was a long period in which I was in analysis, whereas my work on cinema remained non-Freudian.

Q: Similar to linguistics, when you only realized you could work with the two afterwards. ...

Metz: Exactly. Linguistics and cinema also remained separate for a while in my mind (it is a form of resistance). There is also a simpler reason that cannot be overlooked: to undertake a psychoanalysis of cinema, a personal analysis is not enough, you need to immerse yourself in books and it takes years (this is the same for linguistics, it is a disadvantage in regards to real disciplines).

Q: How do you see the spectator? As a psychological entity? As a libidinal economy?

Metz: Yes, like a certain type of economy, but historically-determined. And in a psychoanalytic approach, there isn't just the spectator (you must be thinking about the seminar I presented in 1974). There is also the filmic text itself (= condensations, displacements, primal processes, etc. ...). And finally the institution in its foundations, in its conditions of possibilities, I will say that it is the psychoanalytic constitution of the cinematic signifier, of all the specific codes. At the moment, I am really looking into this in "The Imaginary Signifier" and at this level everything is about the spectator, the filmmaker and the film, it is the psychoanalysis of the cinematic apparatus itself.

I am not really interested in individual differences; I think they are an illusion. They exist empirically, and are of great importance in our practical and emotional life. But in order to understand them, you should not look at them, you should look *under* them. They are due to different forces, and these forces are not individual; they create a socio-psychological space. That space makes these variations possible. You have to study this space directly (or the different variations within that space). This space is the code, it is the metapsychological apparatus and it is also the technology of cinema.

IV – On *Language and Cinema*

The retroactive impact of psychoanalytic work on this book

Q: You are now looking at cinema through psychoanalysis – has it changed the functioning of codes for you, in comparison to when you studied them in *Language and Cinema*?

Metz: It really depends, for there are many different cases. Insofar as I am now studying the spectator's metapsychology, it does not change the issues of codification in terms of classical semiology, for it deals with something different. I look at the relationship between the spectator and the film. I am not studying the internal articulation of codes in a film like I did in *Language and Cinema.* The change lies in an addition. At that time, I was only interested in film from a so-called immanent perspective, rather traditional in semiology, whereas I am now interested in the spectator. If we were using terms from the semiology of communication, we would say that I have passed from the 'message' to 'receiver'. I do not really believe, by the way, in such terms, I use them here to say that there is no retroactive interference with *Language and Cinema.* Apart from that, the 'receiver' that I am currently studying is not a kind of individual variable or a group variable, as it is often done (= different reactions on a film according to different tastes, social and professional affiliations, etc. ...). For me, the spectator is not the real actual person, the person who goes to the cinema, but a small part of that person who attends a screening. In order to function, the cinematic institution requires a certain psychological disposition, but only requires it during the screening. For example, in order for a fiction film to be consumed as a fiction (and this is the same, more or less, for any audience from the same culture), it should not be mixed up with reality, and yet this is less so today: this process assumes a fine-tuning of perception and belief, a psychological (or rather metapsychological) phenomenon, but a psychology related to the cinematic institution and not to its consumers as actual people.

We can say the same thing regarding the psychoanalysis of the code itself, of the cinematic-signifier (not just the fiction film) seen as a specific mix of the real, the symbolic, and the imaginary. And here again, there is no interference with *Language and Cinema*, but another addition (slightly narrower than the study of the spectator). I start with the concept of 'specific code' and the 'relevant traits of the material of expression'. I would like to show that these codes and traits, without modifying their meaning, presuppose the existence of an earlier stage (which I did not look at in *Language and Cinema*), a stage that I now call 'the constitution of the signifier': the specular space of the cinema room, the presence of the photograph, the absence of the photographed object, the games of 'identification' and projections etc. ... In short, all the social and historical processes without which the cinema could not exist and that psychoanalysis seems quite well suited to dismantle. It is the code's condition of possibility, it does not change anything of its *content*.

On the other hand, there is something in my current work that retroactively reflects on *Language and Cinema*, and will necessitates further developments that are still unclear in my mind. I am referring to the psychoanalysis of the filmic text: rhetorical figures (and which ones?), condensations and displacements, the emergence of primal processes and secondary revision, etc. In summary, it seems that all those processes happen on the level of the textual system, and that the codes are, on the contrary, on the level of existing and 'hardened' secondary revisions. Such would be its formulation with *Language and Cinema*, but it is only a general idea, far to general. I still need to work on it.

The difficulty of engaging with Language and Cinema

Q: I had the impression, when reading *Language and Cinema* and especially when I finished it, of finding an impressive apparatus that enables one to engage with textual analysis; a Tinguely-like mechanism,[1] so fascinating that it excludes everything with its perfectionism. There is a fantastic effort to explain, a frenzied policy occupying every inch of its territory, an excessively cautious progress, always careful of returning to its former positions, and when we try to be part of it, we feel a bit left out. We do not know how to employ this knowledge; we are left with fabulous tools but we do not know how to use them.

Metz: It seems to me that you overestimate and underestimate at the same time the tools in question. Firstly, this book does not claim to tell you how to carry out a textual analysis (I seldom do it), but only what the textual approach means in contrast to the analysis of codes. The book deals with cinema, not film (hence the title), and the three chapters on film aim at placing film within cinema.

Q: In my opinion, it feels that we fall short of *Language and Cinema*. We may not be quite ready to see so many complications in cinema, and to take up this book and the analysis following it can be overwhelming. We are dealing with a very complex and immense topic, especially when the later concepts constantly rectify the former ones. When you delve into one code, it is always in a paradigmatic position with four or five others, and it is extremely difficult to start working on that for we are never certain of what the fifth one will mean.

Metz: I think there are quite a few distinct points in what you say. ... First of all, you are saying that 'we are not quite ready to see so many complications in cinema'. I think it is very true and it is a very important statement. The conceptual difficulty that you are indicating, these 'revolutions' that others bring about via revision or new paradigms, often occurs in scientific books. If it was a linguistics book, nobody would be surprised, but since it is a book on cinema, people are not used to it and are somewhat panicked. There is an objective and historical factor that contributed to making this book frustrating and terrifying: adjusting to the expectations of various fields or disciplines. In each field, we are used to reading in a certain way, with certain requirements, accepting a certain degree of restraint. *Language and Cinema* is surely a demanding book, a gloomy book (it is meant to be, it is my very own 'private joke'[2]), but the conceptual torture is not pushed as far as in many other books. It is just that these books do not deal with cinema. Its 'difficulty' lies in the immaturity of the field rather than in the book itself.

In spite of this sociological obstacle, which is considerable, there are researchers, some dedicated to textual analyses, who have used the method

I proposed in my book. I can think of many works such as those by René Gardies on Glauber Rocha, Michel Marie or Roger Odin, or even Geneviève Jacquinot's thesis on instructional films. I can also think of very detailed essays (sometimes critical of my work) by Raymond Bellour in France, Ben Brewster and Stephen Heath in England, and Paul Sandro in the United States. I am very pleased with those interventions, not just for the obvious narcissistic reasons that we have the tendency to deny (who are we kidding?) but also because it highlights the start of a movement that, I hope, will develop: to teach writing on the cinema, open mindedness (rather new and fragile at the moment) at a conceptual level and level of precision that is more accepted elsewhere. Cinema as a social fact is not as simple as one may think.

Another problematic element is that *Language and Cinema* was not appropriately introduced to the public by critics and reviewers (with a few exceptions, but in very specialized magazines). In order for a book to be well received, critical reviews are extremely important but, to write them well, the authors should have been linguists and very knowledgeable of cinema, which is very unlikely. Here again, the historical weight of 'traditional' fields and the division of disciplines had a real impact on the release of the book. Then followed a very strange situation: the book received many commendations, it has been mentioned everywhere and the unlucky journalist covering it did not have to understand what was at the core of the problem, the content of the debate. Most of the time, people settled for: 'Very important work, very new, it is a difficult read but it is so worth it'. In summary, I sincerely applaud the reviewer who communicated to people his admiration and his terrified bewilderment.

The book's distribution is also quite surprising: it is a well-known book, it sold well, is widely translated but it is also an ignored book, is not widely read (even if it is very visible on the bookshelves). This is understandable, for it is not the only example, there is a real issue in regards to publishing, and it makes the 'applications' more complicated.

Understanding the definition, not extrapolating it

Q: At the beginning, I had to struggle a little with the book but now, I feel more and more comfortable with it. I reread a chapter and I started to immerse myself in the book, to adapt it to my own ideas. Then, as soon as I wanted to study a film, everything seemed unclear. ... Because, you speak of codes, you say that there are codes (and we are well aware of that) but we only see their form, not their identity. It is like an aerial picture that does not quite help the explorer.

Metz: First of all, if a lot of people now admit that films are coded, do not forget that it is mostly because I insisted on it, because I have repeated it everywhere and in a great number of ways. Ten years ago, this idea was far less accepted, it was barely accepted. But, deep down, it is normal, it is what I would call the 'scientific struggle' (or an 'ideological struggle'). We seek to conquer more fields and change the intellectual landscape. There has never been a pure science, the influence of the times always mattered.

I completely agree with what you said before (it is actually clearly explained, if I remember well, in my book's last page). Let me use your words: codes are defined according to their form and not their identity. Ideally, there would have been two books to write about language and the cinema, two rather different books. The first one, the one that I wrote, would be on the *status* of codes, on the act of coding in the field of Film Studies where it has not really been explored. What is a code? Why is it cinematic? How 'present' was it before the semiologist's intervention? To what extent is it a construction? What makes it different to textual structures, etc.? In summary: what is the use of codes in an epistemology of film analysis? I wanted to build a cinema-object as a scientific object and create a 'rupture' effect. I would, indeed, need a second book – I will hopefully write it one day or it may be written by someone else, I don't know – that will *list the codes*. It is important to have a book that will list (even if it is incomplete) cinematic codes to categorize them and tell us which are the principal ones. This second publication would come very useful for researchers' groundwork. There is a little of it in my book from page 171 to 175 [*Language and Cinema*, pp. 224-233] and, here you are right, it is very short and insufficient. I think my book can be misleading, in terms of its listing of codes, it deals with something different. This book defines the understanding of all the codes and not their extension.

You never 'apply' anything

Your remark makes me think about something else, something that goes beyond *Language and Cinema*, which is related more to scientific advances in general. I am very skeptical when it comes to the concept of 'application'. If you tell me: 'I've taken this book, and for one of my film analyses, I cannot put it into practice'. Well, for me, when looking further into this comment, I do not really see it as a criticism. I believe you can never apply anything. It has nothing to do with – despite its appearances – the phenomenon of 'influences' I was dealing with before and that I actually find quite real. Influences come into play at the level of general inspirations, mind sets and a few fundamental concepts, but not in terms of application. It is undoubtedly paradoxical since this book clearly aims at founding a theory and, consequently, will be seen as a work to put into practice. But the more informal and diluted 'schools of thought' are, the more realistic and lively they become: It would not, actually, be right to see them as schools. (This is a belief I hold everyday with my students. I accept influence, when it exists, but I do not accept *control.*)

In summary, it was necessary to develop this book as a 'complete machine', with all its inner workings, even the smallest ones, because it is only at this level of coherence that it corresponds to my conviction and can inspire others. At the same time, what will 'remain' of this book in future research (apart from a few people who decided to become my close students) will be the big ideas, some of the main parts, but only in a few cases.

Of course, some could say on this account, that I could have limited myself to the main ideas since they are most likely to 'spread' at a wider level. ...

A necessary loss

... but in fact, it would not mean very much to say: the internal logic of a book's fate does not coincide with this other inner logic that enabled me to write it. What I mean by 'enabled me to write it' is very concrete: the conditions without which the author would not have been able to write the book and, furthermore, publish it. Among these conditions is that the book becomes a complete object of desire that exhausts a topic of interest. We end up with a rather lengthy book, with a hundred or two hundred concepts (look at the index, at the back). And on top of this number, a dozen will be of use in certain research fields: ideas such as 'codes', 'textual system', 'cinema *vs.* film', 'specific *vs.* non-specific', 'pertinent traits of expression', and three or four others. It is already quite a lot, I expected the level of understanding and support of this book to be close to nil. It is through these key concepts that the spirit of the book is conveyed. A book only becomes influential through its main outlines, not its details or specific film analyses. It becomes popular through its broad appeal. And yet, in order for the book to gain in popularity, the author needs to think about the details as scrupulously as the main outlines. It seems that there is a 'lost coefficient' (a little like 'noise' in computer science) that lies in the intrinsic conditions of communication, which consists for the most part of non-communication. What one remembers from a 300 page book is approximately 30 pages, but those 300 pages were necessary to assert those 30 perfect pages.

In fact, this is not only relevant to the difficulties of communication, to the rather low level of most film studies essays, to the 'broken' and erratic structure of the scientific domain, to the high refractive index that must be calculated in advance and integrated into inverse coefficient formulations (with all the consequences that follow and the profusion of misunderstandings that we must prevent). There are also genuinely scientific factors: it is long and difficult to explain oneself precisely, and especially with complex content. In a way, the whole work aims at *explaining* a few important achievements (those which have the chance of 'passing'). The 30 ideal pages would be enough to outline them, which is not the same thing.

V. On Research. On Film Semiology

Research progresses in zigzags

Q: Nonetheless, I fear that certain terms are becoming quite popular even if we don't quite know what they cover and what they mean. Due to the lack of a list of codes, terms are a little hazy, and I was rather astonished when reading several texts to see that the term 'code' was a bit of a magical word. We grasped the general idea but it did not go further than that.

Metz: You are talking about certain words becoming magical. There are indeed academic fashions where a certain amount of misinterpretation comes into play: an idea 'resonates', as if in an empty room, it multiplies itself but does not go further than that. If this is what you are talking about, this popularity, there is nothing we can do. All the sentences we write can have unsettling effects, even if those sentences are not related to the overall content. To write is to have our thoughts stolen from us, and (fortunately, not for all readers, but for many of them) it only becomes a canvas on which they create their desires: they wish they could have written it themselves. One should accept this situation or choose to live in silence.

But your question does not just deal with this. Your last words (= 'it did not go further than that') raise a real issue which is not related to fashion or popularity: *how does research progress?* What I want to say is – if it progresses, how does it actually progress? I am convinced that, in a certain way, it does not progress by going 'further', which would involve a linear progression, but rather it progresses in zigzags. (It may be different in other fields like maths or the exact sciences, for example, but I do not know that enough to develop this point.)

By wanting to progress in a linear way, one is very likely to fall into a rather inhibiting individual or collective voluntarism. In the scientific (or technocratic?) mythology, there is a sort of ideal image: someone publishes a theoretical book, we then apply it and we can then improve and criticize the theory etc. ... It is always represented in a linear manner. In reality, at least in my field, I have rarely observed research happening that way. For example, a book suggests a really difficult concept, the concept of the code. On top of this, some people follow their own research, they carry out textual analyses or they write other books, other articles. Others will use the concept of the code from another perspective, but *laterally*, through a displacement or reframing of meaning. The problem progresses in an oblique and dislocated manner (like crabs!) and yet it surely progresses. Only an ideology of 'efficiency' would be surprised or would denounce such a trajectory, but it is no better than the others. For example, a pioneering book's input in the scientific debate can often be measured – among other influences – by the *unease* that it brings to other researchers, that pushes them to work and come up with new findings. This pioneering book inspires the work of other researchers (which does not mean that they are conscious of this): in numerous cases, research begins with a feeling of unease, or other approaches. On the other hand, other researchers may choose another approach, based on scientific convictions and personal disposition, to explicitly 'extend' the pioneering book, therefore becoming a critical application or series of propositions to directly improve it. This is also a very important approach; both approaches are useful.

Against the official ideology of the research environment

I must say that in our world of research the image of knowledge is rather 'naïve'. It is as if our only aim in life was to do scientific work, as if this goal was not heavily overdetermined, as if we were a group of pure minded people constantly on the same level, whose work fits together perfectly and that we would all work in harmony.

In fact, other types of motivations come in the middle and you cannot keep them from interfering with the purity of scientific discussion. What I am saying is rather obvious and it is the same for other groups, but there is something quite curious (what I call 'naïve optimism'): these factors can never be uttered, it is like a huge taboo or fear, and is in all cases denied. We should not talk about it. And yet, a rational policy of reorganization into teams, collective work, would be very different from what we usually see. Of course, it is desirable to keep one's cool and to keep the scientific debate in one's own field. But in order for every participant to be able to make this secondary effort, one must make sure that there is no (or very little) resistance or emotional short circuit underneath and to pay minimum attention to it. For a start: acknowledge the existence of the issue and do not lie to yourself.

We will not be able to avoid strong antipathy between two people with different theoretical motives who will certainly start hours of confused and hopeless discussions. We will not be able to avoid that Mr. John Doe voices his opinion for nothing, because he has issues asserting himself. But this is not the aim of a discussion. A seminar, for example, is not a therapy group. It does not deal with the participants' personal issues (there are other places for that). I am simply thinking of ways to improve research in its own environment, which takes charge of the emotional urges present in the background. That would help to avoid worsening some situations. It would be a good start if we think that the principal effect of most collective research organizations is to make things difficult via their paperwork, their latent authoritarianism, the time and energy wasted in meetings, writing reports etc. ...

In a way, the policy I am thinking of does not rely on much, but it is rarely acknowledged, let alone practiced: to be ready to speak to people (to listen to them especially), to give people space to talk about their research, to let them speak, give the freedom to choose one's topic of interest, etc. ... It is rather a 'tone', a general attitude, made of various approaches (but specific ones) and various refrains – all of this aimed at creating, not a scientific space (= that can only come afterwards) but a space where you can breathe, something that you rarely find (our research can only get better once we breathe): it is not enough for research to be created out of nothing, for we also need to find ways not to deny or reject it when a row takes place in a meeting.

Q: If you say that this naïve ideology exists and that research can only be done with desire – can it lead to misunderstandings (a few students come to mind), when they are aware that research is transferred, channelled through sciences, rigor and methods?

Metz: Yes, absolutely. ... There is a group of students with whom I can only have a satisfying relation, a rather normal one, after a while, the time they use their initial miraculous scientism and they realize at once (that's why I deal with personal relations) that I am a human being like any other.

There are psychoanalytical factors coming into play, rather obvious ones actually (= the position of the 'disciple' creates a Father Figure), and also institutional ones: we could say a lot about Ph.D. theses (Barthes actually talked about it quite well). It is a possible and impossible exercise, it is writing without writing, it not scholarly enough or too didactic. It really is a subtle adjustment.

When I am asked to be a Ph.D. supervisor, two things very often clash within the student: a real desire to explore object X, and the need to not acknowledge the object as it is (even though it is his best chance to do rigorous work), a need to persuade himself in advance, on the level of labels and procedures (such as semiology) that what he is going to do is really scientific. There is also a real desire for limits, caution and safeguards. In certain cases, the demand borders on pure magic and puts me in a very delicate situation. I had candidates who, while looking anxious for my approval on their research project, were not satisfied with my initial approval (for they suspected it to be based purely on politeness); they expected me to determine the genuinely semiological and scientific authenticity of their work that they had not even started. Or they thought that, when I told them that the topic they chose had to be of interest to them, they were afraid that it was a polite way of saying it did not interest me.

It is much harder than you think to make the candidate admit two issues, the first one as significant as the second and yet so simple (I even failed to do so with certain candidates even if we had two hours of frank discussion): 1. That if the chosen topic was the one that interested me the most, I would have studied it or I would have started to get into it. 2. That the topic interests me as much, and I am glad to see that it is handled by someone who loves it more than I do.

Sometimes a super-egotistical projection is cast onto me (and I assume it is the same with all the rather famous researchers) and that can be quite alienating for the person who does that. Not only do they have to work in the same field as I do, making distinctly different contributions within the same field; they think that their desire should be mine (they seek for their desire an *approved substitute*). In the realm of the imaginary, I should be writing their book or they should write mine. It is an extreme case (in which the physical separation of individuals can be an issue), but it indicates a certain tendency. A tendency that can go as far as the sort of an attenuated hallucination such as when I hear 'But you have written that...' for things that I have never written.

Imprisoned desire is often the main issue of those who start their research. When you have many students, you observe certain patterns, similar to the embryo's development in successive phases, without even noticing that young researchers go through the same phases. When they come and see me at the beginning, their attitude is a mix of unjustified modesty and aggressiveness. And what is going to make our meetings easier and relaxed is that they will learn to know me in my everyday life through seminars or discussions, but what is important, most of all, is their first contact with real work, with their own work (or non-work, in the case of those whose 'desire for doing a thesis' was fundamentally an illusion). Then, little by little, they reorganize their work, and it becomes possible to talk about a 'science' without this stifling defensiveness that they adopt at the beginning. For example, it is now possible to consider that the thesis will have certain semiological aspects but it will also be free to use other methods (I am not joking: this simple prospect is, at the beginning, sometimes experienced as a real heartbreak, as genuine anguish). The situation then becomes clearer and students then decide whether they want to carry on with their theses or not (it is a real choice). On a certain level, these two cases are very similar: it is assumed that the two students have reflected (without me) on their real interest on their thesis topic or their dislike for this type of thesis. Some of my best students, the most intellectually active, have not written a doctoral thesis, and may never do so. There are also some who decide to undertake it without really believing in it; it is, rather, a professional choice. This is again another lucid choice, real progress compared to the initial *pathos*.

In the same way, I have always been amused (and rather saddened, too) by the ready-made expressions that many students bring up: 'I work with Mr. so and so' (a well-known researcher). We all know what this often means: Mr. so and so, notoriously overworked, spoke to them twice for five minutes in the corridor between four phone calls. And yet, these students are not liars, they are not trying to impress their interlocutors, it is much deeper than that, much more sincere and unclear (quite serious actually): they are victims of the constant and stupid psychodrama of belonging and affiliations, and without a 'team' (even imaginary, as they are 9 out of 10 times), they would not feel like a participant, they would not take seriously their desire to work on their interests. Once again we are dealing with imprisoned desire.

A folklore of mythical science exists (but it is waiting for its ethnologist); that is, an alienated scientific imaginary (for the scientific imaginary has another side to it, the one that intervenes in real research). A personal anecdote reminds me of this folklore: on several occasions, researchers who read my work without meeting me in person were surprised to see me on our first encounter because they imagined me to be an old and austere gentleman wearing ties and black suits. (As a result, when I saw their reactions, it was as if they thought I was barely twenty. ...) My writings do not give away anything about my age, my lifestyle, my taste in clothes, but I must say that my methodologies and problems are often rather austere. Here lies the projection made onto the author, a process that is much stronger than you think (it sometimes remains with me for quite a long time, and it is stronger than the visual evidence). It says a lot about people's need for 'roles': they first envisioned, like the scholastic disputations of the Middle Ages, a sort of entity (a physical person) and 'film semiology'. This would be a mere picturesque detail if, unfortunately, it did not go awry: that is, when the medieval entity serves only to interrogate itself, and when the desire for science, imprisoned by images, keeps you from working scientifically. That is why I often avoid using the term 'science': it is not because we are remote from it in our field, but this word tends to have devastating psychological effects.

Quantitative misunderstanding

The alienation of this desire to work takes various shapes. I am in the right position to observe another one that I call 'quantitative misunderstanding'. Over two years, more than two hundred candidates have applied to my seminars (and I could only accept a small number of them for I have already too many doctoral candidates). This situation, contrary to what you may think, is not very pleasant, or at least it becomes unpleasant rather quickly: once you have passed the pleasure of flattery (quite silly, and that does not last very long), you truly understand the real nature of this request and the 'inflated', unhealthy side of it.

If I told you that the University of Pau had received 200 applications for their only Master's degree in Ornithology, you would think, everybody would think, that there is something wrong, something that has nothing to do with ornithology and that there must be in this field a sort of collective unease, whereas the real cause is elsewhere, and that creates a rush into the fabulous representation of this science.

In comparison to the world of research, all the disciplines, the courses, the work that I do or that can be done around me, represents a territory as tiny, as specialized, an intrinsic choice as 'improbable' as ornithology or other similar fields. The only difference is that you cannot really see it, and here lies the misunderstanding. There are magical words such as 'semiology' (the new miraculous gadget for some) or 'cinema' that attract many people because it is 'modern': what a great reason!

Cinema is one research topic among others, semiology is one way to approach it among others and I am a film semiologist among others. (It is true that I am to some extent the initiator of this approach, and I have therefore apparently gained power that I do not actually have. That's another misunderstanding: the desire to work with me, it is as if it could replace the work that everybody will have to do.) In certain cases, the misunderstanding is misplaced: there are many candidates who I cannot take on in my seminar but with whom I am ready to discuss work matters, as long and often as they need it; I tell them that but they remain dissatisfied. Their real desire was to be part of the seminar, it was their goal.

I have caused real damage (and that really disturbs me, that's why I'd like to talk about it) to some students I could not accept on the programme. What I mean is: imaginary damage that appeared to be psychologically real, at least at that moment.

If the misunderstanding has different shapes, it sometimes manifests itself in different ways. For example, some people visit me in an enthusiastic, indeed rather vivacious, frame of mind, yet they disappear three months later and never come back. It is in the second phase of their absence that a certain truth comes up: these people's problems were elsewhere, they were interested in something else. But then, how did they come up with the (sincere and fervent) illusion that it was vital to undertake research on film semiology? Moreover, to undertake it with me? It is another case of intellectual warping of desire.

In reality, I think that once we write, we raise a disproportionate amount of hope, hopes that inscribe within the reader (often momentarily, before they fall for another author) an unfocused ambition or expectation, a dissatisfaction that the goal is remote from what has been written: as much as we are trying to be precise in our writing, it is never enough. We are expected to know everything, to be able to solve unresolved and ancient issues, to answer questions to which we never had the key, questions that never crossed our minds. Here lies the gap, comical and rather annoying, between what the visitors expect from me and what I can provide them with: if I tell them that, in terms of their own confusion, I do not hold any specific key and that we could simply talk about it, nothing else, they do not really believe me; instead, they think that I want to turn them away.

Film semiology is similar to all other intellectual enterprises: there are very few researchers for whom it represents a real and long lasting choice. Simply for statistical reasons, there are a great number of other topics offered to them. But it is part of one of those disciplines (it is not the only one) that attracts uncertain questions, that temporarily deals with uncertainties, researchers unsure of their work. I must admit that it is rather difficult to be a student or a researcher at the beginning (and there the real issue begins). I must also say that, in certain fields, intellectual work is seen as an overrated ideology, a validation that verges on the grotesque (when there are so many different things we can do in life). I have noticed that there is strong pressure – and I could see it in certain distressed individuals who felt the need, often in a real panic – to write something, an intense search for something to write.

Semiology as a universal mill

Q: In regards to cinema, the rise of semiology comes with its frenzied application in film studies, and it tends to rely on exhaustive descriptions. It is the desire to differentiate itself from impressionistic criticism. And finally, this elevated position comes down to a defence mechanism, of the sort: 'At least, for me, no one will ever say that my work is not rigorous' type of attitude that is leaning toward a scientistic approach.

Metz: I also find that there are no general conclusions to draw, when exhausting the film becomes a goal in itself. That is what I call 'slicing semiology': we add everything to a universal mill, all the texts in the world, all the myths, all the novels and all the films etc. ... They come out cut in slices of different sizes, big syntagms, small syntagms, groups of second or forty-fifth articulations. But in the end, we should not be surprised, it can only prove that there are bad semiological studies, just as there are bad historical studies, psychoanalytical studies and so forth. ...

I also think that the answer is already in your question: in the field of cinema studies we have seen so many purely impressionistic and journalistic writings that, when semiology came into play, it brought more rigor; consequently, some have reacted by taking the opposite direction, a very common strategy in the history of all disciplines.

And you know, there are *two* histories in each field, parallel and yet also slightly staggered: the first one, with its own internal evolution, shapes actual research; and the other one, related to taste and desire, to the specific coefficient of adulation, also obeys some sort of rules, like the rule of successive waves. The same persons, those who are lacking a topic, will take care of the succession of consecutive waves. To limit myself to a small spatio-temporal area, I notice that some have first fought with classical semiology, then semanalysis, and now with what Deleuze-Guattari and Lyotard have worked with. Each time, the work is carried out with equal enthusiasm, followed by a painful process of questioning. I have deliberately taken the example of three approaches that seem important, that interest me and that influenced my work. But, to remain open to new contributions, to continue to work in a changing environment, and when we are convinced that there are things to change, we need to remain calm, form an inner resistance to those waves (to the waves, not the authors), an ability to put things into perspective, to determine for ourselves the intrinsic importance of certain tendencies and projects (this determination enables us to relate to them to a certain extent, but it keeps you from getting mixed up, keeps you from discrediting everything).

Honestly, it is very difficult for all of us to find our own approach in the midst of the turbulent intellectual life, especially in Paris. We should read what is published (otherwise we become fossilized) and at the same time not spread ourselves everywhere, or consequently there will not be anything for us to do. We need to stay on our own track, avoid unproductive aggressiveness, even if this path is long and winding, and even if at certain times you feel uncertain or hesitant (you should allow yourself to say 'I don't know' without torturing yourself).

This process is the only one that suits my temperament. But the question goes beyond my personal case and brings us back to what this interview is about. The scientific activity corresponds to keeping a delicate psychological disposition (an economic balance), which cannot develop for some and which can work at the cost of persistent wounds, stresses, a daily suffering (there are shipwrecks on occasions). I am therefore convinced that one of the main difficulties (not the only one obviously) lies in the *confiscation of the desire* I have talked about, a seizing made by scientistic chimeras, by the other's desire (which is assumed), by the entire scientific universe and their stiff self-punitive inclinations, as a protection against ourselves. I have forcefully insisted, in my answers, on the importance of choosing a work topic that we love (and that first of all we have to make sure that we like scientific methods). It may be obvious but the entire scientific machinery tends to make us forget this fact. The dimension of desire has to be reintroduced (a desire that is rehabilitated, accepted), and it needs to be done explicitly, in the field of scientific work. We need to refuse this *artifice* that freezes our fields and harms the most vulnerable of us. We must be simple and that may be the most complicated thing of all.

Interview tape-recorded in May-June 1974.

Notes

1. [The interviewees are referring to the machine-like kinetic sculptures of the artist Jean Tinguely.]
2. [English in the original.]

5. Round Table on Film Theory

Christian Metz, Michel Fano, Jean Paul Simon,[1] and Noël Simsolo

Buckland, Warren and Daniel Fairfax (eds), *Conversations with Christian Metz: Selected Interviews on Film Theory (1970–1991)*. Amsterdam: Amsterdam University Press, 2017.

DOI: 10.5117/9789089648259/CH5

Abstract
In this round table discussion, carried out after the conference 'Film Theory and Research' and published in *Cinéma* 221 (1977), the participants (Christian Metz, Michel Fano, Jean Paul Simon, and Noël Simsolo) reflect on the success of the conference and discuss issues such as the problematic perception of film as an object of study, the role of psychoanalysis in the study of film, and the need to study film sound.

Keywords: Christian Metz, film theory, psychoanalysis, film sound

'Théorie du cinéma. Table ronde.' Christian Metz, Michel Fano, Jean Paul Simon, and Noël Simsolo. *Cinéma* 221 (May 1977), pp. 49-61. Reprinted with the permission of Jean Paul Simon and Michel Fano. Translated by Warren Buckland.

I. Challenging the traditional split between theory/practice

[*Gaston Haustrate*:] Last February [1977], the Office de la Création Cinématographique[2] (Office for Cinema Creation) organized a conference called "Film Theory and Research," which we briefly mentioned in number 219.[3] We wish to return to the organizers and some of the participants in order to identify more clearly their objectives, and hopefully to learn some lessons from them. Can you begin by addressing the first point?

Jean Paul Simon: Our initial objective was to collate research using a location we had available to us (UNESCO). With this in mind, our goal was to allow people, specialists or not, to meet and present progress reports on film theory research, which we knew existed in several countries. But no gathering of this kind and on this topic had taken place before in France, nor, to our knowledge, in other countries. Admittedly, an identical idea had been put to the Office by Joël Farges who was, with Michel Fano and myself, one of the organizers of this conference. Its project was the organization of a meeting about film theory research. We wanted to unite researchers and filmmakers from different countries in order to challenge the traditional split between theory/practice, and to compare different ideas.

Michel Fano: It is necessary to point out that there had been, in January 1976, in Beaubourg, an experimental film retrospective. By proposing this conference with the Office, I wanted to respond to the intellectual zealotry undertaken at this previous event. Indeed, an article in *Le Monde* had referred to the retrospective at Beaubourg as "The History of the Cinema," trying to get people to believe that the history of the cinema was the history of experimental cinema. Admittedly, we were extremely interested in this type of cinema, but we think that between the non-narrative experimental cinema and the commercial cinema, characterized by Claudine Eizykman as N.R.I. (Narrative, Representational, and Industrial), there remains a vast range of cinema to research, in particular, Robbe-Grillet's dysnarrative [*dysnarratif*]. Therefore, without being able to cover everything in this new conference, we wanted to show that theory and research did not apply only to experimental cinema, and that it was false to limit the history of the cinema to it.

Noël Simsolo: As a spectator at this conference, I was struck by its serious approach. There was no hysteria, nor any sneering in regards to the various types of theoretical and practical research presented there.

Simon: By avoiding zealotry, in responding to the limitations of the Beaubourg retrospective in 1976, we also reacted strongly against the traditional unfounded reduction of cinema to the commercial sector. Economically and sociologically, dominant cinema is an important phenomenon that needs to be understood, yet the methodologies for studying it are not necessarily the same as those that drive the very important work on what we call the 'avant-garde'.

Simsolo: Today, researchers realize that their work needs to focus just as much on the films of John Ford or Marco Ferreri as much as the films of [Jonas] Mekas, Michael Snow, or Stephen Dwoskin. This awareness struck me at the conference.

Simon: There are certainly different ways to study film just as there are different types of films made. But, by successively comparing these types of studies, we can begin to see *the film as object*, and determine how to define it descriptively. In a way, this conference wanted to be a beginning and to present a series of questions to be published later.

Fano: To be specific about one of our other motives: we wanted to emphasize research that seeks to show that cinema offers more interesting possibilities beyond films that make the spectator work. After seeing 47 films at the last Cannes film festival, I have noticed that the problem is not so much with the films themselves as with the work spectators undertake in relation to the film they see and hear. Also, one of the objectives of the conference was to try to listen attentively to films because, to a large extent, criticism tends to ignore this type of work. I would like to see this conference as a point of departure for future research that could develop in this direction.

Christian Metz: I was not one of the organizers of this conference, but was an enthusiastic and actively engaged participant. In this respect, my question is: 'Why this conference today?' I have several answers.

First of all, what struck me is that this conference was timely, an historic opportunity in relation to my intellectual work on theory, this new tendency that I instigated and needed to call 'semiology' (a convenient if simplistic label).

This conference was timely because of what we had developed in our semiological 'workshop' in the past fifteen years, where we stayed with our specialized research, despite the international dissemination of some of it.

It is true, an established fact, that this dissemination was limited, making our work inaccessible; but this was necessary in order to develop the discipline. It therefore seems to me that a dialectical interaction exists between the development of the discipline and this conference in February.

Within my area of 'pure' theory – an idiotic term simply indicating that I do not make films – in this area, the discipline made the conference a success – and I insist: it was a success. ...

But in return the conference presented the discipline's specialized research to a wider public. We can even say that, in terms of theoretical research, this conference was a landmark, a step forward, and it opened up the possibility of rich collaboration. This conference represented a major move towards the resolution of conflicts.

II. In general reflections on art, cinema does not merit a place

[*Haustrate*:] Before this event, there had been no equivalent attempt?

Simon: There have been meetings of the same importance but in areas other than cinema, and certain other film events but of limited scope. Here, the event clearly established an international profile with, of course, French numerical advantage due to geographical and economic reasons (because our budget was insufficient) that limited foreign participation, which is important for this type of work.

Simsolo: I would like to reconsider the idea of the spectator's work about which Michel Fano spoke. I would like to say that the idea of work does not exclude the pleasure of seeing a film. It is false to think that a researcher sees a film in an oblique way, with a meta-perception that physically segments the film, which would then become a simple object of immediate dissection. ...

Metz: I can offer some personal remarks on this issue, since I am often labeled an 'extreme theorist' and 'cerebral'. It turns out, for example, that I am an enthusiastic spectator of westerns; when the hero shoots the villain, I celebrate. I get 'worked up', if I want to, without that preventing me from maintaining a critical attitude while watching a film and after watching it. We embody a naïve spectator [*un spectateur de premier degré*] within ourselves and, as Edgar Morin said more than fifteen years ago, *we are all black, we all carry in us our black heritage.* The theorist is like everyone else. ... Lastly, how could we speak about the social phenomenon of cinema if parts of it are not in us? ...

Simon: If one were always located at the meta-level [*second degré*], one would not be able to study the cinema; and this is precisely why many theorists ignore the cinema.

Simsolo: We can get pleasure watching a film and wonder afterwards about the reasons for this pleasure. It can work for everyone. When a film makes us euphoric, we wonder what elements, what type of alienation or which system, generates this pleasure. We are far from the stereotypes that caricature the theorist as a person who, with his head between his hands, seeks while watching a film the reasons the principal actor has so many hairs on his eyebrows or in his nostrils. ... It is necessary to fight against this false image.

Fano: I would like to underline the difference in the general public's approach to cinema and to the other arts. We reflect on music, we reflect on literature, we reflect on painting – it is even very fashionable – but the film must first entertain, make us laugh or cry. For 95% of spectators, '*the film as object*' does not exist: the operation of its text, even less.

Metz: This type of position on the cinema is common. Personally, I am all the more conscious of it, for my books are labeled 'difficult'. If they had been books on linguistics, musicology or sociology, I would never hear this type of comment. It would seem that, in regards to film, the general expectation was that one writes stupid stuff. In this depressing context, my books do indeed appear 'difficult'; in fact *Language and Cinema*, for example, is no more difficult than any basic, serious book on musciology.

Fano: In this connection, it is sufficient to think of Beaubourg, which wants to promote popular culture, but the cinema scarcely holds any real place in it: at most a minor role. This shows that, in this idea of cultural dissemination, of reflecting on art, the cinema does not have a place.

Simon: Therefore, the basis of our conference was to create awareness of the existence of the cinema and of research that studies it, because we are still utterly illegitimate: a film critic cannot – without being laughed at or without facing howls of contempt – use 'complicated' vocabulary; whereas for other arts, it is legitimate.

This absence of legitimation is found everywhere. If, for example, we examine how the cinema entered the university, we see that its legitimation came from politics and not from cinema itself. The cinema is always perceived as secondary. It is placed within 'Broadcasting' or 'Information and Communication' etc. These labels legitimately justify the presence of the cinema in the university, as well as in other places.

Simsolo: The nature of legitimation even covers theses on the cinema! One does not see a thesis on 'the cinema according to Lang' but rather 'the idea of culpability in the work of Fritz Lang'.

Fano: Why a shot has a certain length, how it functions compared to others, or why something on the left of the screen passed on the right: these are issues one never speaks about since one never speaks about the film as object.

Simsolo: However, these are questions that arise in the work of any real director. Apart from the critical texts written by filmmakers, writings on film generally ignore these issues. This is more than an anomaly: it is often incompetence. Generally, the critic of painting knows the object he writes about.

Simon: The art critic is or was informed by preliminary study of the history of art, of aesthetics, etc., whereas a number of film critics simply improvise without any prior study at this level.

III. The urgency to produce real work on the way film functions

[*Haustrate*:] Where exactly do you locate the work of the theorist compared to that of the filmmaker?

Simon: The theorist endeavors to work from a scientific foundation, and his research in semiology overlaps with the filmmaker who works from a material and practical foundation. Their work is complementary.

Fano: I would like to focus more on what we said earlier and to make a statement. In the past I belonged to various commissions: festival selection committees, *avance sur recettes*,[4] etc. In this field, the argument made in connection with films or projects is never done on the basis of film in itself. It is done on the basis of what the film 'says'. The members of these commissions evoke, for example, the psychological approach of the characters, interest in this or that situation, never the film as object.

Simsolo: And look at the result! The lack of analysis is reflected in 'political' films, whose defenders call upon the represented ideas to praise the work, forgetting absolutely 'how it is represented'. And because 'how it is represented' often transforms left-wing ideas into reactionary, alienating films, it is very serious. For this reason, the work of the conference, the work of Metz, and of *Cahiers du Cinéma*, is important. Other film journals, in their way, are taking into account the specific nature of film, and are beginning research in this direction. And, the investigation of film as object becomes critical because the film as object can distort the ideas in the script. Which proves, *inter alia*, that no film exists without its film language.

Fano: And one can readily understand how the problem becomes insoluble for political leaders: how to determine the value of a militant film like *October* [Eisenstein 1928]?

Metz: Political cinema and militant cinema are not the same. This is the problem.

Simsolo: The opposite is the case for Hollywood cinema. Thanks to Raymond Bellour who refused, for example, to be limited to thematic research on Hitchcock in order to undertake an analysis of pleasure in the Hitchcockian film as object, we know that the pleasure of being afraid when watching these films was not only a question of social fantasies, but the result of the operation of images – their framing, their editing, and their duration.

[*Haustrate*:] In this connection, where do you locate the urgency? Is work on mainstream cinema today's priority compared to work on the non-narrative cinema?

Fano: One type of film is not more important than another. The urgency is to be able to listen to a film: How do we practice this listening, how do we open film to new readings, to be attentive to 'other' cinema, to different socio-cultural habits of today?

Metz: For me, the urgency is to produce valuable reflexive work in all areas. I am wary of making demands in terms of content because, even if we prefer not to, the demand quickly becomes extreme. And it is always speculative. The demand is to produce real work, as in Bellour's research mentioned earlier. For years, we were told to attack, criticize, and expose Hollywood. This is true, but it was even more urgent to show how it worked. This is what Bellour achieved by dismantling its machinery and mechanisms, overcoming the manifest level, as for example in the complete denunciation of the dream factory, to show how this dream factory actually worked.

Simsolo: This contributed to opening up different analyses of Hollywood films. When Straub declares that John Ford is a Brechtian filmmaker, the analysis of the film as object justifies his assertion, because the film as object can positively deform what a film 'says'. Certain Hollywood directors achieved this, unconsciously or not: Fuller, Tourneur, Lang, Hitchcock, Jerry Lewis, Billy Wilder, etc.

Simon: It is important to go beyond the simple denunciation of ideology, which says that the dominant cinema is the result of the dominant class. ...

Fano: Let us take for example the case of Bach in music. ... He was kicked out of his church several times when he merely composed masses and cantatas. However, it was felt – rightly – that his technique was untraditional. Of course, what opens less conventionally than the St John Passion, for example? It affects the libido and the German priests of the time, who felt it instinctively.

Metz: The process of deformation of a work by its technique is very sharp, very acute and always very interesting to analyze.

IV. Yes, there is a psychoanalysis of the signifier

[*Haustrate*:] We noticed the prominence of psychoanalysis during your conference. How has it inspired you?

Simsolo: As a participant, I liked this prominence. Up to now, facing the signifier on screen, the spectator took refuge in the signified to justify the nature of his pleasure or his impression of a film's quality. In analyzing the signifier beyond thematic meaning or the screenplay, one realizes that it provides a certain amount of information connected to the new field of psychoanalysis. There, the image functions on another level, which it often tries to erase with an ideological fog.

Metz: This raises an important problem: the completely inaccurate and unbelievable image that many people have of psychoanalysis. People think that to speak about the psychoanalysis of the cinema is to talk about wanting to see buttocks. This is absolutely false. Psychoanalysis is a formidable instrument to analyze the signifier and the relation between image/sound. There is a whole psychoanalysis of the textual operations on the one hand

and, on the other hand, the cinematic institution: a social institution and a cinematic institution. A social institution has its imaginary, its symbolic system, its diluted fantasies. ... Yes, there is a psychoanalysis of the signifier.

Fano: It is the only one that is interesting.

Simsolo: And it is also why it is interesting to analyze the relation between the spectator and a porn film's images, rather than the content. The function of the image is often the only naturalism present.

Simon: Interestingly, it is the excess of naturalism that makes it dysfunctional.

Simsolo: Because the exaggeration of a code subverts that code. But in the psychoanalysis of cinema, there is also the spectator facing the film. Every image is erotic.

Metz: Absolutely! The spectator's look brings the film into existence. And in terms of porn, Bazin noticed that the pornographic film is content to play directly with voyeurism, not sublimate it: it offers an exaggerated version of all film. All film functions on voyeurism, but one should not limit the term to the fact of looking at buttocks. Voyeurism is the passion to see, to perceive; it is one of the foundations of the cinematic institution.

Simsolo: Walt Disney cartoons, for example, are pornographic, and the biggest porn film is undoubtedly *Psycho* (Hitchcock, 1960) which, as Jean Douchet has demonstrated admirably, plays on desire, gratification, and frustration.

Metz: Psychoanalysis is nothing more than a tool. The frustration of the look, for example, poses the problem of the frame, the rectangular screen. Frustration, in the form of concealment, forms part of the scopic play, of voyeuristic play, including ordinary erotic exercises. Concealment, delays, and resumptions play on the scopic regime and on the final pleasure [*jouissance*], which *Psycho* indeed shows magisterially.

On this question, it is necessary to return, *inter alia*, to the research of Jean Paul Simon, [Pascal] Bonitzer, Roland Barthes, etc. They produced texts on the voyeuristic-fetishistic mechanisms at work in the frame, which argue that the rectangular screen has the form of a cut or division that fundamentally belongs to the operation of the fetish.

Simsolo: See the perfection of the frame in the Hollywood cinema and the analysis that could be made – which would be exciting – between the distance produced by this perfection, and the process of identification with the Hollywood hero that tries to produce this N.R.I. cinema (which involves a play with frustration).

Metz: It is Bazin who said that, in *The Blue Angel* [von Sternberg, 1930], the sex of Marlene occupies the diagonal center of the screen in certain shots. It is useless to psychoanalyze Jannings or von Sternberg on this subject. It is the screen that functions as the place of tension and desire.

Simsolo: You spoke about porn but, in porn, there is a loss of spectatorial pleasure [*jouissance*] because of the frame and the cinematic institution.

Metz: Precisely. The issue with pornographic film is not in its content. Pornography is traditionally defined in terms of content, forgetting that it is in the act of looking. The question of the camera's point of view is never posed. This is not pornography, but a meat market [*l'étalage de charcuterie*].

Simsolo: There is no erotic pleasure without frustration and, as such, the cinema of Eric Rohmer is exemplary.

V. The ideological downplaying of the sound dimension in our civilization

[*Haustrate*:] On another level, do you think theoretical work on sound is important?

Fano: I think that the neglected sound dimension is what reaches the unconscious most directly. This dimension was expunged a long time ago by filmmakers who worked exclusively on the image. For sound, one established a system of reassuring clichés which one always finds: for example, what is usually called 'film music' [*la 'musique de film'*]. That avoids conflict.

Simon: Remember that Godard's soundtracks were regarded as obscene.

Simsolo: Even amongst technicians, there is always this idea of 'clean sound' and 'dirty sound'.

Metz: It is a defensive strategy. In the past, when leaving a screening of *Lola Montes* [Max Ophüls, 1955], there were epic fights on this subject.

Fano: The result of this idea about loud sound leads to one not hearing the sound in the cinema. The projectionists seldom adjust sound to a normal level. One hears films at 25 decibels, i.e., connecting to the visual source and not to the ear.

Simsolo: That started when films were screened in Broadway theatres or the Royal Palace. This clean sound is aberrant because it also gives a false idea of the theatre.

Metz: One of the roles of theoretical work is located there. Between 1927 and 1933, this question of sound was frequently discussed. There are numerous accounts of this problem involving Rudolf Arnheim, plus Eisenstein, Pudovkin, and Alexandrov's 'Manifesto for Orchestral Counterpoint,' the Pagnol-René Clair polemic, the theories of the 'asynchronism' and 'non coincidence' of image/sound, the reflections of Balázs, etc.

Fano: Curiously, the "Manifesto for Orchestral Counterpoint," a significant theoretical text signed by Alexandrov, Pudovkin, and Eisenstein, was hardly applied thereafter by Eisenstein who, with *Alexandre Nevsky* [1938], contributed to the design of 'film music'. This difference is surprising.

Simsolo: As a result, the viewer of Robbe-Grillet or Carmelo Bene is furious not hearing clean sound to which he was accustomed. Not to mention that the majority of viewers see films dubbed.

Metz: Dubbing horrified Bresson: "His (untrained) voice gives us his intimate character."[5]

Simon: The cinema creates codes of reading and codes of pleasure, with the result that any attempt to do something else is perceived to be a violation, a transgression. ...

Simsolo: ... Or iconoclastic, which is symptomatic of a self-protective strategy.

Metz: This is not a problem exclusive to film, this downplaying of the sound dimension in our civilization. It is a historical and ideological phenomenon, which is everywhere, including in our own group and inside theoretical work. Except for Lacan and [Guy] Rosolato, no one really speaks of the 'invocatory drive', the mother's voice and the fear of this voice. In psychoanalysis, work on the voice is far behind work on vision.

VI. Not working according to an absurd conference ideal

[*Haustrate*:] Certain participants in your conference pointed out that opera, theatre, the comic strip, were rarely mentioned. Why was this?

Simon: We wanted to, but we were delayed by other things.

Fano: And our organizing work included various tasks that were taking our time: transport, handling, advertising, administration. ...

Simon: Because we were with UNESCO, we believed that we would benefit from its rich, substantial infrastructure. But there was nothing.

Fano: Most of the work was carried out by Jean Paul Simon and Simone Raskin. ... Moreover, we had problems such as Customs blocking films brought in by Annette Michelson. Of course, this conference had flaws. It is true that opera was not mentioned, although this popular spectacle is precisely what cinema replaced. Alban Berg had understood this; before his death, he planned to make a film of [his opera] 'Woyzeck'. He began the *découpage* just before he died.[6]

Metz: Wasn't Diderot's great dream a total art that would include opera?

Simsolo: The popular novel, the comic strip of the Thirties and its relation to adventure Hollywood films, or the Italian comics of today that directly influence popular Italian cinema in terms of eroticism and violence, were never mentioned. The same with theatre.

Simon: There is the issue of animation. We wanted too many things.

Metz: There was also the problem of the large number of important presentations, which left insufficient time for general discussion.

Simon: That said, the many discussions after the presentations demonstrated the positive aspect of the conference.

Metz: Some people criticized the chaotic aspect of the conference. I do not agree. I am a veteran of conferences in various disciplines and, generally, others were much more disorganized than this one. Those who made these criticisms spoke of an ideal, perfect conference, which has never existed.

[*Haustrate*:] How did the working groups function?

Simon: Only one really functioned, the one organized around Noël Burch and Jorge Dana. They analyzed the implicit norms of film production, using a television program and a new film: *Solemn Communion* by Rene Féret [1977]. They worked on this film and on the film's unedited footage with the technicians and the director. This group will continue its analyses.

[*Haustrate*:] How do you see the future of this conference?

Fano: It would be necessary to envisage a new conference in two years in order to fill the gaps of this one. We would focus less on new media because research is very slow in this field. We should direct the conference towards research that advances rapidly, by widening the approaches in order to avoid criticisms we received.

Metz: Taking these reservations into account, we can say that this conference marks a step forward in the *maturity* of the general level of discussion on film. For five days, we heard discussions on the cinema and on films where, of course, we spoke about linguistics, psychoanalysis, theories of ideology, etc. It is not necessary to fetishize it, but this is in fact the work that we do today.

VII. What would contribute to the popularity of theory?

[*Haustrate*:] How do you explain the fact that your conference received little coverage in the press in general and by film critics in particular?

Fano: I believe that the absence of coverage in the press was to be expected for reasons referred to above (working specifically with film); many of your colleagues [film critics], who are to some extent a reflection of the public, did not feel concerned. The majority did not come to this conference so that they would not have to write on something they still barely comprehend.

Metz: I find this quite harsh. I say this calmly, that I often suffer from fatuous attacks or silence from critics. But we should consider the professional constraints specific to this job: seeing many films, working quickly, often under bad conditions. Consequently, to be open to advanced thinking means hard work for many people. Rare are those who can carry it out (there was Bazin, in particular ...).

[*Haustrate*:] It is true that film criticism is practiced under poor economic conditions. But it is also true that 90% of our colleagues' work remains, due to intellectual laziness or neglect, a thematic or psychological form of film analysis, which completely neglects [theoretical] writing, whereas their influence could be great in regards to popularizing theory. Why this gap? Why is there a gulf between high-level theory and routine work in organizations like the IFACC,[7] for example? What solutions do you recommend to reduce this disparity and expand our respective areas of activity?

Simon: These questions are too important to be settled quickly. This gap is also an effect of film's lack of legitimacy. It is also important to avoid a moralizing critical attitude: the defense of a non-legitimate object always leads to strategies of defense and recognition, which leads to innumerable presentations on film as art, passing through types of analysis found in other disciplines (literary analysis, theatrical) that is, thematic analysis (a film will be interesting for its important themes, there exists an implicit catalogue of 'good themes').

Again we are faced with the same problem: the idea that cinema involves a specific type of work, yet access to documents and equipment is still not generally accepted. The result is to carry out work in piecemeal fashion, and without sharing information. Or working in organizations like the IFACC also means, although differently, a break, a gap vis-à-vis usual modes of thinking and working on film. Moreover, experience shows that some theories deemed difficult work remarkably well for non-specialists under certain conditions, as shown in Alain Bergala's experience teaching audio-visual media in secondary education (see Alain Bergala, *Pour une pedagogie de L'audio-visuel*, Paris: Editions de la Ligue française de l'Enseignement et de l'Éducation Permanente, 1975).

Metz: In this matter as in others, I do not believe we should expect an all-inclusive solution. Some film critics work under pragmatic conditions that exclude theory; they lack the minimum level of intellectual training. Sometimes we also come across active 'resistance', a deliberate rejection of modern theoretical advances, an aggressive attitude that comprises a fear of loss. Moreover, these various factors can add up; these are cases where one cannot do anything.

But there remains (fortunately) other cases. Here, it is not hopeless. Instead, a problem – a big problem, but which is a normal obstacle to scientific progress, and which is not exclusive to film studies – a problem of *disseminating* the methods and concepts of recent research.

I do not have a miracle cure. No solution, I am sure, will avoid *a dual approach,* an effort and real work on both sides. Critics must read and study, take time to reflect, remain up to date, take new courses. But theorists, on their side – and this is one of our objectives at the l'Ecole des Hautes Etudes, already partially fulfilled thanks to the efforts of those who work with me, such as for example Geneviève Jacquinot, Michel Marie, Guy Gauthier, Bernard Leconte, Alain Bergala, etc. – the theorists must regularly and frequently get involved with associations and training courses. They must agree to devote part of their time – because this is one of their specific perennial tasks – to write high-level introductions to contemporary film studies research. It is not exactly a question of 'popularizing': this word has an unequal, contemptuous nuance that I do not like. It is a question of *teaching,* dialogue, real circulation of knowledge. What is called 'theory' is not a sanctuary reserved for great minds; it is nothing more than a requirement of rigor and precision, a certain way of posing problems. It is a thing that one learns (as with everything else). It is enough to want it. And to put it to work.

Remarks collected by Gaston Haustrate.

Notes

1. [At the time of this interview, Jean Paul Simon was in charge of the research department of the Office de la Création Cinématographique.]
2. [A public entity set up by the Ministry of Culture.]
3. ["Ephemerides," *Cinéma* 219 (March 1977), p. 3.]

4. [An 'advance on earnings', or government subsidy/loan awarded by a commission to a selected number of films, which is paid back only if the film goes into profit. The funds are managed by the Centre National de la Cinématographie, a public body.]
5. [Both Simsolo and Metz use the term 'post-synchronisation'. Metz's quotation from Bresson is from *Notes on Cinematography*, translated by Jonathan Griffin (New York: Urizen Books, 1977), p. 36. I have followed Griffin's translation. Bresson calls dubbing 'naive barbarity' on p. 25.]
6. [*Découpage* can mean planning a film (breakdown of the script into shots prior to filming) and the editing of the finished film. Michel Fano is referring to the planning stage.]
7. [Institut de Formation Aux Activités de Culture Cinématographique.]

6. Conversation on *The Imaginary Signifier* and *Essais Sémiotiques*

Christian Metz, Jean Paul Simon, and Marc Vernet

Buckland, Warren and Daniel Fairfax (eds), *Conversations with Christian Metz: Selected Interviews on Film Theory (1970–1991)*. Amsterdam: Amsterdam University Press, 2017.

DOI: 10.5117/9789089648259/CH6

Abstract
In this interview, carried out for the journal *Ça-Cinéma* in 1979, Christian Metz looks back over his research (published in the two collections *The Imaginary Signifier* and *Essais Sémiotiques*), the changes his work has undergone, and mentions the latest developments in his research, including his interest in experimental cinema.

Keywords: Christian Metz, film theory, psychoanalysis, experimental cinema

"Conversation sur *Le Significant Imaginiare* et *Essais Sémiotiques*." Jean Paul Simon, Marc Vernet, and Christian Metz. *Ça-Cinéma,* 16 (January 1979), pp. 5-19. Reprinted with the permission of Jean Paul Simon and Marc Vernet. Translated by Daniel Fairfax.

1. Analysis, the cinema and the lost 'object'

Jean Paul Simon: We often hear that 'semiology makes its object disappear', but this phrase seems to rest on a dangerous confusion between the object of common sense as it already exists, and the object as it can be produced in a model of intelligibility by semiological analysis and theory. What is more, it also expresses the idea that any methodology whatsoever can take a pre-existing object and that, at the end of the process, this object will be closer to what it was in 'reality'.

Christian Metz: When film semiology is accused of making its object disappear, the term 'object' derives from the traditional approach to the object. And it is quite true that, up to a certain point, semiology sidesteps this object (but it also opens up a different film-object).

Common discourse deems it self-evident that the cinema is nothing other than a collection of 'works of art' – some successful, others failures – which one discusses in aesthetic or journalistic-impressionistic terms. Semiology, of course, will never encounter this cinema. But it is not *the* cinema. In its definition there already enters, surreptitiously, a good dose of methodology, even if the method, in this case, is rather soft and feeble.

Simon: Another version of the question above is: 'but where is the cinema in all this?' Most of the time this presupposes the existence of films that, by their very nature, are excluded from semiological approaches.

Metz: I am convinced that what we have here is an additional misunderstanding. It is correct that certain films have been analyzed more often than others from a semiological perspective, or according to the various procedures of 'textual' study: whence the relatively widespread impression that there are films that are intrinsically 'semiological', and that they are (*rightfully*) more accessible than others to rigorous decomposition or structural analysis. We sometimes hear this about experimental films, which are supposedly 'non-semiological' (but inversely, let us not forget, other experimental trends, such as 'structural film' or the Werner Nekes tendency, conceive of their productions as being cognitive, self-reflexive and metalinguistic in nature; so the problem is complex even within non-narrative cinema).

Nonetheless, it remains true up to the present, and it would be dishonest to deny it, that the semiological method has been applied more often to films of a largely 'classical' nature (which does not mean that they are banal, or commercial: the list of films most often studied from a semio-textual standpoint includes *North by Northwest* by Hitchcock, *Muriel* by Resnais, *October* by Eisenstein, etc.).

In my opinion, it is purely a matter of circumstance, of the chronology of semiological research, which began, quite naturally, with more or less narrative objects – that is, objects that are socially more common (this is important, to the extent that all semiologies involve an element of sociology, a project of socio-historical critique), as well as films that are 'easier' to analyze (to once again speak hastily); easier, that is, at least initially, for an approach that is still in its early stages.

Today, before our eyes, things are already beginning to change. A true semiology of experimental cinema is in the process of being developed. I am referring, for example, to the research carried out by Dominique Chateau and his colleagues, the work done by Thierry Kuntzel, or the work of Bernhard Lindemann in Germany, who has just dedicated an entire book, based on semiology and textual analysis, to experimental cinema (= Snow, Lawder, Frampton, Emshwiller, *Un chien andalou* by Buñuel, *Entr'acte* by René Clair, *Ballet mécanique* by Fernand Léger), titled *Experimentalfilm als Metafilm* (*Experimental Cinema as Metacinema*), published in 1977 in Hildesheim, by the Olms publishing house.

This evolution is reflected in my own preoccupations. Experimental cinema interests me more than it used to. Whence the long supplementary notes on this subject that I have added to older texts reprinted in my *Essais sémiotiques* (cf., above all, pp. 167-168 and 172-173).

Marc Vernet: In your latest work, you insist that the more semiology advances, the more narrowly it focuses in on its object, only looking at a small part of a film, a small part of a text.

Metz: This is true, but it seems to me that this is the flipside, or the inevitable corollary, of any deeper undertaking and rigorous study. In a recent, short review of my books, you yourself speak, humorously and fittingly, of the virtues of myopia... We cannot study something in depth if this something covers, at the same time, an immense area. This restriction is not specific to semiology, it imposes itself on any serious reflection on any object whatsoever.

Vernet: Here, there is a bizarrely pleasurable process: I launch myself into the analysis of a film that pleased me, I imagine that my analysis will tell me why and how the film is pleasing, but I can only study one small segment of the film – one code, for example, among the multitude of codes that compose the film – and so I cannot really grasp this pleasure. ...

Metz: I readily agree with you, but on the condition of adding this point: the pleasure of analysis is qualitatively different to the pleasure of viewing a film, which first establishes itself at the level of the whole film (or more exactly of the film in its entirety, even if certain parts were not especially 'pleasing' to the spectator) – by this I mean a certain type of affectivity, which sustains cognitive functions (this does not entail falling back into an opposition between the intellectual and the emotional, which is absurd and populist [*poujadiste*]). The pleasure of analysis derives from the act of dissecting a film (then synthesizing it), from the impression of understanding, examining and clarifying it. This is why this pleasure (a different type of pleasure) can be fully felt with a *segment* of the object or problem being studied, at the moment in which this segment has truly been 'mastered'.

2. Cultural illegitimacy and its perverse effects

Simon: Does this not engage the status of this film-object as it is commonly understood (but also what it can represent for the imaginary of the researcher), in terms of its relationship with the legitimate objects that we do or do not feel the need to study?

Metz: I believe that this *deficit* in the cultural legitimacy of the cinema (in Bourdieu-Passeron's sense of the term) raises three kinds of perverse effects that are triggered in a chain reaction, one after another. Each effect is the equal and opposite reaction of its predecessor, over-compensating for its drawbacks.

The first perverse effect of this illegitimacy (and the most quantitatively widespread of the three) is the idea that the cinema is not a serious subject. Serious people do not bother with it, and they leave the job to others who are willing to tackle it. An example is film criticism in the daily newspapers (with, thankfully, a few exceptions).

The second perverse effect resides in those pathological forms of cinephilia. The cinema arouses, among certain individuals, feelings of passionate love, leading to an overestimation of the object (as Freud would say), and an imaginary, effusive, excessive allegiance to it. These are inseparably linked, by a dialectical reversal, to the cinema's status as an unrecognized art form (= it has to be vindicated). This is the source of a certain type of fanatical discourse, which we have all heard. Between weak-minded discourse and fanatical discourse, it is not all that easy to speak of the cinema in a rigorous manner, or even simply in a calm and precise manner. A possible definition of semiology, or at least good semiology (which is not the only type, far from it) is this: calm discussion of the cinema. The aesthete attacks semiology with fury, because the semiologist does not return *his* object to him: the aesthete's object, which the aesthete calls 'cinema'.

The third perverse effect: semiological fanaticism in all its various forms: delirious semiotizations, loose approximations claiming to be Lacanian, heavy platitudes, pseudo-linguistic studies, etc. In a word: *leaden discourse* [*discours plombé*] (which is, by the same token, dispiriting [*plombant*]). This is an awkward, somewhat pathetic attempt to react against the discourse of derision (= level 1) and against the discourse of illumination (= level 2). Semiology thus becomes a miracle remedy, the gadget of the century, the key that opens every door, the raft that rescues us from all shipwrecks. But in reality this discourse is the shipwreck of semiology itself, for what defines the true spirit of semiology is the very opposite of this arrogant, philistine imperialism. Semiology is a modest approach, very slow-moving, patient, constantly open to external relations and constantly placed under interrogation.

Vernet: With the third perverse effect we have a double lover: the lover of semiology and the lover of cinema. ...

Metz: The former risks being doubly mistaken.

3. Linguistics and psychoanalysis as detours

Vernet: There is a double restructuring in your work: a restructuring of semiology, insofar as it must first pass through a certain number of disciplines, which represent detours and sites of investment, and a restructuring of the cinema, which can no longer be envisaged in the framework of a partial approach. ...

Metz: By speaking of investment and detour, you make me think of something else, a point I have not developed very far, and where the situation, too, has not changed much for ten or fifteen years. There was a time when I thought that, in order to do semiology, we had first to pass through a considerable *linguistic detour*, to really learn linguistics, dedicating several years to the project. Later, I had the same feeling about psychoanalysis. But today I feel that if, for me, these two 'detours' were indeed very important, then this is because I find linguistics and psychoanalysis very interesting in and of themselves, and not because a rather strong dose of these two disciplines would be truly indispensable for film research. It is not an unimportant matter to rectify this point, because an overly weighty 'recycling' of disciplines external to the cinema can justifiably frighten away or discourage certain young researchers whose objective is the cinema itself. This is why I have become ever more careful about speaking of a linguistic (or psychoanalytic) 'inspiration' rather than a 'method'.

When it is said that semiology owes a lot to linguistics and psychoanalysis, this is quite true, obviously, in comparison to other types of discourse on the cinema, which owe nothing to these two scientific fields. It is also true when it comes to the guidelines of the semiological method, its founding principles, its major inspirations (I am using this word again, and not by chance), and, I would almost say, its state of mind (and this is of major importance, undoubtedly).

But in another sense, it is false. It is false because, among all the linguistic and psychoanalytic notions and procedures, only a small fraction of them are usefully exportable to film studies (otherwise there is the risk of transplanting, which is the worst of all forms of semiology). Only the great foundational texts of these fields are of use to semiology (but in these cases, one must really know the texts).

In my individual journey, which is not a model for anybody because it is linked to a unique biography and temperament, two quite distinct things have been confused: my adoption of two tutor-disciplines in order to renew film studies, and the very strong attraction these disciplines exerted on me by their very nature, beyond any preoccupation I might have for the cinema. At the École des Hautes Études, before commencing my seminar on the cinema, I taught 'pure' linguistics (to which, even recently, I dedicated an article in *Essais Sémiotiques* and several sections of the other articles in my book). Another example of this: in *The Imaginary Signifier*, when I talk about metaphor and metonymy, a relatively long passage consists entirely of proposing a new theory of censorship [pp. 253-65]: this is a purely psychoanalytic problem, which does not specifically concern the cinema (psychic censorship applies to all of social life).

But those who have the goal of studying only the cinema, even from an authentically semiological point of view, do not have to make a linguistic-psychoanalytic journey as long as mine, because my journey owes much of its length to extra-cinematic preoccupations.

Simon: With respect to this relatively old article from *Essais Sémiotiques* where you say that semiology must be linked to linguistics, would you now tend to think that it is sufficiently autonomous?

Metz: Yes. It is, in any case, more autonomous than it was when I wrote the article you are speaking about (the one called 'Les Sémiotiques,' written in 1965 [*Essais Sémiotiques*, pp. 9-30]). Within this question of the linguistic (or psychoanalytic) detour, we touch on another factor, one that is distinct from my personal tastes: the objective evolution of the field over the last

15 years. Film semiology, whatever its worth, has undergone development; it is a little more sure of itself, it has less need of being vouched for by tutor-disciplines; it continues to borrow from them, but more freely and with less rigidity. I found it striking that the most robust research on cinematic codes and texts are from writers who do not claim any special knowledge of linguistics (e.g., Raymond Bellour) or psychoanalysis (e.g., Michel Marie).

There is also something else, which is that linguistics and psychoanalysis, for their part, have in the meantime pursued their own, autonomous, increasingly technical development, one in which cinematic preoccupations, as far as I can tell, are playing a weaker role. The film semiologist who wishes to really 'follow' all these recent developments runs a great risk of exhaustion, even if only because of the amount of reading he would have to do. Let us take the case of linguistics: three-quarters of present-day research is situated in transformational generative theory, or research that extends and supersedes it, like generative semantics, the grammar of cases, sociolinguistic variation, etc. We cannot wait for all semiologists to become well-versed in this research (even if it is exciting), because it is so difficult. Only a few semiologists are keeping pace with it, those who chose to apply these precise procedures to their object, like Dominique Chateau and Michel Colin in film studies.

That said, I still feel it is impossible to study seriously a social practice of signification like the cinema without a minimal knowledge of linguistics and psychoanalysis. It is with respect to the exact size of this minimum (which should not be too minimal!) and its quantitative determination that I have modified my evaluations, by 'lowering' them.

Simon: I had the impression for a while that 'strictly' cinematic preoccupations were quite frequently excluded from your seminar. Many people thought that it was not useful to go to the cinema; what mattered was the acquisition of linguistic or psychoanalytic competence. The investment in a complete object is transferred to theory and not to the cinema.

Metz: I too felt this about my seminar, but I believe that it was an evolutionary phase, the 'negative moment' if you will: a reactive period where we opposed the dominant aesthetic discourse. At some point, however, we bent the stick too far in the other direction: we stopped speaking about the cinema and semiologists took themselves for linguists, or psychoanalysts, or theorists of ideology and the 'Ideological State Apparatus'. Since then, things have changed, and, I feel, for the better: the participants in my seminar have retained the (salubrious) habit of speaking about a bit of everything, but they are also beginning to speak about the cinema again. Bit by bit, things are being put back into perspective.

In one's personal development, you also find reactive phases. Thus, in the initial period of my project, from 1962 to about 1970, I went to the movies less often than I did during my cinephilic, ciné-club youth. I did still go to the movies, but not very often, about once or twice a week. And then, I started going again. At present I watch four or five films a week. It is also not really a question of the number of films, because this can vary due to external factors (one's work schedule, the neighborhood one lives in, how overworked one is, etc.). What I mean to say by all this is that, once again, I love going to the movies.

Simon: Is there not, alongside this reactive position towards cinephilia, another attitude that involves the desire to acquire competence in linguistics or psychoanalysis, without feeling the need to go to the movies?

Metz: You are right, but there is, I believe, something else that comes into play, and that distorts the problem, which is that *competence in a formalized discipline* and competence in a non-formalized discipline are two very different things. In principle, an apprenticeship is necessary in both cases, but between the two the type of apprenticeship needed is so distinct that we almost have two autonomous definitions of the word 'learn'. Learning a non-formalized discipline, like the history of cinema for example (or staying up to date, even in great detail, with contemporary cinema as it evolves), merely involves recording factual data and general impressions. That is, it involves filling your head with material, but not changing your ideas. On the contrary, someone who starts off without any knowledge of linguistics (or psychoanalysis, which is formalized in its own way), and who sets out to gain knowledge of the field, even if only at a basic level, is obliged to go through a genuine process of apprenticeship: they, too, must ingest factual data (= dates, books, authors, etc.), but in addition to that they are led to modify their mental universe, their habitual ways of reasoning, and to acquire, even if only in summary form, an authentic 'education'; it is not enough for them to gather information, they must change their way of thinking.

This, in my opinion, goes some way to explaining the 'reactive' period we just spoke about: many semiologists, in this period, dedicated their energies to 'real' apprenticeships, everything else was shunted into the background.

4. On classical film theory

Simon: '[Classical] film theory', it seems, is of great importance to your work, yet at the same time it is relatively absent from it. It is present because it is so often cited, but absent because it does not intervene anywhere.

Metz: In the early stages of my work, traditional film theory was of great importance; I am thinking of some of my initial articles, like, for example, "Cinema: Language or Language System?" or my two long texts on Mitry. I spent several years reading the major theorists, and they 'resurfaced' in my work, not only in the form of ritual footnote references, to spice things up, but also because they truly nourished and enriched my own outlook. Film theory was one of the major sources of semiology (by the way, I already said this very clearly; see pp. 92-93 of volume I of my *Essais sur la Signification au Cinéma* [*Film Language*, pp. 90-91]).

But a kind of backlash has also taken place, relating to the very existence of semiology, and more generally modern thinking on the cinema. These approaches are more rigorous, more detailed, more conceptually elaborated and more in step with contemporary science than was classical aesthetic theory. The latter had, therefore, by force of circumstances, found itself somewhat devalued, *obsolescent* – which, by the way, is a common phenomenon in the history of all disciplines (for example: the mere existence of generative linguistics has dealt a heavy blow to structural and distributional linguistics). This effect, of course, is not retroactive, except in the eyes of hurried, muddled minds who merely follow fashions. Eisenstein, Balázs, Arnheim, Bazin, etc., still retain their interest, which is considerable. Nevertheless, it is no longer possible *today* to write a book 'à la Balázs', or 'à la Epstein'.

Simon: Are we not falling back into the same problem we had before regarding film 'culture' – with the exception that, in spite of everything, film theory is more apt to be formalized?

Metz: Quite true. In this respect, [classical] film theory occupies an intermediate stage. Unfortunately, among the various 'fields of knowledge' [*savoirs*] we have been talking about, it is by far the least favored, in my seminar and elsewhere, and in practically every country (it strikes me), apart from Italy. There are people who know linguistics, who know psychoanalysis, who know films, but there are few who know classical film theory, or who even have an inkling of its richness and breadth.

Simon: Has there not been, in your work, a phase that we can locate in other developments in semiology; namely, the phase of critical re-evaluation, which consists of taking earlier texts as a basis for a more 'modern' reflection?

Metz: To tell the truth, in the current phase of my work, I am less often concerned with classical film theory than I used to be, but this is the normal evolution of every author constructing their own discourse. And there remains the fact that, throughout my writings, I have spoken about it rather often.

There is also a remarkable thing (I am departing from your question a little here): certain detractors have accused semiology, or have accused me personally, of giving short shrift to classical film theory. And yet they use it in their own work much less than I do. In certain cases, they are hardly even familiar with it, like the thief who shouts out: 'Stop, thief!' For instance, who speaks about Rudolf Arnheim today? As far as I know, only three people in the entire world, all three of whom are semiologists or 'fellow-travelers': Keiji Asanuma in Japan, Emilio Garroni in Italy, and myself in France. Another example: among those who claim that semiology makes a clean sweep of the past, who has undertaken the work of 'rereading' it patiently and at length, to the same extent as I have with my work on Jean Mitry's two major volumes? [*Esthétique et Psychologie du Cinéma* (1963, 1965)]

In truth, one of semiology's contributions has been to return classical film theory to the agenda, or at least it has done everything possible to make this happen. Even today this theory is poorly known, but 15 years ago it was almost totally ignored.

5. From one logic to another

Simon: It seems to me that there is another source that constantly nourishes all of your texts, namely 'logical competence'. An example of this is your text on connotation in volume II of *Essais sur la Signification au Cinéma t. II*.[1] There is a whole section of the text (which you have not included) that is an analysis of the preceding logics of the notion of connotation.

Metz: Yes, this is true.

Simon: However, in *Essais* vol. II the only part of this text that is reprinted is the part that is directly linked to the semiological analysis of film. Can you give an account of this publication (or work) strategy?

Metz: I think that the first part of my seminar on connotation (which was held in 1971-72, I believe), the part that I did not reprint in the published text, was didactic in nature, rather than a personal research project. It thus had a place in the context of a seminar (which allows room for both new research and historical review), but not in a research book, which by definition excludes the latter (it would only have been publishable in a textbook).

But to respond to your question on a more general level, yes, indeed, a certain logical horizon is always more or less present in my work.

Simon: This is very clear in *Essais Sémiotiques*. ...

Metz: Yes, and to tell the truth this comes from the fact that the linguistic approach and the psychoanalytic approach both constitute kinds of logic. Modern linguistics is close to logic, and it is becoming ever more so, notably with generative semantics (see the notion of 'natural logic'). Psychoanalysis, with its concept of primary and secondary 'processes' – particularly in its Lacanian orientation – also becomes, so to speak, a logic of mental trajectories, or a logic of the 'illogical'.

Simon: All your texts in *Essais Sémiotiques* are very strongly marked by the role of logic, for instance, in the way in which you discuss the work of Hjelmslev and Prieto, who enter into this framework via the logic of sets and problems of formalization respectively. You are probably the only person, along with E. Veron, to try to combine these two figures.

Metz: As a matter of fact, it seems to me that we should make the effort to combine the two aspects: on the one hand, 'secondary logic' with linguistics and logic properly speaking (the logic of logicians), and 'primary logic' with its condensations and displacements, its 'figurability'. ... This is all the more necessary because the primary is constantly present beneath the secondary. They are not truly dissociable from one another.

6. Semiology of communication and semiology of signification

Vernet: What, for you, are the consequences for analysis of the distinction between a semiology of signification and a semiology of communication?

Metz: To tell the truth, I think that the problem is posed with less acuity today than ten or fifteen years ago. In this respect, the situation around us has changed a lot. At a certain moment, these two forms of semiology – the semiology of signification (marked by the decisive influence of Roland Barthes) and the semiology of communication – appear as two options of equal importance; they divide the field in half. The semiology of communication had, for its part (and still does have), important works: especially Bussens, Martinet, Mounin and Prieto. But it has barely gone beyond these works, whereas, in the same period, the semiology of signification developed very rapidly.

Today, the semiology of communication has become a kind of sub-section within semiology *tout court*: a clearly demarcated domain, which I find very interesting, but which has clearly become a minor tendency. This does not mean that it is 'dead': in the case of iconic studies, for example, Michel Tardy's doctoral thesis, *Iconologie et Sémiogénèse* (Strasbourg, 1976, 2 vol.), which I am trying to have published at Klincksieck, is a recent example of an excellent work in the semiology of communication.

Simon: To what extent, however, does the development of this second semiology – where meaning is conceived of as an operation – render completely inadequate this distinction between signification and communication? The communicational model, as you present it, referring to Julia Kristeva, fully inscribes itself into a semiology that has the 'communication' aspect as one of its outputs.

Metz: We are increasingly reaching the point of conceiving of communication as an output, occupying the level that transformational generative grammarians call the 'surface', the ever-provisional effect of a deep level of signification, which is a production and not a product. It is always possible, and of great interest, to learn about the total process of signification through one of its end-points, where an emitter and a receiver are in agreement on the meaning of a given static unit. Hence, everyone in France would recognize that the words *cheval* (horse) and *jument* (mare) are divided along the axis of sex. But this is only the end of a long signifying journey, because it already supposes, in advance, the entire system of *gender* in French.

In all domains, including the cinema, we will find surface units that are codified (I mean codified in the ordinary sense of the word, since for me everything is coded). A semiology of communication can grasp them, enumerate them, classify them – this is important work. It is clear, for example, that certain firmly established film 'genres' – like the classical Western, the musical comedy of the inter-war period, or 'film noir' in the 1940s and early 1950s – offer the analyst a genuinely real catalogue of stable and recurrent filmic configurations.

7. Signification as *deixis*

Simon: In fact, the semiology of communication presupposes symmetry between the level of the signified and that of the signifier. At one point you said, citing Prieto, that there is asymmetry between the two levels. Is this not what allows history to be reintroduced, for the discrepancies [*décalages*] between the two levels must be taken into account? At the same time it enables us to determine what is primary and what is secondary?

Metz: Yes, in a passage from my book *The Imaginary Signifier*, pp. 282-84, and 313n3, I focused on Prieto's article, which was already dated (1957-58). It was one of his first texts, which he himself entitled 'D'une asymétrie entre le plan de l'expression et le plan du contenu de la langue.' He convincingly points to this asymmetry: only the signifier is concrete, manifest, directly accessible. But it seems to me that we can go further (today) and draw from his work an argument for a *semiology of the signifier*. The signifier – which in the cinema consists of images and sounds – is the only instance on which the analyst can hold a *factual*, completely verifiable discourse: a given camera movement lasts three and a quarter minutes (but, by contrast, what does it 'express'?), a given motif recurs 19 times in the film (but what does this assertion 'mean'?).

I do not speak about the 'signified' much (except in the case of fixed surface units: the punctuating fade to black, the shot/reverse-shot in dialogue scenes, etc.). I have increasingly come to prefer expressions like 'significatory pressure', 'signifying circuit', etc. We can never truly know what the signified is. It is akin to a spatial direction, a line of flight, a vector. This is not to say that it is 'vague'. It is precise, in its own way, but it is precise as an orientation, not as an *emplacement*. In this orientation, the path is open to all overdeterminations, signification is always deictic in nature.

Vernet: We must then insist on this idea of signification and deixis as far the cinema is concerned, for what is designated is not the real, the referent, but only a line of flight of the signified.

Metz: What you say makes me think of a line of poetry that I will cite from memory without any guarantee of accuracy. I do not even remember who it is by anymore, who wrote it, nor who, in the discussions between Lacan and Lyotard on metaphor and metonymy, cited it and commented on it. This line, therefore, in my memory (or in my imagination), is as follows: '...medusas [jellyfish] of the dream in flowing robes...'.[2]

This is a good example of a significatory pressure. This is obviously a metaphor: medusa/woman. And also a condensation, because the metaphor is tendentially concentrated into a single image (= flowing robes). Nonetheless, the line does not mean that medusas 'are' women, nor that they 'resemble' women, nor that their bodies are 'like' a robe. This line functions more as a monstrative gesture: it indicates to us a *dream space*, a path along which the figure of the woman and that of the jellyfish can be associated with one another or superimposed on one another in a hundred different ways. And all this, at the same time, is very precise: we have a genuine logical operator, the word 'robe', which is the logical lever of a phantasmatic drifting [*dérive*]. Classical rhetoric would recognize, in the element 'gown', a *tertium comparationis*. This is, to a degree, what I call the circuit of signification, this mixture of the logical and the phantasmatic. ...

8. The problem of cross-classification

Vernet: One thing that strikes me in *The Imaginary Signifier*: the articles it includes are very often imprinted with what you call 'cross-classifications'. Does this not represent the abandonment of a purely taxonomic activity, where things would be monolithic, with a correspondence between a 'nice' name and a 'nice' phenomenon, in favor of the affirmation that everything is mixed, which was already apparent in *Language and Cinema*?

Metz: It seems to me that we are of necessity arriving at cross-classifications and formalizations presenting a certain degree of entanglement, for this alone responds to the complexity of facts, the filmic material itself. A very simplified example, but one that is at the heart of the problem, is that of the combination between two distinctions, paradigm/syntagm and metaphor/metonymy. I see no other solution than cross-classification (with, as a consequence, in this example, four major types of figures), for the simple reason that the two axes do not coincide: if the link between two elements of a given film is of a metonymic nature, there remains the fact that these elements can both be present on screen (= metonymy, syntagmatization), but also that one of the elements can very well be the only one expressed in the film, evoking the other element which remains implicit, in which case we will have the same metonymy, but this time in the form of a paradigm. How can we do otherwise, given that the two 'entries' (metaphor/metonymy and paradigm/syntagm) are independent of each other?

Simon/Vernet: But is there not a risk that the inattentive reader will believe that as a result of an excessive desire to classify things, everything ends up becoming mixed up?

Metz: Like you, I have indeed noticed this type of reaction in seminars and other discussions, which proceeds from a frustrated expectation. Some listeners would have preferred a simpler, more brutal, more easily applicable and thus more reassuring 'grid'. But I cannot give it to them, for it would be utterly false. Some would have found it more gratifying for me to decree a general coincidence between the axes, which would have permitted assimilations by entire series. Deep down, I know very well, from the numerous discussions I have had with very diverse audiences, that what anxious readers *expected* was for me to say: 'On the one side, we have metaphor = paradigm = condensation = *découpage*, and on the other side we have metonymy = syntagm = displacement = montage'. The only thing is that this does not hold water, it is a caricature of semiology. ...

This said, my cross-classifications are nonetheless less complicated than people sometimes claim. When we find ourselves before a specific filmic moment, we situate it *successively* on the different axes, we have no need of keeping everything in our heads at the same moment. I have tried to show this with respect to the lap-dissolve, in pages 274-80 of my book *The Imaginary Signifier*. The only, singular *place* in which, by definition, we must mentally 'keep together' all the threads in the tangle of notions, is my book itself.

Vernet: You say somewhere that there is a possible way of speaking didactically about things, which sheds light on one point while obscuring another. And yet it seems that this is an attitude you refuse in *The Imaginary Signifier*, where you strive to hold all the elements together.

Metz: I have tried to be as clear as possible, since for me it is a question of honesty, or even, I would almost say, of professional morality *vis-à-vis* the reader. The more the material is complex, the more we should strive to give a clear exposition of it.

However, I do not believe that this effort from me has been able to completely annul the effect of an objective law, which you have alluded to, and which I speak about on page 268 of the same book: in order to shed light on one aspect of the problem, we are sometimes *forced* to obscure another aspect. In every book that is densely constructed, even to a moderate degree, and in any discipline, the successive chapters, at the same time as they add to one another by mutually clarifying each other, also *destroy* each other. There is nothing we can do about it, it comes from the fact that the signifier of written discourse is linear. It also relates to the fact that nobody's minds are unlimited places: the chapters 'follow' each other, and it is difficult for everybody to think of the whole work simultaneously. For some people it is even impossible. In the latter case, it can happen that the feeling of inferiority in the reader is transformed into aggressiveness. This is one of the sources – but not the only one – of the hostility towards semiology.

9. The primary and the secondary in language – The two 'depths'

Simon: Finally, what is the current status of the cinematic signifier, viewed both from linguistic discourse and psychoanalytic discourse, via Lacan's theories of linguistics? How are the pairings verbal/iconic and primary/secondary imbricated with one another?

Metz: This problem is obviously rather complicated. On the one hand, there is Freud's position on 'thing-representations' and 'word-representations': the unconscious only knows the former, whereas the pre-conscious incorporates both. Language [*langage*] would therefore be clearly on the side of the secondary process.

Lacan hit upon this point, arguing that the unconscious is itself structured like a language. At first glance, of course (and people have been ready to exploit this fact), the two positions seem contradictory. But as soon you explore a bit more deeply, I am convinced that they are much less contradictory than they would seem.

Firstly, something that everyone forgets is that 'language' for Lacan consists of processes, sequences of movement, and not necessarily elements, that is, representations. The latter can be verbal, but also iconic, or even 'mixed' (= ideograms, hieroglyphs, etc.). Nothing is opposed to images associating with one another following trajectories that are more or less linguistic in nature.

Subsequently, and above all, when Lacan is accused of this type of anti-Freudian *coup de force* that would (it is claimed) consist of making the unconscious secondary by treating it like a language, this is because *language itself is considered to be secondary* (otherwise the objection makes no sense). And yet, if anybody considers language to be secondary, then it is Freud – among others – but certainly not Lacan, to such an extent that it is difficult to see an internal contradiction in the latter. For Lacan, the unconscious is structured like a language but (and these two things go together) language is largely primary. Moreover, it is not by chance that the Lacanian notion of '*lalangue*' (in a single word) groups together the most secondarized aspects of language (that is, the language system [*la langue*] in two words, that of the positivist linguists) than other, 'deeper' or 'overdetermined' phenomena, like metaphor and metonymy, which are associative trajectories that do not come within the rubric of 'pure' linguistics, but which are much more closely tied to rhetoric and poetics (or an enlarged linguistics, which would in fact take the primary process into account).

In other words, what induces an error in many readers is the fact that Freud and Lacan do not have the same linguistics 'behind' them. Lacan is the first to have noted this, on page 676 of his *Écrits* [trans. Bruce Fink (New York: Norton, 2006)]. Freud had a relatively poor and restricted conception of language, in accord with the linguistics of his day, which was much less developed than today. Lacan has a wider, richer vision of linguistics, which excludes any reduction of the language-phenomenon to a secondary status.

Vernet: You should then clarify what you mean by deep language, or the depth of language. Are they operations that must be realized before we can even arrive at a definitive formation?

Metz: Yes, precisely. For example, the *work* of metaphor or metonymy (like we say the 'dream work' or the 'work of mourning') is a work that takes place in the history of the language system. It *is* the history of the language system; it is a work which displaces words, leading them to change meaning, and which consequently precedes a given, provisionally fixed, signified.

Simon: Is there not the possibility of confusion between the metaphoric sense of 'depth' as the site of something hidden that we need to reveal, and, on the other hand, depth in the sense given to it by generative linguistics, where we have a certain number of rules and transformations to carry out? It seems to me that sometimes, in "Metaphor/Metonymy," there is a certain fluctuation between the two meanings of the word 'depth'.

Metz: In terms of whether or not there is in my book any fluctuation between these definitions of 'depth', this is not for me to judge, but is up to the reader. There *is* fluctuation to the extent that I have not been clear and rigorous enough.

By contrast, I can give you an answer as to what was, in this respect, my objective (which in practice was attained to varying degrees). 'Depth' in the first sense you mention (= the hidden, the buried, etc.), and depth in the second sense (= the 'deep structure' in a generative logical process), which you correctly distinguish from the first, may well be two very different things, but they still have a relationship with each other. And in particular, if we want to try to understand and analyze depth number 1, we will end up proposing *dispositifs of knowledge*, which bring about depth number 2. It was in this spirit that I conducted my study of the lap-dissolve in the book. So as to better distinguish its multiple overdeterminations, I tried to situate it at the intersection of several logical matrices (syntagm/paradigm, metonymy/metaphor, etc.).

It goes without saying that I do not use the words 'generate' and 'deep structure' here in the technical sense that they have in generative linguistics, but there remains the fact that, even in their broader sense, they designate operations of a logical type. In sum, the reciprocal interlacing of the primary and the secondary does not only characterize text-objects, but also the very approaches taken by the analyst.

Conversation tape recorded in December 1977, and subsequently re-worked by the three participants.

Notes

1. ["La connotation de nouveau," *Essais sur la Signification au Cinéma t. II* (Paris: Klinksieck, 1972).]
2. [The line (originally 'Les méduses du rêve aux robes dénouées') comes from Victor Hugo's poem 'Dieu'. See, Victor Hugo, *God and The End of Satan/Dieu et La Fin du Satan: Selections: In a Bilingual Edition* (ed. and trans. R.G. Skinner, Swan Isle Press, Chicago, 2014), pp. 34-35. Trans.]

7. The Cinematic Apparatus as Social Institution – An Interview with Christian Metz

Sandy Flitterman, Bill Guynn, Roswitha Mueller, and Jacquelyn Suter

Buckland, Warren and Daniel Fairfax (eds), *Conversations with Christian Metz: Selected Interviews on Film Theory (1970–1991)*. Amsterdam: Amsterdam University Press, 2017.

DOI: 10.5117/9789089648259/CH7

Abstract
In this interview, carried out for the journal *Discourse* in 1979, the interviewers question Christian Metz on the value of conceptualizing the cinema in terms of psychoanalytic concepts (the Oedipus complex, castration complex, fetishism, disavowal, the Imaginary, the Symbolic). Metz also discusses the concepts of the look, primary identification, sexual difference, the cinematic apparatus, and briefly mentions his interest in metaphor and metonymy, as well as the semiotics of C.S. Peirce.

Keywords: Christian Metz, film theory, psychoanalysis, the cinematic apparatus

"The Cinematic Apparatus as Social Institution: An Interview with Christian Metz." Sandy Flitterman, Bill Guynn, Roswitha Mueller, and Jacquelyn Suter. *Discourse,* 1 (Fall, 1979), pp. 1–35. Reprinted with the permission of Wayne State University Press.

Question: Do you feel that psychoanalysis is a necessary component of historical materialism when one attempts an analysis of the complex structure of the social formation? If you agree with this assertion, as put forward in the *Screen* introduction to your "Imaginary Signifier,"[1] do you also agree that the Oedipus Complex, and its essential moment, castration, is central to the formation of the unconscious? Do you feel that there might be a contradiction in the fact that historical materialism and psychoanalysis view different categories as central (For historical materialism, labor is the primary category, while for psychoanalysis, it is the Oedipus Complex)?

Metz: Well, some analysts think that the Oedipus Complex is a very general feature, common to all cultures; some think not. I think not. I think that it has to be studied case by case, culture by culture. In any case, the Oedipus Complex in its classical form, the one which has been studied by Freud and elsewhere within the field of psychoanalysis, seems to be obviously related to the concrete social structure in which Freud lived. That is, the Oedipus Complex is connected to specific historical phenomena, such as the restricted nuclear family, the bourgeois family (the mother, father, and children) as opposed to many other possible – not only possible, but really attestable – forms of family life, or of non-family life. It would be unthinkable for me that the Oedipus Complex and castration had no relation with this very precise, restricted (temporally and spatially), cultural form that the nuclear, bourgeois restricted family is. The relation between the Oedipus Complex and the social formation seems to me to be very close.

Q: Then, once we locate the Oedipus Complex within the specific historical instance of the bourgeois nuclear family, do you agree with the theory of Jacques Lacan that the phallus is the primary signifier by which the small human being enters the order of culture and of language?

Metz: You know, I am not a Lacanian. There is a misunderstanding about my position, because I borrow some concepts from Lacan's work. I use three or four words taken from Lacan, and I am considered in some places as a Lacanian, but I am not. To be a Lacanian in Paris means a very precise allegiance – it is a formal group. What was interesting for me was to take, within Lacan's work, certain concepts which I think are helpful for me in studying cinema and studying such phenomena as metaphor and metonymy. The point whether I am faithful to the deep thinking of Lacan or not is not a problem for me. I think that ideas have no owners when they are published, they are common property. And so, I think I have a right to take certain ideas in Lacan – very few, in fact, when compared with the total number of Lacanian concepts. I really think Lacan is a genius, and certain of his ideas do concern me very closely: metaphor, metonymy, Imaginary, Symbolic. But these are *certain* ideas, as opposed to the major part of Lacan's writings, which in fact I didn't use. In Paris, no one would consider me a Lacanian.

Q: To follow up the question about the nuclear family: do you think that in societies where the objective familial structure has changed (for example in communes which have tried alternative forms of child-raising) the fundamental psychic structure has been altered?

Metz: Oh yes, but of course it depends on the duration of these kinds of experiments. They have to last a very long time before they can deeply change the structure of the ego. It's a question of time. But nevertheless, if such experiments would last a very long time, I am convinced that it could deeply change the psyche. But it takes a great amount of time to interiorize the objective, exterior conditions.

Q: Do you think that film has some specific function in this? Or, more broadly, is cinema as an institution[2] capable of changing certain social patterns?

Metz: Not the cinema specifically, but all cultural forms. But I don't see any reason for the cinema as such to be specifically involved in such a process *more* than t.v., the novel, or theater.

Q: In your talk at the Alumni House (U.C. Berkeley, May 1978) you stressed that the cinematic institution has three aspects: the semiotic, the economic, and the psychoanalytical. How are these three instances to be articulated? How does one relate the objective, concrete reality of the social relations of production with a theory of the subject as it is produced in the cinema?

Metz: Cinema studies – not exactly the cinematic fact – has three kinds of main entrances: the linguistic one (cinema as a discourse, history, or story, editing patterns, etc.); the psychoanalytic one; and the directly social and economic one. And perhaps on this point I could add something: the relation is not the same, not completely parallel, between these three kinds of studies. It seems to me that it's easy – at least possible – to work out some, or many, articulations between the linguistic studies and psychoanalytic studies – because both are sciences of the very fact of meaning, of signification. While the articulation with the socio-economic bases is much more difficult – I don't say it is non-existent, but much more difficult to work on. It is a very practical problem. It is possible to have a certain degree of competence in linguistics and in psychoanalysis – it is possible but it takes a lot of work. But to have, on top of that, a real background in economics – is a science; *économie politique*, I would say, is a science and very, very separate from the humanities. The only way to seriously study this one aspect is to be an economist. You have to study the statistics: how many people go to the cinema, how much money it makes – it's very specialized, otherwise you are only talking generalities. Cinema is a commercial industry, but this fact is not very elaborated. You have to be a real economist, like, for instance, Mercillon in France.

Q: Nonetheless Comolli makes an attempt to articulate these kinds of things in his study of the history of monocular perspective.[3]

Metz: With technology rather than with economics.

Q: Do you think there's a possibility of articulating the type of study that people like Douglas Gomery and Russell Merritt are doing on the economic history of the development of the industry with the metapsychology of the spectator?[4]

Metz: Possible, yes. Difficult, surely! The existence of the relation between the base and superstructure is certain, but very hard to study accurately. If you take a specific instance, how can you demonstrate precisely that certain relations of forces of production, of investment, or of a given country's economic development has this or that influence on this or that editing pattern, or on the flashback? *That* would be a study of the relation between the elements. And so, you realize the difficulty.

Q: One way of relating them is not in terms of economics but in terms of social structures, such as the family.

Metz: Oh yes. Certain relations, such as the point of circulation of money within the cinema industry and the problem of the motivation in the spectator-motivation to be willing to pay to enter the cinema. ...

Q: This brings up the metapsychology of the spectator, which relates to a point that we mentioned before – the question of the relationship of sexual difference to spectatorship. If Freudian and psychoanalytic theories chart the development of the subject in language and culture, and if that subject is male, what are the forms of viewing available to women? As a further question, how does the notion of sexual difference become inscribed in current theories of the cinematic spectator as a viewing subject? Is ascendancy to the Symbolic order based on recognizing a position in relation to castration?[5]

Metz: My answer would be "yes." Yes, insofar as sexual difference is, *to some extent*, a physiological problem – to this extent only. But sexual difference doesn't mean sexual inequality, it is not necessarily tied in to the form of sexual difference we are living in our society. But I think it would be necessarily tied with some kind of sexual difference – *difference* – that would be the general idea of my answer. I don't see any means of escaping the very fact of sexual difference. But I do see means of escaping the form of sexual difference – and not only difference, inequality – that is the feature of our society; that is no longer a physiological problem – it is a fully sociological problem. I think that the subject in Freud and in psychoanalysis in general is a very strange mixture of really human features and of male features. This is a difficult point. According to the social and historical context within which Freud's discovery was made, he was not able to distinguish between certain features which are proper to the male and other features which are proper to human beings in general. And so I feel that the very difficult point that we have, and especially the feminist movement has, is to make this distinction which is totally unclear in Freud. The problem always remains: which part of what Freud attributed to human beings is, in fact, male, and which part is really human? It's an open problem, an open book. I think that it's up to the women's movement ... I think it would be to some extent ... how could I say ... *unfair*, dishonest, when a man takes a very publicly and openly and overtly feminist position, because men have no right to speak for women, at their place.

Q: What you seem to be saying is that this kind of concern wouldn't inform your work on the place of the spectator. You feel that such a position would involve a male appropriation of feminist issues and that it would be dishonest to attempt to define the role of the female subject in the audience, because you can't put yourself in her place.

Metz: Yes, that's the problem. It's really difficult for a man to take a feminist position here; not exactly 'feminist', rather *feminine*, because man is not woman.

Q: But it's not a question of what your personal situation is, it's rather a matter of scientific understanding. One thrust of the argument about psychoanalysis is that it gives you tools to overcome the determinations of your own sex.

Metz: Yes, but it is also a personal question. In every kind of analytical study, you have a sort of auto-analysis within it, or it's not serious.

Q: But then, once you recognize the fact that every ideological /critical position must acknowledge one's own psychic position, you still have to deal with the question of sexual difference in relation to spectatorship.

Metz: You know, certain features of the situation are clear; many others are not. What is clear, for instance, is that in the majority of films being shown in cinema theaters, the place of the enunciation, the place of the 'look' is a male one – that is very clear. But it's not the whole of the question.

Q: This question of the 'look' brings up certain parallels you make in "The Imaginary Signifier," equating the fetishistic situation with the cinematic apparatus.

Metz: Oh no, no, I don't equate. What I was saying in "The Imaginary Signifier" is simply that the cinematic situation has in it *some features* of what Freud has described under the name of 'fetishism'. But it's not an equation. I took two features: disavowal (the structure of *je sais bien, mais quand même*), the structure of disavowal as re-analyzed by Octave Mannoni,[6] the problem of belief/disbelief – but it is only a part of the problem of fetishism. And secondly, I took another feature of the fetishistic situation, that is the apparatus itself as a kind of substitute for the penis. These are only some features of fetishism. The problem of fetishism in Freud is much wider.

At this point, I should like to add something which I hope could clarify our discussion, something about the psychoanalytic fetish in general. It is not exactly the substitute for the penis, but for the *absence* of the penis (or of the phallus, in Lacan's formulation). The point which is common to women and men is castration, is that both do *not* have the phallus: hence anxiety (for both), hence the difficult access to desire, hence the difficulty, for each of us, female or male, to find out within herself/himself the things which really interest her/him, etc. But it still remains a difference between the sexes: they do *not* have the same way of living, of experiencing this common absence of the phallus, and here the socio-political factor (I mean: the objective oppression of women) plays a determinant role. The ideological pressure makes it possible for men to imagine, to hallucinate that they have the phallus, whereas this illusion is more difficult for women. Of course, the ideology of inequality between the sexes makes use of pretexts, alibis, false 'reasons' borrowed from 'nature', or 'anatomy': men have in their body a physical organ which can be hallucinated as being the phallus. But the reality is much more social: there are different organs in men's bodies *and in women's bodies* which could be hallucinated as being the phallus, and society arbitrarily reduced them to one organ of the man's body.[7]

Q: This brings up another question in relation to Freud's theory of fetishism. In Freudian terms, the fetishistic situation as a substitution for the penis has to present specific objects, like a foot or fur. How do you relate this to the different levels of primary and secondary identification?

Metz: Primary, as far as the apparatus and the love for the apparatus is concerned. In *my* terms, at least, all these problems of falling in love with the apparatus itself would be related with what I call primary identification – the identification with the apparatus itself as a fetish.[8]

Q: So, you are broadening Freud, then, in terms of the variety of things that could substitute for a penis?

Metz: Oh yes, I think it *has to* be broadened because fetishism means, *at least*, two things. You have a quasi-medical definition of fetishism, and in this case it was a foot or a shoe. It's fetishism as nosography. And you have fetishism in social life and everyday life which is much wider, and which has no reason to be restricted to the shoe or such accessories.

Q: You are speaking of fetish-as-process rather than fetish-as-object.

Metz: Yes, exactly. A process which can extend to very different objects insofar as they become substitutes for desire and not necessarily tied to certain objects (a very restricted number of objects) because Freud was dealing principally (not only) with fetishism as a nosographical fact, or at least, as characterologic. He was treating a very precise type of conduct, not necessarily pathological, but directly erotic conduct. And of course if you switch to cinema problems, the fetish can become a very different object.

Q: Just another question to follow up on this: In Freud, fetishism seems to be connected with castration anxiety – how does that relate to your definition of fetishism on the primary level? On the primary level of identification with the cinematic apparatus does the spectator experience anxiety?

Metz: Oh, yes. The feelings (whether in the spectator or in the filmmaker) devoted to the apparatus are related to the very fact of the image – the image is a present print of an absent object.

Q: So that would necessarily cause anxiety in the spectator?

Metz: A kind of anxiety, yes. Not necessarily a conscious anxiety, of course. But it has to do with the very fact of the image – the image is something very strange – it's a mixture of presence and absence. And so, it re-plays the game of castration: "to be or not to be," death, anxiety. I think that the image is very important for a particular status, precisely because it is a specific mixture of fulfillment and lack.

Q: Are you saying that this doesn't necessarily depend on a signified of the image, but on the very fact of the image as a signifier?

Metz: Exactly. And, of course, the precise nature of one image or several images *can be* a re-doubled form of fetishism. I think if you have directly erotic sequences or pornographic sequences, in such cases, the content of the particular images redoubles the whole process. But in ordinary sequences, in the very fact of the image itself, you have an obvious fetishism already. The process, in fetishism, is disavowal, and the object would be the fetish itself.

Q: But there is a distinction between identification with the operation of seeing (i.e., with the camera) versus seeing an object on screen that is fetishized. When you referred to Thierry Kuntzel's article, 'Le Défilement,'[9] you seemed to make a distinction between latent process, which we assumed was the identification with the operation of seeing, and the manifest materials, which are conspicuously placed on screen as the form of the fetish or the phallus. Would you comment on this?

Metz: Yes. I think what I would call the process, in fetishism, is the whole problem of belief, disbelief, splitting of belief – in a word, 'disavowal', *Verleugnung* in Freud.[10] And what I would call the object is the fetish itself, some substitute for the penis – not exactly for the penis, for the *lack* of the penis, for the absent penis. And so, you can have in a given scene or sequence a precise filmic object which takes the place of the secondary fetish – fetish on the level of secondary identification. For me, then, you have the process, the object, and inside the object you can have the primary object of fetishism and a secondary object of fetishism, according to whether this fetish relation applies to the fact of the viewing spectator (to the cinematic apparatus itself, i.e., primary object) or applies to a precise object being viewed – being shown within the filmic given.

Q: To shift the terms of the discussion a bit, earlier we pointed to the fact that if certain structures (like the nuclear family and the relations of the means of production) were changed, the filmic image would still be the present print of an absent object. The structure on which the apparatus is built, or in which the apparatus is completely interlocked, would remain. I take it that when you said that the phenomenology would remain the same, you meant that the kind of process that goes on between the spectator and the spectacle (the film) would remain the same in spite of changes in the social formation.

Metz: I think so, but it would no longer re-activate the same past – the same childish past, the same memories. It would not re-activate the same situation, the same background. So, *even if* the phenomenological aspect of the thing remained unchanged, what it does re-activate *would* be changed – deeply. And a second point: in my opinion, social and familial changes would actually change, in the long run, the apparatus itself, the cameras, the ways of using them, etc..., and, hence, the psychical relation to this apparatus.

Q: I would like to continue the discussion of the image as a presentified absence. Both the theater and the cinema operate on a process of disavowal. What characterizes the particular type of disavowal specific to each mode of representation? If all fiction making can be seen as an oscillation of belief/disbelief, how do you differentiate fiction in the cinema from fiction in the theater?

Metz: The difference lies, I think, in the balance of forces between the two aspects of the split. Whenever you have a split, you have two sets of forces, because a split means that the subject is in some manner divided into two parts, two subjects. I think the difference between the cinematic and the theatrical situations lies in the relation of forces between these two agencies, or, more precisely, the balance of forces between the material of the representation – the material of the signifier – on one side, and the specific strength of the signified, what is being represented. Fiction is a very important historical phenomenon and can be dealt with by a great many different signifiers. I think you have two elements in every fiction: the very fact of action, and the different signifiers which are able to take in charge the fiction. You have a fiction in the novel, a fiction in the film, a fiction in the theater: a real material – the material of the signifier – is utilized to represent something else.

And this "something else" is the represented, the diegesis.[11] And in terms of belief, I think that the balance is not the same in the cinema spectator, because the material of the signifier in the theater is *completely* real. The material which is used to depict the diegesis in the theater is real persons actually present during the performance. In the movies, the actor is absent during the screening of the film; he was present during the shooting of the film, but no longer. So, the material of the signifier in the theater is part of reality: real space, binocular space, the same space in which the spectator is at the same moment. In the theater you have a very real signifier which is busy (if I may put it so) imitating, representing a diegesis – representing an unreal. While in the cinema, you have the impression (and that is dream-like or fantasy-like) of being faced with that unreal itself, because the material of the signifier is no longer a completely real one. It is no longer a present actor – it is an absent actor, and a monocular space. The material of the signifier in the movies is much more unreal, which makes the diegesis much more real in terms of belief. I would say that the balance of forces between representation and what is represented leans much more to the side of the representation in the theater, and much more to the side of the diegesis – the imaginary presence of the unreal – in the cinema. Is that clear? For me, it's a matter of the balance of belief and disbelief, a question of economics in the Freudian sense: relations of forces.

Q: What about the role of diegesis in psychoanalysis? I'm thinking of Freud's case histories: the patient comes with a sort of jumble of phenomena which can't be put into temporal order, and the process of analysis is the construction of an explanatory diegesis. How would one articulate the relationship between the role of the diegesis of the film, or theater or novel, and the role of diegesis in psychoanalytic therapy?

Metz: There is one main difference, I think, between diegesis in the cure itself and diegesis in fiction. It is a difference between the texts. In a cure, the text has no boundaries. The text is being augmented, is being built, constructed; it is being led further during every session of the cure. It has no existent boundaries – it's not a closed text the way it is in a film.

Q: But that's only if the analysis is interminable.

Metz: Yes, but Freud means terminable in a very relative sense. In fact, all cures are interminable. I really think it is part of the very definition of the cure to be interminable. Of course you can make a distinction – and Freud made it – between so-called terminable cures and so-called interminable, depending upon *to what degree you meet the problem of castration*. In any case, there is an essential difference, a second one, between diegesis in the cure and diegesis in the fictional arts. When an analyst begins to work on the diegesis in a work of art, the work of art is already finished. So, its literal manifest content is predetermined, it precedes the work of the analyst. Whereas, on the contrary, when the analyst begins the work in a cure, he has an actual influence on the very literal content of the text – text of the cure. And he has a real subject who is able to react, to respond to the fact of the cure, while the literary or filmic text doesn't respond to the act of the filmic analyst. It's a huge difference.

Q: Perhaps we could talk about the articulation between the Imaginary and Symbolic axes. There are two ways in which the Imaginary and the Symbolic can be seen to intersect: in the spectator's relationship to the film and in the analyst's relationship to the film. What interlocking relationships of the Imaginary and Symbolic axes come to the fore when film is analyzed in terms of these concepts? Some theories of spectatorship in the cinema deal with the situation in the Imaginary which is reconstructed – the Mirror Stage, the specular relationship, the duality – in the film viewing experience. And yet, cinema – the film – is a Symbolic construction – it's a discourse, and it is understood because the spectator/subject has acceded to the Symbolic. There's a complicated relationship between these two regimes.

Metz: But I think this complicated relation is not part of the cinema alone. It's the very problem of the imbrication of the Symbolic as such and the Imaginary as such. The Imaginary doesn't properly exist without a *prise en charge* [assumption] by the Symbolic. In Lacan, the Symbolic is nothing else but the *prise en charge* of the Imaginary. It is the distinction between levels of functioning, not a distinction between several facts. You never find the Imaginary without the Symbolic *prise en charge*, certainly not in cinema nor anywhere else. The Imaginary has to be told, has to be communicated – hence the status of language. I think this complicated problem in the movies is not more so than in everyday life.

Secondly, if you can see those links in the importance of the reactivation of the Mirror Phase (Mirror Stage) in the movies, you have, nevertheless, the difference between the mirror properly speaking (the mirror of the child), and this kind of second 'mirror' which the cinema screen is. The difference is that the cinema spectator is an adult, so he has already gone through the real Mirror Stage, and the Symbolic already functions in him; while in the child, it has yet to be constructed. In fact, it's a difference of age (that is of degrees of socialization), simply, but it counts. That would be the very point – the only one, I think – on which I would disagree, to some extent, with Jean-Louis Baudry.[12] I think he has underlined very smartly the likenesses between the Mirror Stage and the cinematic situation, but that he has underestimated the *differences* between the mirror stage and the cinematic apparatus. One difference is very important: the cinema spectator doesn't look at his own body's image. Exactly as in the question of fetishism, I think that the cinematic situation has only *certain features* of the Mirror Stage. But, you know, more generally, the idea of equating the cinematic situation with anything is impossible. You can't equate things – you can only find out that certain features of the cinematic situation have something to do with the Mirror Stage, the Imaginary, the Symbolic. A kind of socially imposed under-motricity (lessened motor activity) and over perception devotes all the spectator's forces to seeing, watching, and hearing.[13] So, over-perception and undermotricity – these two features are common to the cinematic situation and the Mirror Stage. But a third feature: I mean the presence of the spectator's own body's image, which accompanies the real Mirror Stage, is not available in the cinematic situation. It's a big difference.

Q: If the Symbolic register is a *prise en charge* of the Imaginary, it would seem that this process would vary according to the degree to which a discursive model re-played the imaginary coherence of the Mirror Phase. More specifically, if a discursive model departs from conventional narrative structure and editing modes (which suture the spectator/subject univocally into the signifying chain)[14] would this model be an intervention on the primary level of identification?

Metz: I think that the process of suturing involves primary and secondary identification at the same time. Perhaps the best example would be the character who is looked at by another character who is off-frame. This off-character is a kind of substitute for the spectator, because part of the definition of the spectator is to be off-frame. And so the character-off shares a given 'off' position with the spectator. In this way, then, the process of suturing has to do with the primary identification, because the character-off is really a substitute for the spectator. He *is* a spectator – a spectator within the spectated. But in these shots, you *also* have characters who are not off, but who are looked at by the character-off. And so you have a secondary identification at the same time.

Q: Some theorists have argued that ruptures in secondary identification can break down the pure specularity of the spectator-screen relationship and displace it onto relations which are more intra-textual. In this instance, the spectator's primary identification would be broken down and dispersed between the relationships among the shots. So, the specularity of the image would vary according to the range of different possible identifications available to the spectator at any given time. Could you comment on that kind of movement?

Metz: I would answer "yes" and "no" to this question. Yes, insofar as a breakdown of secondary identification would change a lot, of course, in the concrete functioning of the primary identification, because this primary identification would no longer be 'blocked' – given a massive character. On the other hand, I would answer "no" because I really think that there is a danger in experimental films in that the quasi-vanishing of secondary identification can, as a result, raise or augment the primary identification. Secondary identification is then disappointed by the absence of characters to identify with – disappointed by the sudden breakdown of a whole part of the imaginary fulfillment. So – you have a phenomenon of disappointment, and all these forces within the spectator or filmmaker which no longer meet their secondary identification goal can reinforce primary identification. Hence, the possibility of a sort of idealistic aesthetic in certain avant-garde experiments. It's not a criticism against people who try this way of filmmaking, but I think that they have to be very aware and conscious of this problem. How is it socially possible – in our circumstances, now – to break down the secondary identification without falling in love with the apparatus itself, without reinforcing the stages of the apparatus as a fetish? It is a question of the equilibrium of forces. If you weaken one of the forces, it's difficult to avoid reinforcing the other one, because there is a balance of forces and because the desire remains. It's difficult, but not impossible.

Q: Do you think that a film like *Jeanne Dielman* [1975] is successful in the attempt to articulate a new discursive structure without reinforcing primary identification?

Metz: Yes, no problem. I strongly appreciate this film.

Q: In extreme examples of the breakdown of secondarized identifications (such as Peter Kubelka's *Arnulf Rainer* [1960]), what often happens in the practical viewing situation is that the spectator simply walks out. Thus, this decision would seem to indicate that the spectator has a certain degree of control over his/her desire to be a complete 'seeing' subject. Do you see a problem here?

Metz: This problem of the spectator walking out seems to be a very simple matter. Most people are simply bored and they walk out. The fact is that you have two different kinds of people: those who walk out and those who work with the film. And the danger I was speaking of in reducing secondary identification concerns only the people who work with the film.

Q: But you seem to imply that, by de-emphasizing the secondary identifications, primary identification would somehow be reinforced, and that there would be a psychic process that would satisfy the desire of the spectator who *is* there. Are you saying, then, that it's not possible for a given spectator who is unaccustomed to a milieu of experimental films to change the kind of desire he/she has?

Metz: Yes, the kind of spectator who walks out has a different internal functioning. His secondary wishes and secondary expectations are strongly disappointed, and so he is no longer able to maintain his primary wish-fulfillment. But you have another type of person, who we all know, who is very enthusiastic about experimental cinema and does not have the same reaction. And for this second kind of person, there is this danger of what I call idealistic aestheticism. But a danger does *not* mean that you automatically fall into this danger.

Q: You're pointing, then, to a non-recognition on the part of certain abstract theorists and filmmakers. They deceive themselves into thinking that they are disrupting something when they are actually reinforcing it.

Metz: Yes, the danger of this non-recognition exists, but it doesn't mean that the reaction of the people who walk out is better, by any means. I only mean that nothing can be done (at least in the short run) about those who walk out.

Q: But it does point to a very important factor which is the viewing contract (an idea advanced by Jean-Louis Comolli).[15] If the viewing contract does not take place or is terminated, then the whole thing doesn't even occur. If somebody walks out or if somebody doesn't see the film, then neither primary nor secondary identifications are set in motion in any sense whatsoever. The notion of a contract is central, because it places very definite limits on the workings of the cinema.

Metz: I agree completely. And I think that this notion of a viewing contract is very important.

Q: If you accept the premise that knowledge is also a function of desire, and if the object of desire is a fantasmatic lost object, what are the epistemological implications?

Metz: I think the searcher is trying to find or to re-find (hence, the lost object) a kind of security by the very fact of giving a very precise description of the given, by a pathetic attempt to master the material. And so I am convinced – not only am I convinced, I feel it in my close relation to my work – that it's a kind of internal endeavor to re-find some sort of very ancient security, *even if* illusory. And so, yes, I think that knowledge has much to do with the search for the lost object, but in a very transformed way.

Q: You are talking about the knowledge of the intellectual for whom pursuit of knowledge is a profession (the scholar, the student, the critic, the analyst). What about knowledge of the spectator?

Metz: Ahh, in the spectator it's very different. I think in the spectator the lost object and the search for, the re-finding of the lost object, has more to do with voyeurism. On this question, I would agree nearly completely with Melanie Klein's position, according to which epistemophilia is a transformed form of voyeurism. And I think the only difference – a very small difference in fact, and a very important one at the same time – between the spectator and the scholar is that the former occupies a more privately voyeuristic position, while in the latter the voyeuristic position has been transformed. 'To know' is a transformation of 'to see, to look'.

Q: You have spoken of the notion of drives at a distance: the scopic drive (the desire for pleasurable looking) and the invocatory drive (the desire for pleasurable hearing), and of their special relationship to representation. Would you speak some more about this?

Metz: First, you have the very important difference between the biological instincts or biological needs and the drives. The difference is that, with the needs, there is a very strong relation with the object. Hence, the absence of sublimation, or the absence of real 'repression' in the analytic sense. Drives have a much looser relation with their object. According to Lacan, that is one of the points of definition of drives. The object can be replaced through the process of displacement, through substitution, which is impossible when you are hungry – if you are hungry you have to eat. The drives can be repressed – hence, the very possibility of repression – without putting into immediate danger the life of the subject. Point two: among the drives themselves, some drives, it seems to me, the ones which are related to the senses at a distance, have this sort of *mise en scène*: a spatial invocation, a spatial designing of this loose relation to the object, which doesn't happen with other drives which are related to the sense of contact. The best example, I think, would be the anal drive or the oral drive, which are based on the sense of contact: the distinction between the goals or aim of the drive (to use Freud's words) and the source organ tends to disappear, because the very aim of the drive is to obtain some pleasure on the level of the source. While in the other drives, such as the drive to see or the auditory drive, you have a spatial *mise en scène*. In the arts, painting, theater – in all arts which are related to the senses at a distance (seeing and hearing) – you have this spatial gap, this *mise en scène* of the distance. The very fact of looking implies a distance. If you are too close to an object, you no longer see it. The very fact of hearing implies a distance. So, I think that all drives are based on this loose relation with the object. With certain drives you have a concrete spatial *mise en scène* of this loose relationship. With other drives, related to the sense of contact, you can more easily have the illusion or impression of another kind of relation with the object. You can more easily have the *impression of fulfillment of the gap* between object and subject with the senses of contact; even if it is an illusion, it's more easily producible, while it's more difficult to produce even the illusion with the sense at a distance. Personally, I would add that the difference between these two kinds of drives plays a very important social role by the very fact that the main arts, which are socially accepted, socially legitimate as art, are based on the sense at a distance, not on the senses of contact, which are socially *illégitimes*, as we say in French, which have a weaker social estime, like the art of cooking, for instance, or the art of perfumes.

Q: So far our conversation has emphasized the psychoanalytic aspect of 'new semiotics'. Does your current work constitute a major break with your previous work in linguistics? For example, how do you see the work of primary and secondary processes in film analysis?

Metz: The central notion in psychoanalysis is not so much a sort of simple binary opposition between two terms (primary and secondary), but rather the notion of the *degrees of secondarization*. It seems obvious – obvious and, hence, not so interesting – it's obvious to notice that the unconscious is more primary than the conscious discourses or the conscious conducts in life, like language, film. In fact, Freud already said it, for instance, when he emphasized that the dream has no syntactical markers, no separators to indicate an opposition, a consequence, a cause. The dream has no separate words to express, to carry the logical relations between the elements in the images. The dream expresses these relations by the very dispositions of the images themselves, not by separate markers. The whole level of the cinematic discourse is secondary, or has a high degree of secondarity (to be more exact). And *on this level of relative secondarity* the linguistic notions are operational. But on the other side, the more primary roots of the filmic discourse, the primary sources of the filmic discourse, *remain* behind it, being an initial point of departure for the forces, importantly affecting the forces involved in filmic discourses. I see no contradiction here, because one of the definitions or features of the primary is that it never appears. It appears only through its more or less secondarized forms. It can be established or guessed at or incited only through more or less secondarized material. I see no reason why it would be contradictory to use, at the same time, some linguistic notions and some analytic notions in the study of cinema. What I think is even more general: it is the same situation in the study of other fields. You could use linguistic and analytic notions to study spoken language, to study everyday life, to study all kinds of institutions. For me it's not a choice, because both are operational. You can study the game and the functioning of metaphor in cinema, and metaphor is already a very secondarized process, but behind metaphor there is condensation, which belongs to primary process.

Q: In his book, *The Dynamics of Literary Response*, Norman Holland discusses the concept of the 'willing suspension of disbelief' and suggests that if the reader thinks that a text speaks the truth he/she will check it for its verity, as in the case of non-fiction. But if it's presented as fiction, the reader will not even consider the text's verity. In other words, it is precisely our knowledge that we are dealing with fiction that enables us to experience it more fully because we do not feel that we have to test its verity. Do you agree with this analysis?

Metz: Yes, I agree totally with this point of view. I think that is another form, a precise sub-form (which I personally did not study, but a very interesting one) of the phenomenon of the splitting of belief. It's always the same question, this balance of forces in the splitting: security about 'it doesn't have to be checked'. And so, you can put a lot stronger belief in fiction because 'it doesn't have to be checked'.

Q: In the case of cinema, is not the process of identification affected in a similar fashion when the spectators assume that they are viewing some version of social reality in the form of the documentary or docu-drama, as opposed to spectacle as fiction? Doesn't the verifiable nature of the referent in the case of the documentary and the docu-drama prevent the screen from becoming the mirror that it does in connection with spectacle?

Metz: My answer would be yes, it does, to some extent. And perhaps I should explain this "to some extent." The main problem, with respect to this question, is that the fiction regime, in many cases, remains dominant, *inclusive within non-fiction films*, because people are used to it. Fiction is not only certain films, as opposed to non-fiction films; it is not only the nature of the particular films. Fiction is also a socially coded regime of viewing, of looking, the internal economic condition of the spectator. And so, in many cases, the fiction regime remains dominant in non-fiction films, because of the way they are consumed. And, in some cases, even because of the way they are constructed by the filmmaker himself. Even if you wish to break with fiction, it still remains that you have to do it from within, and it's always a problem. I am struck by the many cases in which, for instance, a documentary film remains constructed in the main patterns of editing exactly as a fiction film. The main difficulty for me is the very presence of the dominant fiction regime within the non-fiction film. There's always this very important difference between wishful thinking – a wish to break the fiction regime – and *achieving* it in making a film, or in viewing a film.

Q: In terms of this breaking of fiction, the project of the avant-garde seems to be directed against the Imaginary or against belief in the diegesis in order to shift the balance of forces toward knowing. Is your objection to aesthetic idealism that the avant-garde identifies with technique primarily?

Metz: It's not exactly that, it's a danger within this orientation. A danger these people have to be aware of. But not an objection; on the contrary, I think they are bright. They are courageous, but they have to be aware of this problem.

Q: A film like *La Cecilia* (Jean-Louis Comolli [1975]) is criticized because it doesn't point to its fictionality in an obvious way, whereas a film, say, like *Tout Va Bien* (Jean-Luc Godard [1972]), which actually inserts posters and direct address – a certain battery of techniques – is considered by some people as a radical film. In your view such a film would actually be less radical because it would maintain the fiction with a greater hold.

Metz: I am not sure I understand the second part of your question, but in fact, I disagree with the beginning of what you were saying. I think that in the precise example of *La Cecilia* it is a big mistake to miss the marks of enunciation[16] because they are not obvious. That would be the real problem with *La Cecilia* for me: the marks of the enunciation process are not obvious, but they are there, very subtle, very sophisticated, and certain people miss them. And so they condemn the film as not radical, whereas I think it is.

Q: That's why I used that example – I think you misunderstood me. I was saying that at an obvious level, it is criticized for *appearing* illusionistic when, in fact, it is working at a more subtle level in terms of the contradictions it poses.

Metz: You have different forms of radical films. A film can be radical in its very concrete and punctual commitments. You can shoot a film of a strike and it can be a really radical film. But a film which would be radical in the sense you mean would be a discourse with the marks of enunciation in evidence, in *La Cecilia*, for example, the way the sound is used and the way the spatial relationships are organized within the static shot.

Q: But does the ordinary spectator observe these very subtle marks?

Metz: I think you have a real, directly political problem with the radical films. If you try to shoot a radical film in the sense of inscribing the marks of enunciation with the enunciated, you have no audience. And so, in another sense, the film is not radical. I think that a real choice has to be made by each person, each filmmaker. If a given filmmaker wants to have an immediate, practical influence, he has to know what kind of audience is the target, and to use the editing devices and the lighting devices according to the expectations of this precise audience.

Q: Do you accept the critique of naturalistic reproductions of reality as being misleading because they presuppose that the world can be discovered by just looking at it? Would you accept, for example, that a documentary of a strike could be misleading insofar as it assumes that knowledge is unproblematic and on the surface?

Metz: If the film has a very precise, political, immediate aim; if the filmmaker shoots a film in order to support a given strike, for example, and if the film actually supports the strike... what could I say? Of course it's O.K.

Q: I think it's a question of levels of complexity. If a film produces a particular effect for a strike, if it mobilizes workers to support a strike, then I don't think that theorists who are involved in more subtle levels of film analysis are going to denounce the film. But I think that they are not going to stop working on those other levels in their own work. What concerns us, however, at this point is to correlate your theory with the practical task of film criticism.

Metz: Perhaps I could take a concrete example: the film by Barbara Kopple, *Harlan County* [1976]. A very, very good film – I loved this film. It was a big hit in Paris – a real success – three months in two cinema theaters – thousands and thousands of spectators. It is the kind of film that has nothing really new on the level of primary/ secondary identification, but it's a very good film. I could find no reason to criticize the film or to say "oh well, you know, it doesn't elaborate the secondary identification." This is obviously not the purpose of the film. It is unfair, in a sense, to call a film into question on terms which are not within the filmmaker's purpose. She intended to make a ... I don't know whether you would call it radical . . . but she intended to support the strike and she did it. It's a marvelous film, and I support it.

Q: Am I correct in saying that your work is not oriented toward values, ethical or aesthetic, but toward description, exposition and a science?

Metz: Oh yes, a science, except that science is a big word. You know, in physics, in chemistry, the people who are really informed are not sure that what they are doing is science. So, how could I be sure that what I am doing is science? Science remains the goal, but I would hesitate to use the word science except as a very far away target – a direction of mine. Personally, I would prefer to put it another way – to say: "I try to be precise; I try to be rigorous." Only that, that would be enough. It has something to do with science, but … .

Q: But your project is not so much polemical or critical; rather it is a work of clarification, precision, description of 'what is cinema?' From my past reading I know that you work on codes, on the spectator, but your recent lectures on figuration seemed to center on the actual generation – the actual mental processes that generate what cinema is. Is that accurate? Have your interests extended to the actual generation of the cinematic text?

Metz: To some extent, yes, my interests have switched to the spectator, in which I was not interested in the beginning of my work fifteen years ago. It has switched also to the process of … not exactly generation … perhaps figuration of the deep processes of … .Yes, generating in a sense – not in the precise sense of generative grammar in linguistics, but in some sense… . For instance, the problem of condensation and displacement as deep matrices – generating in this sense for the textual linking – textual links between two images in the film. So, in this sense, yes, generative.

Q: There are many operations at work at different levels in a single figure. For example, what mental processes produce a lap dissolve? In your lectures you gave extensive example of analyses of the different axes of these processes of figuration: metaphor/metonymy, primary/secondary, condensation/ displacement, paradigm/syntagm. I think you mentioned other work on camera angles, close-ups, and other aspects of specifically filmic codes to which you had applied this kind of analysis. Is that correct?

Metz: Yes, that is correct, if you mean by that that, in my long article entitled 'Métaphore/métonymie ou le référent imaginaire,'[17] the idea of a single surface figure as being the terminal result of several mental processes (more precisely four: metaphor/metonymy, condensation/displacement, primary/secondary, paradigm/syntagm), this idea is applied not only to the particular case of the lap dissolve, but also to several other figures in different films, or in advertising posters, or in poems by Victor Hugo, etc.

But if you mean that I have in preparation, in this moment, another article on this kind of problem, the response is: no. When I finished the long article we are speaking of, I temporarily stopped – not working, I am still working – , but I temporarily stopped writing, because in a scholar's life (or in everybody's life) you need from time to time periods of rest, of reflexion, on non-immediate production. Probably, I think, I will begin my following book (or long article?) in the middle or end of 1979, and I do not yet know on which topics. And so I have no secrets, I have nothing in my pockets. All is available in my last two books (or in the previous ones).

Q: It struck me, though, that if you continued, if you analyzed figures along these different axes and analyzed not only lap dissolves and some others but *all sorts* of other specifically filmic codes, that you would have the other book that you were talking about – that you would have not only the *comprehensive* book of cinematic codes, but the *extensive* book.

Metz: Hopefully! But if I write this book, it will be a lot of work. So I feel unable to promise that I will write it. I don't know.

Q: We understand that you have been working on Peirce in your seminar at the Ecole des Hautes Etudes this year, in February and March 1978.

Metz: Yes, I am very interested in Peirce. I think that Peirce describes three levels of signification, or three semiosis to use Peirce's word, rather than three different kinds of signs.[18] I really think that Peirce was very often misunderstood and was forced into a very positivistic interpretation, mainly by Charles Morris. The very famous distinction between symbol, icon and index – the famous tripartition – is very often interpreted as a distinction between three separate materials, separate kinds of signs. Between three sets, in terms of the set field, which would be exterior to each other. So you could put one sign into one box (index), and another sign into a second box (icon). I'm really convinced ... and there are a lot of remarks in Peirce's writings which very clearly indicate .... For instance, when he speaks about photographs – it is an example that Peirce takes very often, and he says it explicitly – he asserts that photographs are, at the same time, index and icon. Index by some features of the photographic process; icon by other features of the same photographic process. And so I think that the interesting way of using Peirce is not a typological one – the need for making boxes and a typology of signs. Peirce is generally considered a typologist of signs. But I think the more interesting way of understanding Peirce is to consider that he tried to describe three levels of *every* act of signification. And that is what he finally intended to say: in each semiosis – each signification act, signification event – you have a functioning level which is indexical, a functioning level which is iconic, and one which is symbolic – symbolic in Peirce's sense, that is totally socially coded, without contiguity, without a basis in contiguity index, without a basis in any similarity which would be icon. And so, I think that Peirce can help a lot and has already helped a lot in film studies. In Peter Wollen's studies,[19] for instance, and Gianfranco Bettetini's in Italy. Bettetini wrote a whole book (Gianfranco Bettetini is an Italian cinema semiologist) called *The Index of Realism* devoted to the so-called realistic films: *Nanook* [1922] by Flaherty and *Greed* [1924] by Stroheim, which he describes as being, to some extent, indexical. And obviously, I think Peter Wollen's work is very important in this. But the main point for me is that Peirce is not a typologist. And if you read Peirce carefully, he did explicitly say so, but people have forgotten this aspect of Peirce. He was forced into a positivistic typology of signs with three boxes.

Q: Would you like to make a closing statement?

Metz: Yes. That I like speaking with people and making communication, and so I am very glad for this conversation between you and me.

A number of people participated in this interview in its various stages. The major work was done by Sandy Flitterman, Bill Guynn, Roswitha Mueller, and Jacquelyn Suter.

In addition, our thanks go to Margaret Morse, Ann West, Bertrand Augst, Barbara Freeman, David Miller, Francia Friendlich, Joel Fineman, and Tom Andrae.

Notes

1. Vol. 16, no. 2 (Summer 1975), translated into English by Ben Brewster. Originally appeared in *Communications*, no. 23 (May 1975). Also appears in *Le Signifiant imaginaire* (*Psychanalyse et cinéma*) (Paris: Union Génerale d'Editions (10/18), 1977).
2. " ... the cinematic institution is not just the cinema industry (which works to fill cinemas, not to empty them), it is also the mental machinery – another industry – which spectators 'accustomed to cinema' have internalized historically and which has adapted them to the consumption of films ... [T]he institution as a whole has filmic pleasure alone as its aim." *The Imaginary Signifier*, pp. 18–19.

3. Jean-Louis Comolli, 'Technique et idéologie,' *Cahiers du Cinéma*, nos. 229 (May /June 1971), 230 (July '71), 231 (August-September '71), 233 (November '71), 234–235 (December '71/January '72), 241(September / October '72). Partial translation in *Film Reader*, no. 2, 1977, p. 128–148. [See also Jean-Louis Comolli, *Cinema Against Spectacle: Technique and Ideology Revisited*, trans. by Daniel Fairfax (Amsterdam University Press, 2015).]
4. Anthologized in *The American Film Industry*, edited by Tino Balio (Madison, WI: University of Wisconsin Press, 1976). See also *Quarterly Review of Film Studies*, vol. 3, no. 1 (Winter 1978).
5. The 'Imaginary' and the 'Symbolic' are terms introduced by Jacques Lacan to describe two fundamental registers of the psychoanalytic domain.

   Most broadly understood, the Imaginary is the order of relationships to images, conscious or unconscious, perceived or imagined, which are the basis of the ego. The term first appears in one of Lacan's earliest theoretical articles, 'The Mirror Stage as Formative of the Function of the I as Revealed in Psychoanalytic Experience,' (1949), translation in *Ecrits* (Norton, 1977). Here, Lacan proposes that the ego is formed through the infant's identification with the image of its own body as perceived, for example, in a mirror. This narcissistic identification is based on the child's misrecognition (*méconnaissance*) of himself in a unified image, which is external and objectified. This constitutes the basis of all later identifications, which are in principle, fantasmatic. However, Lacan insists that the formation of the human subject is not to be reduced to the Imaginary relation, and he introduces the Symbolic register.

   The Symbolic is the order of pre-established symbolic social structures, for which language is the model. Lacan builds his notion of the Symbolic on F. de Saussure's linguistics and Lévi-Strauss' anthropology. Subjectivity is constituted through the child's accession to language by which he transcends the dualism of imaginary identifications as someone who can represent or designate himself as an 'I,' thereby assuming a position in the symbolic order of culture. For a more detailed discussion of these terms, the reader might refer to the headings: 'Imaginary,' 'Symbolic,' 'Mirror Phase,' in *The Language of Psycho-Analysis*, J. Laplanche and J.B. Pontalis (New York: Norton, 1973).
6. *Clefs pour l'imaginaire ou l'autre scene* (Paris: Le Seuil, 1969). This important work on fetishism and disavowal unfortunately remains untranslated. Mannoni analyzes the situation of the fetishist who oscillates between knowledge (as confirmed by sensory evidence- "I know" that the mother has no penis) and belief (the wish to deny this fact – "but nevertheless" I believe she has one). Mannoni, and Metz, see this process at work in the spectatorial situation, positing the structure of fiction as a structure of belief.
7. For a useful discussion of symbolization in relation to the phallus and the position of women in this construct, see Parveen Adams, 'Representation and Sexuality,' *m/f* no. 1 (1978).
8. "I just wished to show that in the end there is no break in continuity between the child's game with the mirror and, at the other extreme, certain localised

figures of the cinematic codes. The mirror is the site of primary identification. Identification with one's own look is secondary with respect to the mirror, i.e., for a general theory of adult activities, but it is the foundation of the cinema and hence primary when the latter is under discussion: it is *primary cinematic identification* proper ('primary identification' would be inaccurate from the psychoanalytic point of view: 'secondary identification', more accurate in this respect, would be ambiguous for cinematic psychoanalysis). As for identifications with characters, with their own different levels (out-of-frame character, etc.), they are secondary, tertiary cinematic identification of the spectator with his own look, they constitute together secondary cinematic identification, in the singular. ..." *The Imaginary Signifier*, pp. 57–58.

9. 'Le Défilement: A View In Close Up,' translated by Bertrand Augst, *Camera Obscura*, no. 2 (1977). Originally appeared in *Revue d'esthétique*, special issue (*Cinéma Théorie Lecture*) (Paris, 1973).
10. "Term used by Freud in the specific sense of a mode of defence which consists in the subject's refusing to recognize the reality of a traumatic perception – most especially the perception of the absence of the woman's penis. Freud invokes this mechanism particularly when accounting for fetishism and the psychoses." 'Disavowal (Denial)' in J. Laplanche and J.B. Pontalis, *The Language of Psycho-Analysis*, pp. 118–121.
11. "[Diegesis] describes the film's represented instance (which Mikel Dufrenne contrasts to the expressed, properly aesthetic, instance) – that is to say, the sum of the film's denotation: narration itself, but also the fictional space and time dimensions implied in and by narrative, and consequently the characters, the landscapes, the events, and other narrative elements, in so far as they are considered in their denoted aspect." Metz, *Film Language*, translated by Michael Taylor (New York: Oxford University Press, 1974), p. 98.
12. 'Ideological Effects of the Basic Cinematographic Apparatus,' translated by Alan Williams, *Film Quarterly*, vol. 27, no. 2 (Winter 1974—75), p. 39–47. Originally appeared in *Cinéthique*, no. 7/8 (1970).
13. For a discussion of this idea, see Christian Metz, 'The Fiction Film and Its Spectator, A Metapsychological Study,' *New Literary History*, vol. 8, no. l (Autumn 1976). Originally appeared in *Communications*, no. 23 (May, 1975). Also appears in *Le Signifiant imaginaire* (*Psychanalyse et cinéma*) (Paris: Union Génerale d'Editions (10/18), 1977).
14. The 'suture' is an immensely complicated theoretical notion which has recently been analyzed in detail in an effort to specify the processes at work in the cinematic viewing situation. The concept is borrowed from psychoanalytic theory (particularly as elaborated by Jacques Lacan and Jacques-Alain Miller) and is used to describe one of the processes by which the spectator/subject is inscribed in the cinematic discourse. It emphasizes the functioning of the unconscious in any spectator-screen relationship. A special dossier on the suture appears in *Screen*, vol. 18, no. 4 (Winter 1977–78). Two articles that first introduced this concept to American readers are: Daniel Dayan,

'The Tutor-Code of Classical Cinema,' *Film Quarterly* (Fall l974), pp. 22–31, and William Rothman, 'Against the System of the Suture,' *Film Quarterly* (Fall 1975), pp. 45–50. (Both articles are reprinted in Bill Nichols, *Movies and Methods* (Berkeley, CA: University of California Press, 1976), pp. 438-59.)

15. 'Machines of the Visible,' conference paper presented by Jean-Louis Comolli at the International Conference on the Cinematic Apparatus, University of Wisconsin, Milwaukee, February 1978. A book including some of the papers from the conference is forthcoming. [See Appendix II of Comolli's *Cinema Against Spectacle.*]

16. Enunciation is to be distinguished from the enunciated (the utterance, what has been stated). It is not the manifestation of discourse (*parole*). It is the very act of producing an enunciated in which the locutor mobilizes and appropriates language (*langue* i.e., elements and rules underlying and assuring individual messages) on his/her behalf. The individual subject enunciates his/her position as locutor by means of specific indicators: personal pronouns (*I-you*), ostensive indicators (*here, there, this*, etc.), the system of tenses (the present coinciding with the moment of enunciation), etc. Enunciation implies the discursive relationship between locutor and allocutor, the structure of dialogue. In the classic narrative film, the marks of enunciation (i.e., indicators of the presence of an enunciator and hence of the discursive situation) have been effaced. According to Metz, the classical film presents itself as *story* rather than as *discourse*, to use Emile Benveniste's distinction. In analyzing enunciation in film, one must take into account various interlocking systems which work together to produce the textual system of a particular film. The marks of enunciation can be said to designate the place from which the cinematic discourse proceeds. However, this place is not to be confused with the author or the individual filmmaker. For a detailed discussion of enunciation, see Benveniste, *Problems in General Linguistics* (Coral Gables, FL: University of Miami Press, 1971). Originally published as *Problèmes de Linguistique Générale* (Paris: Gallimard, 1966).

17. In *Le Signifiant imaginaire* (*Psychanalyse et cinéma*) (Paris: Union Génerale d'Editions (10/18), 1977).

18. Charles Sanders Peirce (1839–1914) was the founder of American semiotics. For a description of his taxonomy of different classes of signs, see 'Logic as Semiotic: the Theory of Signs,' in J. Buchler ed., *The Philosophy of Peirce* (London, 1940). For an extensive critique of Peirce's theory, see Umberto Eco, *A Theory of Semiotics* (Bloomington, IN., and London: Indiana University Press, 1976), p. 178 *passim*.

19. *Signs and Meaning in the Cinema* (Bloomington, IN., and London: Indiana University Press, 1972).

8. A Seminar with Christian Metz: Cinema, Semiology, Psychoanalysis, History

Chaired by Rick Thompson

Buckland, Warren and Daniel Fairfax (eds), *Conversations with Christian Metz: Selected Interviews on Film Theory (1970–1991)*. Amsterdam: Amsterdam University Press, 2017.

DOI: 10.5117/9789089648259/CH8

Abstract
In this seminar discussion, published in *Media Centre Papers* in 1982, the participants investigate with Christian Metz the viability of analyzing film using psychoanalysis, the difference between Freudian and Lacanian psychoanalysis, and the role of sociology in the theoretical study of film. Metz also mentions that he is beginning a new study, a psychoanalytic analysis of the joke.

Keywords: Christian Metz, film theory, psychoanalysis, film and sociology

'A Seminar with Christian Metz: Cinema, Semiology, Psychoanalysis, History.' Chaired by Rick Thompson. Published in *Media Centre Papers* 16, introduced and edited by John L. Davies (Bundoora, Victoria: La Trobe University, 1982), pp. 16–46.

Those identified in the discussion are:
Metz – Christian Metz
Thompson – Rick Thompson
Freiberg – Freda Freiberg
Rohdie – Sam Rohdie
Flaus – John Flaus
Davies – John Davies
Routt – William Routt
Martin – Adrian Martin

Thompson: Tonight's guest is Christian Metz. Professor Metz' new book has just arrived in Australia. It is called *Psychoanalysis and Cinema: The Imaginary Signifier.* I think it would be appropriate to begin by asking Professor Metz about the current direction of his work – I understand there has been rather a significant change in the direction of your work at the moment: perhaps you could speak of that?

Metz: I would say rather a significant intermission in my cinematic work. I'm just now in the process of writing a book on jokes, on wit (*witz*). I started this book two years ago and I think it will take me another one and a half or two years. After that I intend to return to my cinematic interests which still remain active, but I felt the need to change the subject-matter, if not the method of my work, because when you have worked for a long time – twenty years in my case – on the same subject, you are in danger of repeating yourself. Very often people expect you, or invite you to repeat the same thing, and so I felt the necessity to, let us say, break with myself momentarily, and to produce a semiological and psychoanalytic book on another subject-matter, namely 'wits and jokes', starting from Freud's book, 1905 [*Jokes and their Relation to the Unconscious*], and criticising and developing it in a more elaborate way.

Well that is the first answer I can give before receiving other questions.

Thompson: You have been at the centre of both the first semiotics and the second semiotics; could you summarise your views on the state of French semiotics at the moment?

Metz: Yes. The current state of semiotics in France now is characterised mainly by a sort of hollow period. A coming down which is not necessarily a decline – I cannot predict the future – but what is sure is that we are inside the hollow period. This does not mean that semiotics has disappeared. The situation is somewhat different in France from other countries; in France semiotics has already become a part of the general culture and education so that it is a part of all sorts of studies – painting, literature, cinema, and it can remain very strong, in a sense, influencing all kinds of studies without remaining a separate school of semiotics as such, as we had in the beginning of the sixties. At the beginning things take the form of a school, very formal, and then it becomes more informal and diffused.

There is an exception, an important exception. There is one person in France who is continuing the semiotic undertaking as such, general semiotics which has a vocation for replacing all the previous sciences, the knowledges, which is Greimas. Greimas is a very important semiotician with whom I don't agree, but he is continuing a school of general semiotics as such with a number of disciples, and he is continuing with the idea of semiotics covering the whole field of knowledge. So he has sub-groups in seminars, at the Ecole des Hautes Etudes, in the semiotics of painting, of semiotics of music and so on. The idea is to cover all things. Personally, I don't stand for this imperialist conception of semiotics because I am sure that semiotics cannot replace the other kinds of knowledge – but can only collaborate with them and bring its own enlightenment as a part, as one method among others.

Thompson: Can we open for questions?

Freiberg: In what way do you mean that semiotics is in a state of decline?

Metz: I'm not sure it is in a state of decline – it could be, I don't know, but I was speaking only of a 'hollow period' and what the future will be I am frankly unable to answer you. To some extent I'm sure that a certain number of basic concepts will remain because they are obvious – when we speak, now, in 1982, of signifier, signified, connotation, denotation, code, system, text, etc., it's no longer semiotics, it's obvious, we cannot do without them. They were brought in by semiotics in the sixties, so this part will remain, I'm sure, because everyone uses it and needs it.

Rohdie: While they have become part of the common speech they have also become less precise ...

Metz: Yes ...

Rohdie: ... so that their analytic strength – I can't say is less than void, but in one sense is very confusing. Words like 'text' or 'the textual' are used very loosely now, whereas at one point there were attempts to specify not only what those terms meant, but also they had a polemical and political edge attached to them. Notions of 'text', for example, were not simply descriptive notions, but brought a certain purchase on the way in which you conceptualised works, on the way in which you analysed works, and so on. Once that language of semiotics – and, indeed, at some prior period the language of psychoanalysis – became a common speech it also became de-natured and almost less useful.

Metz: Yes, I agree, it is a danger every time something diffuses. I see no means to avoid such a danger because it is the other side of 'working out', you know, of success. Except when you are a serious writer, a serious researcher, to make precise in every case that I am taking 'text' in the sense used by Hjelmslev, or in the sense of Kristeva, and so on, you can do that and it is better so. Nevertheless, when a notion diffuses there is a danger that it becomes more vague.

Rohdie: On the other hand the terms themselves are by no means fixed and as you said there is 'text' according to Hjelmslev and 'text' according to Kristeva and, indeed, most of those terms are subject to considerable debate depending on what theoretical position you might take, either towards various objects like the cinema or painting or various critical positions you might take with regard to semiotics. The terms on the one hand might be denatured but there is no fixed sense to exactly what they mean or what they refer to – or is there?

Metz: What is the danger exactly, in your opinion?

Rohdie: It is not exactly a danger. When one speaks about semiotics and if I think of a lot of your work, which has been concerned with defining, to a large degree, terms and concepts and fixing them in their relationships with each other, from the point of view of, say, cinema studies, teaching the subject or relating to your own work, I often feel there is an impulse towards a scientific description, and a setting aside of those terms, outside the polemic. From other positions the terms you seek to fix are the subject of quite serious debate and some kind of polemical edge. I was not implying any danger but responding to that question about semiotics in decline. The terms are by no means clear within the subject itself, but are also used in a sloppy and unclear fashion in an ordinary sense.

Metz: I am unable to answer you about the situation here or in other countries, but in France they are to a certain degree fixed and are no longer so controversial. There were very important controversies, but not now. This is for the very good reason that the notions of semiotics can be used by its enemies for their own purposes to the extent that the terms are formal ones and can be used for different political intentions.

Rohdie: Is that a notion that somewhere there exists a space in which the terms and concepts of semiotics are clear and precise, and another space where enemies and friends are using these terms for various battles – is that the sense you are suggesting?

Metz: Yes, but that you cannot avoid. It is not confined to semiotics. ...

Rohdie: Perhaps one could take the position that the terms have no fixity, and that the assertion about their fixity is a political position, and they have to be seen, for example, to have a certain lack of fixity. In so far as there is a debate about those terms, you seem to be saying that there is some space in which they are clarified and precise.

Metz: Yes, there is some space, but it is not much. It seems to me you are confounding two different things. On the one side to propose a fixed definition for those terms, and on the other side to demand from everyone that they take the terms in this very sense. It is quite different. I have devoted an important part of my work to conceptual definitions but I do not demand from any of my students that they take the term in this sense, only that they define in which sense they use it, in order to make things clear. It is not the same thing to propose a fixed definition as to impose it. The whole thing is about proposing/imposing.

Flaus: Let me offer you a possible example for your jokes. I am hearing you using the word '*defusion*' and I think you are intending the word 'diffusion' – diffusion, a spreading, and 'defusion' a taking away of meaning by force?

Metz: I was thinking of diffusion with an 'i'.

Flaus: I am hearing you also as de-fusion, taking the explosion out of it. Let me ask it this way – diffusion of the usage of the term, that it is passing from a smaller elite to a larger, less privileged ...

Metz: Oh, it is not at question, the beginners ...

Flaus: ... once the terms become accepted in the intellectual life of a community then they have passed from being in the sacerdotal domain, that is belonging to the priests and acolytes and they are then passed down to the faithful – and I understand that is what has happened to those terms – but I understand there to be a diffusion in the users and not a diffusion in the terms. Would that be so? It is not that the number of things they may be said to mean has increased but the number of users?

Metz: I do not understand what you mean by 'users'.

Flaus: In the sense that we say 'usage', users of any language, any system of communication. The number of users has increased which amounts to a diffusion of the usage, but not of the terms. Correct me if it's not what you intended, but in the distinction that Lévi-Strauss makes between nature and culture, that terms such as the ones you mentioned, let us say 'text', has passed from being seen as part of culture and it is now accepted as part of nature.

Metz: I would not agree. It has passed from a section of culture to another section of culture but it still remains social: the whole story remains social.

Rohdie: I wonder if I can ask one thing concerning the previous issue. If I took a set of terms which were now part of a semiotic, psychoanalytic, linguistic vocabulary – things like fetishism, sadism, scopic drive, or the signifier, and I looked at a work like *S/Z* [Roland Barthes, 1974] that employed those terms, and I looked at your own work, which also employed those terms, I would be very hard put to construct any kind of meta-language in the case of *S/Z* because the terms within that semiotic vocabulary would shift, within the work, as I was reading it; they would not have any secure place within the work itself. In the way that they were used I could not find some model which I could take out of the work and find meanings for. When I look at *The Imaginary Signifier* and the earlier 'first stage' semiotics, the more linguistically oriented semiotics of *Language and Cinema*, the impulse is towards constructing a meta-language of the cinema. They are not exactly definitional, but there are terms which form themselves into relational complexes so that you can speak of the cinema semiotics of Christian Metz as a system of constructed terms that can be re-applied and used.

Rohdie: When I was suggesting that there was something of a polemic, there is obviously a different impulse in the use of semiotic terms which in the end lose all their stability to one that is concerned with their stabilisation. If I compare one with the other there seems to me to be a whole position, not only about semiotics, but about their use, about texts and their function, and indeed about the function of the cinema. It would not surprise me to hear you argue that there is a systematic relational place for terms within a cinematic semiotics – but some would argue that there is not, that these terms cannot have any fixity, argued from similar positions to you. For example, they might argue it from their reading or understanding of Lacan. In so far as writing would involve them with desire the signs and signifiers they use would necessarily shift their meanings, change and alter.

Metz: Yes – you know, what I took from Lacan was only a general inspiration, very little. I have been reproached for using many psychoanalytic terms – whereas, in fact, I have taken from Lacan only four or five ideas – the Mirror Stage, metaphor as condensation, metonymy as displacement, only very well-known concepts. In Paris no one would call me a Lacanian – no one.

In my opinion we have a whole range of semiologies, more or less scientific, more or less literary. Roland Barthes' semiology was literary – he was a writer, a great writer, so the way he uses semiological concepts in *S/Z*, is arbitrary and this book is impossible to apply – but why should we apply it? That would be my question. It is a wonderful book and why should someone, anyone, apply it? Why should there be things to apply? I am very sceptical about the very notion of 'applying' because we are not in the domain of the physical sciences where you can really apply something.

I think that even the scientific side of semiotics is only an attempt to be more rigorous. In my books if you notice, I never use the word 'science' or 'scientific' – only the French word 'rigorous' – so I am very sceptical too, about semiotics being able to be a science because it is confusing to say 'science'. When we say 'science' we think of physics or chemistry where the degree of precision, of accurateness, of fullness or predictivity have nothing in common with semiology.

So we have many semiologies, some of which are more literary like *S/Z*, which is impossible to apply; some of which are applicable, such as my first books – if people wish to apply them. But – they were not written to be applied. They were written to clarify some problems and notions of cinema. This notion of applicability is possible only when the discipline has reached a very high degree of scientificity, then you can apply them.

Davies: Could I take this a little further and suggest that, at some level, you do seem to apply Lacanian theory to the study of the cinema. Maybe you will say that you only picked out what you need to?

Metz: Yes, exactly.

Davies: It is what you picked out that I find very interesting because this has been a problem for a number of years in understanding your intellectual development. For example, in *Film Language*, the first book of yours that I read, there was a very convincing argument against taking the iconic sign as being 'similar' to the linguistic sign – an argument that can be used just as convincingly in, what to me, is a battle between Freud and Lacan. This seems to hinge over the one word 'pictogram' – whereas Freud thinks the pictogram is the initial way the primary processes become inscribed in the unconscious, Lacan seems to need to translate 'pictogram' in a linguistic sense; he really wants to call it a 'hieroglyph', and that very arguable hinge obviously cannot be open to any scientific or perhaps conceptual argument. Lacan is then able to later claim that the "unconscious is structured like a language" and we get a very linguistic view of the whole theory that traces its path back to Freud. If I am right in suggesting that Freud may well have been more correct than Lacan in that the initial inscriptions on the unconscious are iconic, only later to be transposed into some form of language, that seems to have grave implications, in, for example, how we see a film. I wonder why you found it necessary to import Lacanian theory – only "five or six concepts from Lacanian theory," but they are integrated concepts which back each other up all the time – they come out specifically in *The Imaginary Signifier*, I think fairly uncritically on that point about iconic inscription. I wonder if you would like to comment?

Metz: There are at least two points in what you said. There would be a whole discussion about the relations between Freud and Lacan – it is a very complicated issue. Freud thought that the language system – not the language but the language system – was inscribed in the preconscious and that the unconscious had only icons, images. Whereas Lacan seems to say that the language – not the language system is the unconscious. What Lacan means by that is no longer the language system but what we call the 'deep language' – the language of poetry for example. We could be referring to the unconscious even in Freud because he very often speaks of wordrepresentations translated into thing-representations which is the equivalent in Freud of the Lacanian theory of language. Am I making myself clear?

So I am not sure – it would be another discussion – but as to the fact that Lacan and Freud disagree on this problem of language, I'm not really sure. I think that Lacan is confusing because of his presentation, his language which is very difficult to understand, but I'm really convinced that Lacan is totally a Freudian – behind each line of Lacan you have a sentence by Freud. Of course the style, the words, all is changed – it is hard to recognise and it takes much study.

On the disagreement about the level of language – whether preconscious or unconscious – I think that in reality both agree, but not as to the presentation.

Davies: There is another difference, I think, between Freud and Lacan concerning the exact boundary between the conscious and the unconscious which has implications on your later work. The way I characterise it Freud sees the unconscious/conscious boundary as a semi-permeable membrane through which concepts may pass via dreams, hypnosis or free association, whereas for Lacan it seems to be a much firmer juncture through which only desire can penetrate with meanings. You talk a great deal about the power of desire in terms of the cinema, especially in the latter part of *The Imaginary Signifier*. What would happen, for example, to instinctual identification, in a film that does not really address the concept of desire specifically, let us say, in a film that only addresses the instinctual forces of aggression? Can we do the same kind of thing for aggression that you have done for desire?

Metz: Oh no, it is not so. For Freud it was desire – it was no longer libido, but it was still desire.

Davies: Is not, for Freud, aggression still an instinctual drive?

Metz: Yes, it is.

Davies: So can we not, in theory, have a film that talks about aggression rather than desire?

Metz: I do not understand 'rather' because aggression is a desire. When you desire to aggress somebody ... or perhaps I misunderstand you?

Davies: So the model we have is of desire, as the boundary, and after that we have desire in its sexual form and in its aggressive form?

Metz: I am not convinced, you know. I feel the opposite – that the borderline between conscious and unconscious is stronger in Freud, which is natural because Freud began, and so he was thinking in stiffer terms, whereas Lacan explicitly says that, roughly translated by me, that 'behind each conscious phenomenon or action or discourse you have the active presence of the unconscious'. I think, on the contrary, that in Lacan the borderline is more flexible. It is not an obvious point, you know, you have to study the text of both, but I feel so.

Routt: The goal of psychoanalysis is a cure. One psychoanalyses a patient and the idea is that something will change and there will be a cure. The language and the method has been derived towards that goal. What happens when one takes those concepts, those ideas and begins to apply them to something else – or – is there a patient to be cured in the analysis of cinema that you propose?

Metz: Yes, that's a very central point – an interesting question. Firstly, what you say represents, in my opinion, the limit to applying psychoanalysis to cinema, because psychoanalysis was conceived mainly in relation to therapy. Applying psychoanalysis to cinema has its limit, like everything. Secondly, you can apply psychoanalysis to film in many different senses. You can attempt to analyse – to psychoanalyse – the film-maker, it is a possible research. I am sceptical for the reason that you mentioned, that the film-maker is not in therapy and he cannot answer, he cannot react to what the analyst, in this case the film analyst, says. You can apply psychoanalysis to the filmic text where it becomes easier, but this also has its limitations because the text cannot answer, as you said.

What I am doing is a third kind of research which is to apply psychoanalysis to the code – to the social institution of the cinema. So it depends on where you apply psychoanalysis – to the film-maker, to the film, to cinema, to what?

Routt: To the institutional object, is there the possibility of some kind of therapy?

Metz: Oh no, there is no answer.You have the limit which was my first point – except when experimental films, for example, inspired by this kind of theoretical research begin to change the cinematic institution itself.

Rohdie: There is surely something of an answer because, as I understand it, one impulse for using psychoanalytic terms and in particular, Freudian and Lacanian terms, has been to see the subject as being formed and constructed by language, in this case, perhaps, the language of the cinema or within representation. There are places, for example there was at some period in *Screen* an impulse to demand a change in practices of representation in order to shift the position of the subject which had ideological and political implications, so that psychoanalysis was to a degree a political weapon aimed at a transformation, both a transformation of representation and of people's relation to that representation. Now, it might be stretching a point to think of that as a cure – it is not exactly covered by those categories that you presented – it is a slightly different impulse.

Metz: Yes, it is.

Rohdie: Both semiotics and – it is hard to say first stage and second stage of semiotics – but both linguistic concepts within semiotics and psychoanalytic concepts within semiotics have been used in part as a kind of descriptive discourse – not perhaps scientific, but it has been used as a weapon in different times and within different cultures. I think within that notion of it as weapon there is some notion of it as a cure involved. At least if not cure then at least change – and not simply as description?

Metz: Yes, but to start with, you were saying that psychoanalysis teaches us that the subject is formed within language. I would not say so. I would say that psychoanalysis teaches us that the subject is formed within society. This is how I understand psychoanalysis. The subject is formed by Oedipus – to make things simple, too simple – which has an obvious link to the restricted family and the restricted family has a very obvious link with certain periods in the economic evolution of the world, so for me – you have sentences in Lacan which are very clear – for me, psychoanalysis is the study of the imprinting of society in the person. You have the exterior society, the society proper, and you have the society imposed by force within the inner constitution of each person, and that is the very meaning of the Oedipus complex. Oedipus complex is a kind of symbol – for Freud it was too – a symbol that means that society imposes its patterns within the mentalities, the feelings, from childhood on. Of course, I know that many analysts in different countries – in the U.S.A., all; in France, many – who are convinced that the Oedipus complex is eternal and universal. But simply they are wrong – because it is impossible to think that Oedipus complex can have no relations with the social organisation of family structures.

Rohdie: But how do you know they are wrong?

Metz: Because it is obvious. How could you have an Oedipus complex – at least in the sense that has been described by Freud – in a community where the children are raised by several parents?

Flaus: There is research on this in Oceania where the function of both the repository of affection and also the administration of discipline is carried out by the brother of the father and in a matriachy, where one finds that families were organised and the State similarly, that such complexes would be absurd in relation to the mother. That is not to deny the system which claims that one of the manifestations of it in our societies is universal. I do not think you were saying that the notion of complex as a system is untrue, but that its application in our society as a universal is untrue?

Metz: Yes. It depends on the conventions you adopt when defining the Oedipus complex. Whether it is a different pattern, but still Oedipean, depends on the conventions. In all cases when society changes over a long time the Oedipus complex changes or it could disappear – I do not know the future. If the family disappears in the long run Oedipus complex would disappear – or, perhaps, deeply changed.

Flaus: I understand that this was the root of the disagreement between Freud and Adler?

Metz: Yes, yes.

Flaus: Can I return to something else that was asked in relation to the question on psychoanalysis and cure. When we say cure we make certain kinds of judgements from the centre of the culture in which we live and perhaps 'adjustment' is a less committed way of describing that. We have in the literature of American psychoanalysts the work of Robert Lindner – who is perhaps known to the Cineastes here because he wrote *Rebel without a Cause*, even though they bought the rights to the book, used the title and threw the text away, that Lindner argued, in *Prescription for Rebellion* that 'adjustment' is the goal of so-called successful psychoanalysis and the notion of cure ought to be applied to the society rather than to the patient. I ask this question – and I'd like to think of it as an example of metaphorical thought – that perhaps there is a cure. This is where I would support Sam, in the notion of application, that if we can say that we apply psychoanalysis to the study of a particular film or film-maker, is every hermeneutic exercise itself an attempt to make a cure – because there is an area of disturbance or maladjustment between the knowledge held now and the knowledge we believe can be acquired. Each exercise to explicate is itself impelled by a need to cure – in other words, a cure is acquiring the knowledge not now held.

The awareness that there is some knowledge as yet unidentified, in which the search to find it and the finding are like an analogue of a cure – and in that metaphorical usage, yes, there is a cure going on in the psychoanalysis applied to film.

Metz: Yes, I agree with your second point. As to your first point, the question of the therapy, the cure being a kind of adjustment, it depends a lot on the countries – that is the American way of doing things. It is not the French one. It is the very reason why Lacan was ejected from the International Society of Psychoanalysis – refusing the adjustment – and in France this notion of the adjustment of the patient – so-called patient, he is not a patient – is foreign to a great number of analysts. In Lacan's school, and around it, recovering itself is considered as a 'secondary gain' (incidentally, it is a danger, the opposite one). But, is it because of poor adjustment that a person in the audience is unable to follow the action on the screen?

Flaus: That's a point about the process of perception, within identification. In the last decade or two we have seen a semantic shift in the word 'empathy' where 'empathy' and 'identification' have come to be the same thing.

Metz: Absolutely, yes, we too, use the word 'empathy' but mainly in relation to 'the cure'. It becomes close to 'identification', but nevertheless not synonymous.

Rohdie: Do you mean any polarity with the term 'projection' which [Edgar] Morin uses almost with projection?

Metz: Yes, yes, I know – no, in Morin's theory, which is very interesting, and a pioneer work, 'identification' is opposed to 'projection', but not in my theory. Only that this identification – to use the word – has both aspects and I make them precise, the introjective one (in Klein's sense) and the projective one. That would correspond to Morin by bi-polarity.

But to turn back to the question of an articulation between semiotics or psychoanalysis and the social or historical dimension, I think that the difficulty is that this linkage, this relation is very mediated, through many stages. Let us take an example – it is very easy to make a relation between sociology and semiology, at a trivial level. If you say, for instance, that films of the bourgeoisie have a bourgeois content (you have many books which say only that) – it's very easy. But if you study 'crossing-up montage' or 'fades', 'dissolves', precise things in the filmic chain and if you think how to relate these fades, dissolves and wipes with the bourgeoisie – well? There is a relation, but the chain is long and indirect and mediated – that makes it difficult.

Flaus: As a model for this, if I might suggest, we could study the shift from harpsichord to piano and the relation between this shift and what was the incipient bourgeoisie of the late eighteenth century, there is a model for us to follow that has not been applied to the cinema – in works which are accessible to us in English, anyway.

Rohdie: If you only look at the articulation between linguistics and psychoanalysis as opposed to the articulation between cinema studies and economics, or linguistics and sociology, I guess it has probably come about through – as you say, unconscious forces. There were certain problems set within semiotics generally and also within the concentration on language, coming from Lacan, which brought one to the necessity for psychoanalysis in order to solve a particular set of problems. Psychoanalysis will continue to be used so long as those problems seem important and so long as psychoanalysis continues to yield the kind of results one wants. I would have thought there are reasons why linguistics and, say, for example, sociology or linguistics and economics have not been articulated with one another, as opposed to its articulation with psychoanalysis precisely because the way in which problems have been developed have not required that move. Perhaps the lack of this articulation requires an explanation, not of unconscious forces – or is it? – in such a large group of people? It seems quite clear that the articulation between linguistics and psychoanalysis is far from accidental. There were certain crucial problems within semiotics as well as attempts to – subvert isn't quite the word – it's too strong, but some way in which one could dismantle certain problems within semiotics. Psychoanalysis undercuts (by introducing notions about the subject and desire) much of the logical problematic that linguistically-orientated semiotics presented by introducing notions about the subject and desire. As soon as you presented the 'subject' and 'desire' representation took on a very different look. I am to a degree surprised when I read *The Imaginary Signifier* for, on the one hand what seems to me the maintenance of a semiotic project consistent with that of the earliest works concerned with specifying the cinema and defining its terms, and, on the other hand, a kind of language which is more rhetorical, more metaphoric, more self-referential, playful, and not exactly aligned with the project – the language is apparently there to explicate. If the language is to give certain rigorous clarity to specific notions about the cinema it avoids – I'm not saying that the language is not rigorous or clear – but it avoids some of that categorisation precisely because it is rhetorical, metaphorical and playful. It is not the language of Barthes but it is not the language is of an earlier Metz, either.

Metz: It is hard to answer. First, I have the right to change my language ! – I know I am joking – but this book, *The Imaginary Signifier,* is composed of four articles and they are not on the same level. The three other essays are more rigorous and, I hope, more scientific, – at least they were written with this intention, especially the study on metaphor and metonymy. The first one is conceived in a more playful and 'literary' way – you are quite right.

Davies: I wonder if you would like to comment on the notion that, at least on one level, the choice of psychoanalytic theory was not an accident or a phenomenon of the collective unconscious but was a fairly decided political step because it presented people with a materialist analysis of the psyche alongside what had up to then, hoped to be a materialist analysis of the social sphere of the cinema.

Metz: You mean that it was not accidental in that it provided us with a materialist theory of the psyche – yes, in this sense, yes.

Davies: I think that might have something to say about a materialist analysis of jokes – is that what you are doing now?

Metz: Oh, I do not know if it is materialist – we'll see.

Flaus: May we ask, is it mechanist?

Metz: (Laughs) Hopefully not!

Davies: I said materialist, there, because I was thinking of another work that re-runs Freud's book on jokes by Timpanaro [*The Freudian Slip: Psychoanalysis and Textual Criticism*, New Left Books, 1976], the Italian, who has a particular and possibly quite different definition of materialism to the one that's accepted within semiotics. I find it incredibly complicated to delineate where these two views of materialism come from – sometimes 'materialism' seems like a portmanteau word to cover the interests of Marxist theory.

Metz: I don't think so. The difficulty is that materialism is often being confounded with Marxism, whereas Marxism is one very important form of materialism. For me, exactly as for you, there is no doubt that psychoanalysis is a materialist conception of the psyche. Freud was explicitly materialist, he thought that all so-called psychological phenomena were ultimately derived from the body. He took his ideas from Fechner – it was mechanistic materialism.

Davies: The problem then is how Timpanaro can write a profoundly anti-Freudian book about Freud's conception of jokes and still call himself a materialist and – it seems to hang together, too.

Metz: An anti-Freudian book?

Davies: It's not a critique of Freud's materialism but it is a critique of Freud's paths by which he arrives finally at the joke, the parapraxes. In other words we have a 'slip of the tongue' and a materialist conception of how to analyse that, while 'the slip of the tongue', itself, according to Freud, is overdetermined. Therefore, you can get to it through linguistic analogies, through geographically similar names, and so on, through many different paths – and the path that Freud chose is not the only path – Freud, in fact, says this quite often but forgets this after a while, and it becomes a single slip, slip, slip to the final joke. He was, of course, more interested in the system being constructed than the final punch line. I do not know how you handle that in terms of materialism, because Timpanaro's other book available in English is about his particular viewpoint on materialism [*On Materialism*, New Left Books, 1975] – or whether its inherent in the kind of pathways, the choices of multiple pathways in the unconscious to arrive at the single symptom that comes out.

Metz: But you have not multiple pathways in a real situation of therapy, of cure – you have no choice. I was seven years on the cure. You have choices in books. There is a materialism of the signifier – there is, a very strong one. Theoretically, you have two paths. One of the two paths produces no result – no result at all, while the other path makes you upset immediately and produces a heavy symptom – so you have no choice, and no hesitation about the right one.

To turn back to the first part of your last question, the articulation between linguistics and psychoanalysis. I think it was rather easy, many reasons which we have heard – I would add one more, both sciences, linguistics and psychoanalysis, share the particularity which is very rare, unfrequent, to be involved with the very fact of meaning and it alone. To be involved with, let us say, the 'meaning of meaning' – to use the title of a famous English work – they are the only two sciences (we have no third one) which are involved only and directly with the very fact of the meaning, as such. I think this is a further reason which made this articulation rather easy, and even the main reason, by far.

Rohdie: I have a quote to ask you about ...

Metz: Please do ...

Rohdie: It is from Christian Metz – I am not quite sure I understand it.

Metz: Perhaps neither do I?

Rohdie: It comes from *The Imaginary Signifier*, I shall quote it to you: "Phenomenology can contribute to knowledge of the cinema [...] in so far as it happens to be like it, and yet it is on the cinema *and* phenomenology, in their common illusion of *perceptual mastery*, that light must be cast by the real conditions of society and man" [p. 53].

Metz: Ah yes – that was my personal Marxist revolution. (Laughter). I mean by that to take Hegel and put him on his feet, you know? Yes, but seriously, I was thinking of Bazin, when he speaks of the cinema as a kind of cosmo-morphism, a revelation in a nearly religious sense, a revealing of the world, a kind of cosmophany, so the revealing of the real world, which we do not see in our real life and all-day perception, but when watching a film we see it – that was Bazin's theory. That can, perhaps, explain the sentence. I think that when we are screening a film we have the impression of perceptive mastery, and it was precisely that impression of mastery that Bazin felt, and expressed, but in fact he was victim of a kind of lure, a deception, a delusion because this impression is the very mechanical, materialist result of the functioning of the objective, of the apparatus.

Rohdie: There is also a notion there of making strange too. There are film-makers that he would champion, like Bresson with those who use the cinema to make things strange.

Metz: Yes, but it was impossible not to support Bresson – obviously so important. Bazin was very, acutely intelligent and he was able to support film-makers very different from his point of view because he knew that they were important.

Routt: Is this 'casting a light on the illusion of perceptual mastery' part of the sadistic project of the film theoretician to which you refer once or twice, but do not really go into much detail about that aspect of film theory? You say it is a form of sadism, once or twice playfully, but perhaps it is worth saying more about it?

Metz: The theory is sadistic? Of course it is, yes (laughter). I mean by that when you analyse something, film or literature, you are pushed by the desire to take apart the object, of de-mounting, de-constructing the object – the word of Kristeva, 'de-constructing', is very expressive in this sadistic sense. It is not my idea – it is the idea of Melanie Klein – epistemophilia is linked to voyeurism, and voyeurism is linked to sadism. I think she is obviously right, in some sense, because in an imaginary way, to analyse an object is to destroy it – even if you do not destroy it physically, of course, but it means to destroy it phantasmatically.

Rohdie: What about playing with it?

Metz: Another way of dealing with it.

Rohdie: But would that be sadistic?

Metz: No, no, it would be the other drive, love drive, libido –

Rohdie: But it could also produce knowledge?

Metz: Oh yes, yes. But not exactly analyse, you know? To analyse is to take apart, to divide in two parts, to cut. If you think, what I mean is very simple. To analyse is to cut, to divide, to hurt, to symbolically destroy the object. Analysis is not the only form of knowledge, but it is a kind of sadism. The Greek word 'analyse' means to destroy, in Ancient Greek, to dissolve (verb: *Analuein*). You know in chemistry to analyse a given substance means, very precisely, to destroy it.

Flaus: Yes, in literature, Wordsworth said "we murder to dissect."

So when you turned Bazin upside down, you were suggesting to us that Bazin's claim that what we are getting there is the pleasure of being possessed by something greater than ourselves – that is the form of masochism. In other words, Bazin's way of seeing what the cinema does to us is the pleasure of being taken over?

Metz: Yes, in reality. But what we feel is the imaginary pleasure of mastery – it could be an unconsicous masochism. Masochism is linked with sadism, so it would be compatible, but the point is: the sadistic level is conscious while the masochistic level is unconscious – in this case. In other cases it is the opposite.

Martin: I would like to ask you, when you look back on *The Imaginary Signifier* whether there is a strong link – or the possibility of a link – between Lacan with Althusser, with certain kinds of Marxism and linguistics. Now, do you think that move is so strong? I am thinking about the critiques of, say, Lyotard, Deleuze, Guattari and Baudrillard. Do you think they have affected the intellectual climate in which you work?

Metz: Oh yes, inevitably.

Martin: Is the status of that marriage between psychoanalysis and Marxism so strong now? What position do you think it is in?

Metz: It was never very strong – it is an illusion of perspective. It was never so strong because it is difficult to link up everything, but it is true that this move has weakened now. Among other causes are the effects of these critiques that you mention, they were important.

Flaus: Not so much a marriage as an affaire?

Martin: Do you think this has greatly affected film criticism and theory?

Metz: Not especially in film criticism. It has a consequence – and a happy one – in film practice, in film-making. It has been responsible for the small beginning of experimental French cinema with the influence of Lyotard, and with people such as Claudine Eizykman and Guy Fihman. Experimental cinema was very undeveloped in France, and it really progressed with the influence of Lyotard – a very positive influence.

Flaus: How recent was that, please, we do not hear much about French experimental cinema at this distance?

Metz: Oh, very recent, within the last five years. Cinema has to manage with the demands of the film industry, which needs to have paying customers. It has to rely on the money circuit of the bank, the producer, the distributor, and so on, the most important of whom is the spectator, who pays to enter the cinema. If he has to pay, it means that he wishes to see the film, he has the desire to see the film, and so, here, you have another example of a meeting point, a crossing between the psychoanalytic problem and the social, economic problem.

Rohdie: How do you see those articulated? The social and economic situation, during the history of the cinema, would have altered considerably. For example, you have a period when there is no sound and another period when there is; a period when the construction of the cinema is basically artisanal, another when it is highly capitalised; you have another which goes through the crisis of the depression and another in which there are world wars and fascism. I am not sure how the narrative codes of the cinema, through, say, the twenties and thirties and fifties, could be articulated with socio-economic circumstances within this structure. You are right to say people are paying for their pleasure and desires. ...

Metz: It means that the affective, psychoanalytic machine is part of the film industry, that is very essential.

Rohdie: Yes, but it is still unclear how, beyond that, those socio-economic issues are articulated with that area that is ideological. That is the area of the position of the spectator and the pleasures which the spectator receives, in exchange for payment. When you talk about a socio-historical critique of the cinema in which it is necessary to concern oneself with economic, social and political structures, it is not clear how the articulation works – because in practice, though one asserts that the concepts are social and therefore subject to historical investigation and we use semiotics that involve linguistic and psychoanalytic representation, most analyses of the cinema in that area have not articulated their discussions of the spectator and questions of representation with those social, economic and class structures. Is it because it is impossible? Are the kinds of expertise required to make an analysis of economic structures at the same level of ideological structures, and to articulate them, are so vast no one can do it – or is it involved with something about the current analysis of the cinema, which genuflects towards the need for socio-historical critiques, but fails to practice them?

Metz: Yes, you know it is so. This lack of socio-economic study of the cinema, in certain works, is so by definition, because, as you said, we are not sociologists, we are not economists. I never pretend to study the sociology of the cinema. You have others who are sociologists of the cinema. You are correct, but it is so for the good reason that the articulation is extremely difficult to realize, intrinsically.

As to economics, there is something to add. Economics is science, real science that you need ten years to study. There are such studies of the cinema, very good ones, Mercillon, for instance. You have sociologists, such as Sorlin in France.

Rohdie: Yes, but within your particular concerns, you can presumably set problems which you, yourself, cannot answer, for sociology or economics?

Metz: Yes, that's right.

Rohdie: What would those be? If, for example, I think of works within that area of semiotics that might genuflect towards the necessity for further articulations with other structures, if they want to explicate something within the cinema they always have their own terms, within a structure of ideology, for answering problems. They never pose any questions outside this infrastructural route. They never pose any questions to economic or social practices. It seems utterly self-sufficient. They say they need articulations elsewhere yet there seems to be no need for them, in many of the works from, roughly speaking, a semiotic point of view, because the answers and the problems mesh with each other. You don't need to ask questions about social practices outside the very specified realm of the cinema – they never enter into it.

If one says they ought to enter into it – and I am not pretending to be a sociologist or an economist – presumably one would be in a position to say that there are certain limits, there are certain problems that I cannot answer and yet need to be answered, need to be articulated with other structures – that does not seem to occur?

Metz: Yes, but you know, it's not my fault. We semiologists achieved some work in the last ten or twenty years, in France, while the sociologists of the cinema did not follow. So it's up to them – I cannot do it all by myself.

Rohdie: You might, for example, find over a long historical period in the cinema that narrative codes have remained relatively stable, and you seek the reasons for that stability. ...

Metz: Oh yes, I know the reason. The reason is that the film has had to reconquer by its own specific means of expression, the flexibility, the spatial-temporal flexibility, the ubiquity of the classical novel of the nineteenth century. It has to reconquer the favourite art of the bourgeoisie – that is clear. But semioticians have studied that, not the sociologists, they don't care. From this point on the sociologists have to take the relay, the historians have to pick it up, because I have no competence to go further. In the absence of the necessary competences, the wish for articulations becomes wishful thinking.

Routt: To focus on one example, it would seem that French cinema before the war there was a certain currency of representation in the working class and it seems that after the New Wave that begins to disappear. A number of explanations might be offered; I would be interested, if you would care to hazard an explanation based on your topographical analysis of film pleasure, based on the notion of the richness of the diegesis based on the Id, and so on. I don't know whether I am pushing you into something too large?

Metz: No. My explanation would be – I have made no precise research, so it is only an opinion – that the objective achievement of the New Wave in France, without knowing it – unconsciously – was to conquer the bourgeoisie for film. Before the war the French bourgeousie did not see many films – it was rather a populist entertainment – and so, as the diegesis became more subtle and rich the bourgeoisie became interested. The plots, the subject-matter of the films deeply changed – it was no longer a question of the working class, the Prévert, the Carné, they disappeared. Then there begin the stories on an executive who is divorced and who fell in love with a second woman, and so on. At the same time all the diegetic details became more subtle, more elaborate, so it was more appropriate to an educated audience. The audience has shifted.

Routt: What would have been the unpleasure of the pre-war audience for that kind of cinema, what would have been the source?

Metz: Ah, the 'false theatre' – it was a kind of cinema which remained very theatrical, but this impression works only for people who are used to going to the real theatre, that is the point. Whereas for the workers, for whom theatre is too expensive, they did not notice anything special – it was their theatre, and it was cinema.

Flaus: In a study of American drama, the observation, say with the rise of the tele-film there is a much narrower range of styles, the codes that are used are purer and simpler, the problem of the diegetic exercise is less pleasurable, to us anyway. The point where the cineaste would stop would be the point where he or she would say that economic pressures in the television industry require that budgets must be one-tenth of what might be spent as a theatre release. As a tele-film, the budget would not only control the questions of casting, which reflects on the box-office, but that rehearsal times are much shorter, directors must use close ups and intercut between close ups instead of wide angle, long takes, and so on. The result of this narrowing down can be stated, by cineastes, to be a return to lower-budget tele-films, and it would be left there. The cineaste would say 'right, economists and socialist audience, find the data for us and put it together'. In my practice that would be a matter of economies – but I do not presume to go any further into that investigation.

Metz: Yes, I agree.

Rohdie: But you might start from the position of a loyal semiotician, and you pursue certain loyal semiotic projects, and you find that it does not answer your questions. You have to find out about other things because your desire to know a specific thing is not served by this collection of theories or concepts.

Flaus: That is where your first question came in, Sam, why is this not being done or is it impossible? Perhaps the gathering of the data is so diffuse.

Rohdie: I think it also has to do with the statement of what the problems are. The problems are stated in such a way that they are only soluble within the discipline, and the professional academic then says 'I can't go any further, this is the end of my expertise', rather than take a political position.

Metz: It is, it is.

Rohdie: But while your expertise might end, the problem might continue. You might have to say 'Well, I'm not going to be an expert any more, I'm going to take a risk'. Go somewhere where no one has been before because the problems require one going further, rather than taking a stand which is basically a particular kind of professionalism which says 'I don't know any more' but it is also saying 'I don't choose to know any more'.

Metz: It is not so, Sam, you know. In my life I have learned linguistics, semiotics, film theory and psychoanalysis and I can tell you that I am tired. I can't go further, it's the human capacity that has a limit.

Freiberg: But why chose psychoanalysis rather than say, sociology or economics?

Metz: Oh, that is the problem of human choice, you never can say 'why'. It is a deep choice made by the unconscious.

Flaus: Yes, why chose one lover rather than the other?

Metz: Yes, if I had chosen the opposite you would have asked me the opposite so ... (laughter).

Freiberg: I would like to continue this point, though, because at one stage early in your career you did try to specify what was essentially cinematic or filmic, what was the specific domain of film studies, and in doing that, it would exclude some of these other areas. In doing that you went on to concentrate – or validate, the area of psychoanalysis.

Metz: Oh no, I don't exclude anything. I say: '*For me*, I study this and that, but other people can study other things'. In all life you have to make choices – but excuse me, I interrupted you?

Freiberg: Some of your previous comments about the French New Wave vis-à-vis the 'thirties' suggest that you do have some interest in sociology –

Metz: But of course, but interest and research, which takes thousands of hours, are two different things. Of course I have an interest, yes.

Freiberg: Do you think sociology has a significant contribution to make to film studies?

Metz: Oh yes.

Routt: It was said that one place where semiotics and psychoanalysis came together at the moment around the time of "Imaginary Signifier" appeared in English [1975], was that it provided the possibility of a theory of the subject in cinema. I was wondering if this was part of your conscious project in that paper, or whether it has been a by-product? The first time I read it, it seemed to be a traditional example of the cinema object in which the subject slowly becomes more paramount – one discovers one cannot discuss one without the other. I wondered how far you intended the theory of the subject in the cinema to be the central aim of this work – as it has been taken to be, in English and American circles?

Metz: Yes. This part of my book was conscious. It was a conscious project, because I was thinking about my former research and its lack of a theory of the subject – that had to be tackled. You have to deal with the problem of the subject, with the spectator; in my earlier research the problem of the spectator was *too* absent, it went too far. That was the beginning of my book and then the rest came less consciously.

Flaus: The Pleasure Principle stated in terms of the Reality Principle?

Metz: Yes, exactly.

Martin: I'd like to ask a question about a detail in your article, "The Imaginary Signifier," where you discuss the nature of identification in the cinema and their types. You distinguish between secondary types of identification that would include identification with a character and primary cinematic identification which is identification with the camera. It also seems to me you are arguing there is an identification with the film system as a whole – the filmic system.

Metz: That would be the primary one, part of the primary one,

Martin: If one considers the model of the spectator in the cinema, would one always talk about the spectator as in a position of identification? For example, if one thinks of a model of a game where one was a spectator, where you are following the game, would you say one identifies with the game or sport in order to follow it? If one does not, maybe one does not in relation to the cinema, and it is more like understanding a set of rules by which one can follow a set of discourses.

Metz: Yes, I agree. In your example it is quite possible that the spectator has no secondary identification with the football game – if he is not at all involved with 'footy', if he does not know the rules of the game. You have the precise conditions which can frequently make this impossible. Only the primary identification is inevitable.

Martin: Why would one want to call that identification, and what is one's definition of 'identification' under those circumstances?

Metz: Because you have to identify – I speak now of the primary one – your own personal look, your eyes, your watching, with the camera, with the projector, with, finally, the whole cinematic apparatus. If you don't, you no longer understand what is going on. It is an objective condition of the subjective possibility of screening – is that clear?

Flaus: I think the problem is that we don't use the term 'identification' in that sense normally in English.

Metz: Ah you mean, perhaps, identification would be only with persons? It is not the French meaning of the term you know? 'Identification' means to confound oneself – or one's self-look or self-hearing with something, anything, a person, an object, an apparatus, a political regime. That makes it difficult to understand. I meant by that the fact that you are identifying your look with the cinematic apparatus – and most of all with the camera and projector.

Thompson: I am sure we would all like to thank Professor Metz for a most interesting and enlightening session, and, perhaps, continue to discuss some of these issues more informally. Thank you very much.

Transcribed at a seminar held in the Media Centre, La Trobe University, 27 April, 1982.

9. Responses to *Hors Cadre* on *The Imaginary Signifier*

Christian Metz

Buckland, Warren and Daniel Fairfax (eds), *Conversations with Christian Metz: Selected Interviews on Film Theory (1970–1991)*. Amsterdam: Amsterdam University Press, 2017.

DOI: 10.5117/9789089648259/CH9

Abstract
Christian Metz responds to a series of questions presented to him by the editorial board of the journal *Hors Cadre* in 1986. The questions seek to determine Metz's use of psychoanalytic concepts, especially the notion of the 'Imaginary'. Metz broadens out the debate by discussing narrative and fiction, as well as condensation/ displacement and to metaphor/ metonymy.

Keywords: Christian Metz, film theory, psychoanalysis, fiction

'Réponses à *Hors Cadre* sur *Le signifiant imaginaire*', Christian Metz. *Hors Cadre* 4 (1986), pp. 61–74. Reprinted with the permission of Presses Universitaires de Vincennes. ©PUV, Saint-Denis, 1986. Translated by Daniel Fairfax.

1.

Hors-Cadre: *The Imaginary Signifier* discusses the cinematic signifier by using concepts from psychoanalysis. Do the analyses you carry out modify the psychoanalytic concept of the imaginary? In particular, does the application of Lacanian concepts to the cinema lead to a certain number of displacements in the analytic domain?

Christian Metz: On the whole, I do not think that my psychoanalytic study of the cinema has had a significant retroactive impact on my understanding of psychoanalysis itself, nor has it displaced such concepts in my mind. In any case, for me, the effect is more general: as film theory is less advanced than many other theories, it can be enriched through contact with them, without the opposite being the case. (I am not talking about *initial impressions* or question setting, which the cinema and the image have in abundance; I am thinking of reflections that have already been developed.)

An example that plays an important part in my book is the role, and the modalities, of voyeurism for the film spectator. If we admit that my description is correct and useful for understanding the functioning *of the film*, then we must ask what it can contribute – apart from, perhaps, a modest change – to the very notion of the scopic drive in psychoanalysis, founded on a substantial and already long-established accumulation of observations and research, which, nourished by the fundamental contribution of clinical analysis, takes things back to their embryonic roots, and which, even when it is problematized, does so in the name of arguments and contributions situated in this field. The fable of the lion and the mouse[1] does not apply to all domains of knowledge, because each domain is not equally applicable to other domains.

Subsequently, I do not believe in interdisciplinarity, in exchanges, in the frequently promoted activity of *borrowing*. This emphatic declaration may be surprising, coming from a researcher who has spent his time applying linguistics and psychoanalysis to the cinema. But this is precisely where the misunderstanding lies: I have not applied anything, I have positioned the study of the cinema within more general concepts, which fully involve the cinema just as much as they involve other objects: the general processes of signification (whence the use of the term 'denotation', etc.), or of the imaginary subject, with concepts that have come from psychoanalysis but that are today, as with their predecessors, circulating far beyond their place of origin. In short, I wanted to place the cinema in the conceptual spheres it already belongs to, and which for a long time have only been kept separate from it by the fanatical or ignorant isolationism of its proponents, who are themselves guilty of the same imbecilic and arrogant contempt in which the intellectual Establishment held the cinema. After all, what is so extraordinary about observing that the cinema depends (to a large extent) on scopic passion, that it pushes this passion to a very high degree, and that we should therefore take a look at the only science that has reflected on this passion at length? And what does it mean to claim that the cinema 'is' psychoanalytic, which, by the way, does not mean anything? Does it not, as it happens, possess many other characteristics? And are there not many other characteristics that give prominence to scopic passion? Will we say that the human being is 'chemical' because we are governed (in part) by (some of) the laws of organic chemistry, that also apply to numerous animals? Well, my work can certainly be related to organic chemistry. It is applied, and sometimes more than one would like. We never apply anything.

But I shall return to your question, or at least to something you said: no, I do not have the impression that my work on the cinema has 'modified' the psychoanalytic concept of the imaginary. As you know, in Lacan's thinking, it is closely tied to the concepts of the 'symbolic' and the 'real'. It has a distinguished history in psychoanalysis itself, and its influence reaches everywhere within the field. In order to displace it, more will be needed than my book. Although I had no particular desire to use the concept, I found it to be entirely satisfactory. It helped me to understand better the fundamental seduction of the spectator's position in the cinema, and enabled me to 'make progress' (?) on one of the two fronts that were present (namely, the film); I could not and would not do so on both fronts at once.

But I begin to understand the reasoning behind your question, especially if we apply it to concepts other than the 'Imaginary'. In the last text of my book, 'Metaphor/Metonymy, or The Imaginary Referent', which occupies half the volume, there are passages that belie the preceding remarks. Either they no longer treat the cinema, or they only reach it at the end of the road, after the core of the 'work' is over, in order to draw didactic illustrations from it. These passages tackle the 'internal' discussion of properly psychoanalytic problems. Thus, we find propositions for a new theory of censorship, conceived as the very *gap* between the secondary process and the primary process, and not like a barrier or dyke separating them. Yes, it is true that this idea is born from my work on cinema, where the supposed barrier is particularly intangible, the oscillation of the primary processes are unstable. But the same text also speaks of language systems, etymology, rhetorical figures (overused and fixed, or, on the contrary, more or less new), and directly interweaves the two aspects in its very composition, in such a way that it is not always easy – even (or especially?) for me – to know *what* has displaced what.

Your question also leads me to think about the ideas I developed in the same section of the book on the subject of the famous homology between metaphor and condensation, and metonymy and displacement. In Lacan, there is a kind of flash of brilliance, a quite astute intuition, which he has not developed, clarified, or 'followed up on'. And yet, when we look at it in detail, we encounter difficulties relating to the very nature of the signifying material, in particular the danger of confusing those relations that are specific to the referent (metaphor and metonymy) and those that are specific to the discourse (paradigm and syntagm). Most frequently, the latter disappear and are 'merged' into the former. Thus, we often speak of a simple syntagm as metonymy. In fact, however, metonymy, when it truly does arise, can take the form of either a syntagm or a paradigm, based on whether its two terms are explained, or whether one of the two terms is left to mental association. I have tried to shed light on these different cases, as well other difficulties of the same type, in order to respond to the meticulous and obstinate demands of textuality, which is not content with two major axes, in order to draw out from Lacan's homology some of the consequences about which it is silent.

At the end of the day, I believe that something of my work is re-inscribed in the psychoanalytic field. But this something is rather small when compared to the set of psychoanalytic concepts I had available to me. And then, is it really necessary to speak, as the agent of this re-inscription and this partial displacement, of my 'work on the cinema'? It is more general; it is also my work on the figural, my linguistic reflections and, at times, my direct interventions in the psychoanalytic field. And yet, all this is done in the framework of a book on the cinema. The *weight* of the cinema has certainly played, for me, a driving force at once more diffuse and more permanent than what I am clearly aware of. At bottom, your question has slightly 'displaced' my initial impression...

2.

Hors-Cadre: What exactly does the term 'imaginary signifier' refer to? To the imaginary character of the material base and/or the perceptual regime that the cinema imposes on the spectator? Does this Imaginary Signifier suppose the 'Imaginary Referent' that you define by analytic and linguistic categories, or would it admit a different type of referent? And which one?

Metz: For me, your question is very central. In effect, I chose the term 'Imaginary Signifier' because I found in it the merit of referring to both traits that you indicate, the imaginary characteristic of the material base and the perceptual regime that the cinema privileges in the spectator (I will not adopt as my own view what you say: '*imposes* on the spectator').

Hence, the regime of belief is influenced by the nature of the signifier. But it is also dependent on other factors, because the fictional target, the consensual credulity, the 'temporary suspension of disbelief' of Anglo-Saxon literary theory, can also appear in the reading of a novel or in a theatrical scene. Fundamentally, the phenomenon is always identical: a mix of belief and disbelief, a split in perception, vividly evoking what psychoanalysts call fetishistic disavowal ("I know very well... but all the same..." [Octave Mannoni]). The attitude of the film spectator is also partly modeled on the Western (Aristotelian) tradition of art as imitation (the imitation of everyday life, or of a mythical universe). On the other hand, we see that this psychic splitting, which defines fiction as such, takes substantially different forms when we pass from one fictional practice to another. We are not astonished when a room has three walls instead of four in the theatre, nor when objects in the cinema are made out of light and shadow. This is how the characteristics of the signifier currently work, and they have been fully internalized by the public (the Signifier is social and historical). Thus, in each narrative and figurative art, the exact proportion of belief and disbelief is different, as is the *line of demarcation* between them. We accept the immobility and the silence of photographed characters; we are more likely to protest against their being out of focus.

It seems to me that if the cinema frequently tells stories (in good or bad films), then this is for three principal reasons: 1. The great cultural tradition that I have just spoken about, which represents an enormous pressure. 2. The exceptional wealth of the signifier in its *indices of reality*: sound, movement, color, the capacity to record practically anything whatsoever. 3. The ostensibly imaginary character of all this wealth. The 'imagic' is denounced, exploited, and only made possible by the *act of montage*. Whence its power: we cannot 'edit' the real, but what we do edit in film truly resembles it. The imagic, in one fell swoop, turns everything into narrative, and transfers to its credit the guarantees of reality that it employs. Otherwise, for example, the theatre – where the signifier is even richer in its allusions to reality, because it consists in a portion of the real itself – should have a stronger belief effect (I have in mind, of course, the belief in the story, not the belief in the spectacle; they are inversely proportional). The mode of cinematic belief has, as its essential trait, this double and remarkable movement: to make the real function to the benefit of the imaginary, to weave from compelling likenesses *the very thread of the fable*, and to thus awaken our old desires, to awaken the enchanted child who wanted to be told stories in the evening.

The cinematic signifier is imaginary because it is photographic. It is an imprint, a duplicate, a 'reproduction', the reflection of something else, the necessarily unreal correlative of a given referent. We have here one of the great difficulties that experimental film encounters in its experiments, to which I pay more attention now than I did before. Even if it abolishes all narration, which happens a lot, its frames continue to represent something (even if this something is greatly *diminished*): reflections, rapid and illegible editing, long, immobile, empty shots. It must reckon with the weight of the *dispositif,* which single-handedly sketches vague narratives at every moment. There is, of course, as in all of these problems, cases that border on the limits, which we still do not know if we should class as cinema – at least in the ordinary sense of the word. Examples include films made by directly scratching the celluloid (when they do not reconstitute, by this very means, a figurative picture), the camera-less films of Giovanni Martedi, etc.

As for the imaginary referent which your question raises, it is the (imaginary) bloc of reality the spectator supposes that the story has been *taken* from. 'Suppose' is not the right word; it is more a case of a diffuse but potent feeling that presents itself as an obvious truth. Literary theory prefers to speak of referential illusion. In Combray, there is a man named Legrandin, and Proust relates some (but not all) of the episodes of his existence: this, in effect, is a veritable *inverse illusion*, because, in reality, Legrandin has no existence other than a textual one, and he in no way 'transcends' the novel, the only thing to speak about him. But this illusion is also a fundamental intellectual *and* affective need. '*Later*', we will say, 'Legrandin became incapable of hiding that he was a snob': but the principal function of this 'later' is to cover the text's momentary silence on Legrandin and his disappearance *from the page*, to make this hiatus resemble those in life, by mentally interpolating into the text the passage of time that would have elapsed. Every narrative proposes that, in some *elsewhere*, the things narrated have really existed. Here, the referent is an effect of narration, and the fictional narration (even if there is another one) does not escape it. Certainly, it leaves us (by definition) very divided as to the reality of the referential real, but not as to the existence of a layer of deduction – one that is still, however, imaginary – which is indispensable to the comprehension of the simplest sequence. If we see the heroine at the top of a stairwell, and then, in the following shot, at the bottom of the stairs, we suppose that, in some enigmatic (and familiar) temporality, she has descended the stairs and that 'we have only been shown' the beginning and the end of the action. We reason as if this woman had an existence beyond her filmic existence, an existence authorizing inferences analogous to those of everyday life. This effect also plays a major role in the emotions provoked by fiction films, when they provoke them. We are not attached to characters in the same way we are to flesh and blood creatures; nor, however, do we see them as mere creatures of celluloid. They are more like those beings that appear to us in a memory or a dream – the unreal real.

For me, the domain of the 'fiction', 'narrative' or 'diegetic' film (I am provisionally employing these terms as equivalents) is not reduced to a completely linear narrativity (closed in on itself, depending on the story and on it alone), nor to 'chubby' or rounded [*mafflue*] narrativity, as Dominique Noguez humorously puts it. I do not see why *narrative* should become a synonym for *merely narrative*. Eisenstein's films are diegetic, those of Ruiz and Straub are also partly diegetic. In this problem, there are two common reactions I have difficulty understanding. Firstly, if a story is disordered, erratic, unraveled, when and how does it cease to be a story? Take *Détective* [1985] by Godard, for instance: four different narratives, all curtailed; but there is the grand hotel, the aviator and his wife, the prince and the young girl, etc. In short, a place, a time, and characters. Evidently, the fiction is not sutured, not 'filled', the film plays on its gaps and defective links. Its imaginary referent, it is true, is less complete and consistent than in a commercial film; it is weakened, assaulted. But it is there. In a more general way, I have the same impression when watching the films of Bergman, Resnais, Antonioni, Eisenstein, Welles, etc. – that is, films of a self-aware, emancipated, 'intelligent' type. Often, the ingenuities of enunciation, montage, recurring motifs, complex layering, etc., make us forget the story to a significant extent. But it has not disappeared, it is even indispensable to everything else. In short, to answer your question, it seems to me that the domain of the 'imaginary referent', of the fiction, is much vaster than we sometimes say, when we reduce it to the model known (God only knows why) as Balzacian. For me, it does not correspond to a type of writing [*écriture*] but takes numerous, diverse forms. It translates a general tendency of the cinema, unevenly affirmed by the films.

Is this equivalent to saying that the cinema (and, by extension, the imaginary signifier) never escapes narrative, and that the nature of the 'medium' determines that of the product without any leeway? No. There are, firstly, variations that I have just mentioned, and which are important. Filling a film with a diegesis varies enormously, even when the fiction is strong. A narrative film like *Citizen Kane* [1941] says at the same time plenty of other things; it is not overwhelmed by its story. Very often, it is 'from within' that fiction films escape from the fictional regime, even in the classical American cinema, which 'works' more than we say it does. And there have also been, with Anglo-Saxon experimental cinema (the London Film Co-op, Michael Snow, Hollis Frampton, Ernie Gehr, etc.), radical attempts to compromise the very functioning of the referential illusion, thanks to the Franciscan, minimalist impoverishment of the profilmic, or by disrupting the process of filming. The film is reduced to a flicker effect, or to a panoramic to-and-fro movement on a banal, unrecognizable object. In order for the diegesis to disappear entirely, it would be necessary for the film to show *nothing* (certain films by Peter Gidal are not far from this). In general, there nonetheless remains something and, as I said a short time ago, the phantasy of the spectator – both the *desire of the narrative* and the *need to understand* – can take a hold in order to enlarge and embellish it. Films also become fictional (more or less) through their reception. Here, we encounter the problem of social demand: experimental films, in spite of their interest, may well be condemned for a long time yet to minuscule audiences. In any case, they show that the imaginary signifier is capable of completely ridding itself of the imaginary referent. The film itself becomes the referent, with all its techniques commenting on the act of filming. These films are self-referential, or 'comparative' (if you like) when they allude to the procedures of conventional cinema by re-presenting and deforming them.

In sum, if you 'add' radical films and the ultra-narrative operations of narrative films, you will perceive that my 'imaginary referent' leaves a lot of room around it. But at the same time – a minor paradox – it is omnipresent, for everything else is almost always articulated around it, since its role (even on a manifest level) is considerable in the great majority of films, and also because it corresponds to a socially dominant regime of reading.

3.

Hors-Cadre: What is the 'imagic' and how does it favor the functioning of the imaginary?

Metz: The imaginary does not have an unlimited choice from among the sensory organs susceptible to using it. The so-called proximal senses (touch, smell, taste, if we adopt the categorization currently used) are strongly attached to reality, to the oral and anal drives. They give rise to poor, unfocused 'images' that technology has not undertaken to reproduce, at least not on a major scale. So, we are left with the superior senses classified as 'distal': hearing and sight. The cinematic imaginary largely rests in these two senses. However, for reasons that do not apply to the cinema, the visual register seems closer to the phantasmatic realm than the auditory register, except, of course, in the case of spoken language. The dream, although populated with spoken words, is above all a succession of images, as is daydreaming. Ardent passion passes through the desire to see (*nudity* is, by the way, a state without any acoustic expression, a purely visual notion), while the innumerable games of exhibitionism and voyeurism do not have equivalents on the auditory level. Perhaps it is necessary to attribute this striking discrepancy to the fact that the eye is much more precise than the ear and depicts objects better to us, as is the case with erotic representations of phantasies. The acoustic register – in everyday life, as well as in modern technology – has the misfortune of being caught between two extremely powerful neighbors, both capable of exact *expressions* and not only impressions: namely, the image and the language system [*langue*]. All this is, incidentally, only a difference of degree (see the importance of Lacan's invocatory drive); similarly, the cinema frequently has recourse, not always imaginatively, to the resources of sound.

There is another factor, specific to the cinema and to it alone. Sonic data are reproduced with all their phenomenal properties. If the sound engineer has done a 'good job', nothing distinguishes the sound of an airplane in the cinema from its equivalent on an airfield. 'Sounds have no image', said Balázs, referring to sound cinema. Filmic sounds are not reproductions but real sounds, or, if you prefer, reproductions, secondary productions of the same perceptive nature as the primary productions. The image, on the contrary, is immediately demarcated from its model by the absence of the third dimension. It records a permanent phenomenological deficit in comparison to the object which, due to this fact, it can only 'imitate'. *It is an effigy*, whereas sound is not. It is thus the most apt to lead the entire film toward the imaginary, the tale, the narrative. It is a very lifelike imaginary, one which is *furnished*, 'realized' earlier, but to which the specific coefficient is selectively absent. And it is through this 'default' that all the powers of the dream and desire come into play.

In short, the 'imagic', for me, is the adjective that, contrary to the 'imaged', corresponds truly to the *image*, with the same force and the same polysemy.

4.

Hors-Cadre: You insist on the importance of substitutional pressures in the psychic functioning of the spectator. Would the specific function of the cinema in this domain not be, under the force of the imagic flux, to exacerbate these substitutional pressures by prohibiting them from being fixed at any moment? Would you go so far as to speak of film as a support for desire, which could also mean a corset, substitute or third leg?

Metz: Yes, I think that film *can* play the role of a support for desire, when desire is deficient in those who go to the cinema because they do not know what to do. It can equally exacerbate a desire that is already strong, which would just about define cinephilia: this is your third leg...

The cinema is much less suitable than photography at *fixing* desire, or more exactly the phantasy of desire. As you recall, projection – the constantly changing audiovisual flux – renders the emergence and stabilization of a *fetish* difficult, a role that the photograph, by contrast, easily assures. The specificity of the cinema lies in *fetishistic activity*: modifications of framing, camera movements, etc. Change counts more than control, as when erotic passion impatiently delays its own satisfaction.

But film, which is mobile, is also fixed: fixed *in relation to the spectator's phantasy*. It is *this* film, and not another one, that we cannot change. We cannot lengthen by a tenth of a second the troubled gaze of the character, or add a little gray to the overly vivid color we feel assailed by. The film might be a dream, but it is somebody else's dream. There is thus always a distance, one that stands in relation to a fixed point: the film in itself (which switches over to the side of the real). On this basis, there are several – or at least two or three – possibilities. If the distance is too great, there is rejection, boredom, filmic displeasure. If, on the contrary, it diminishes, identification and projection can make up for this, at least during the film: the spectator is as ecstatic as he would be if his own phantasy were being told to him. Without going quite this far, he can receive and sustain exchanges with his own images, a foreign but sympathetic daydream, or can intermittently project himself into the film, or only in certain of its motifs, etc.

In sum, if the film 'fixes' the phantasies of us all, it confronts us with a phantasy that is now fixed. Fixed but mobile. This is why everything depends, as in friendship, on the relationship of forces in each singular *encounter*. Depending on who the spectator is, the moment, the film, the imaginary of the cinema can be a prison (or a corset, as you put it) or a springboard, or it can play these two roles at once.

5.

Hors-Cadre: What relation does the imaginary have with the image of the ego in the interpellation of the spectator? Does the spectatorial imaginary only develop through the ego-image? More broadly, what is the status of the signifier in the imaginary of the spectator?

Metz: The signifier is inscribed in the imaginary of the spectator with significant force. It is fundamentally important, and this occurs on at least two levels: the signifier of the *cinema*, common to all films (= Jean-Louis Baudry's '*dispositif*'), which, as if to answer you in advance, I call the imaginary, and which I will not discuss at present. And then there is the *work* of the signifier in each film. Spectatorial reception is all the more permeable, all the more vulnerable if it is not aware of this work. Textual analysis unearths a part of it, but at the same time it creates a new frontier and opens the way to infinite analysis, which is, incidentally, the most beautiful of all things. We will never know that what has moved us in a particular on-screen face, which we declare to be 'harmonious', is, in reality, the combination of framing and lighting. If the beautiful shot of a landscape we speak so much about had lasted 40 seconds longer, we would not have spoken about it. A particular shot/reverse-shot, banal at eight frames, becomes patently leaden on the ninth frame. Our imaginary is happy to record the effect, and it is the sum of these 'details' (which are mentally tied to the diegesis, that is, *fictionalized* [*romancés*]), which is very largely responsible for our overall reaction to the film.

Certain films, including the most admirable works, seek to *inscribe* these effects, rather than abandon them to secrecy and manipulation. But since the procedure of inscription is itself an effect, nothing has been fundamentally altered, apart from the fact that the augmented complexity of the *dispositif* offers an intrinsic interest.

In my book, the ego-image is given as *absent*. I describe the filmic screen as a specular space where we can see everything except our own image. This, of course, only applies to the physical appearance of the subject. As for the image of the ego in the psychic sense, it is a point that, until now, I have barely discussed. But it seems to me, in fact, that the filmic imaginary can only be developed in close relation to the ego-image of each spectator. The ego-image is deep down the only thing I *bring* to the screening (along with my own phantasies, but there is no real difference between the two). We have other strong images, like those of beloved people or places, but they do not stay with us. The ego-image is the only one that walks along the street with us (as in *Lady in the Lake* [Robert Montgomery, 1947]), the only one which is directly (and *continuously*) sustained by that of which it is an image, even if it is to restore a somewhat distorted event. It is also the only analogical instance we have to *follow* what the on-screen characters are doing. For example, from what other source could we draw any kind of knowledge on what it means for a character to *cry*? How to understand the acts of the villain, if not by mobilizing our own real or virtual evil side?

This option is most often unconscious; we encompass it in the very notion of *understanding*. It relates, I should stress, to the ego-image much more than the ego (we do not truly know ourselves), unless we define the ego, in the spirit of Lacan, as a *flight of images* [*fuite des images*]. This is also why the same film can be interpreted in an infinitely diverse manner: each one has assembled major pieces of its being, which itself escapes into multiple images...

Note

1. [In Aesop's fable, the small mouse is able to help the mighty lion.]

10. Interview with Christian Metz

Michel Marie and Marc Vernet

[The interview took place after the conference 'Christian Metz and Film Theory', held at the Cerisy Cultural Centre in 1989.]

Buckland, Warren and Daniel Fairfax (eds), *Conversations with Christian Metz: Selected Interviews on Film Theory (1970–1991)*. Amsterdam: Amsterdam University Press, 2017.

DOI: 10.5117/9789089648259/CH10

Abstract
In this wide-ranging interview published in 1990, Christian Metz speaks about his early work on film semiology and discusses his more recent work on impersonal filmic enunciation, and a future project, a study of jokes. He also makes a series of positive remarks on Gilles Deleuze's two books on film (*The Movement Image* and *The Time Image*), books usually regarded to be at odds with Metz's semiological and psychoanalytic approaches to film.

Keywords: Christian Metz, film theory, enunciation, Gilles Deleuze

'Entretien avec Christian Metz', Michel Marie and Marc Vernet. *Iris*, 10 (1990), pp. 271–296. Translated by Daniel Fairfax.

I. Semiology and Film Theory

1. On the Conference

Michel Marie: The conference 'Christian Metz and Film Theory' has finished. I would like to know what impression you have had of it.

Christian Metz: I really liked the atmosphere of this gathering, and I consider you to be largely responsible for it: the organizer of a conference, who has worked on it for a whole year before proceedings even begun, has a major influence on the style of the discussions, even if this is only due to the tone he adopts when talking about the simplest matters, like when the meal breaks are. In this case, you had a tone that was both serious and 'cool', not without humor, an imperturbable and amusing tranquility, in short, a good mix. And then there were the relatively short sessions, allowing plenty of time for conversations, and downtime. All this resulted in a certain spontaneity in the interventions and discussions during the sessions, and the absence of this stodgy and verbose theater that permanently threatens meetings, even interesting ones.

I am also persuaded that the opening address by Raymond Bellour, due to his intellectual generosity, his agility and his refusal of hackneyed clichés, also greatly helped to get the conference off to a good start.

Marie: It is also due to the place, and the format. The participants were present for several days in a row and were far from Paris. So we had the good fortune to be shunned by the professional conference-goers, who make remarks just for the sake of it.

Metz: In fact, I noticed that all of the 'speakers' talked about what they were actually doing, what was in their hearts, and also that they had all worked on their 'papers' – either well beforehand or (for those who kindly replaced absentees at the last minute), right here, in the château, and losing sleep in order to do so. In short, we escaped from those talks where the speaker is simply showing off. What is more, the level of discussion was very high, and remained high from start to finish: this should be noted, because, in general, having a large number of talks gives rise, through sheer probability, to uneven talks that are facilitated by being drowned out by the others. I will also take advantage of this interview to thank all the participants for having consistently maintained this high quality. The organizers (once again) have notably played a part here: by dedicating an entire session to each paper (or at the very least half a session), you allowed them to be genuinely listened to, something I observed with pleasure and surprise, and which 'obliged' everyone to give their most.

In a sense, of course, I could not avoid being satisfied with this conference, because it focused on my own work. But this personal, narcissistic aspect had a potential counter-effect: it made me more sensitive, because I was directly concerned; it made me desire a 'perfect' encounter, of a sort that I could just as well have been very disappointed with it.

Marie: Do you think that there were real debates, exchanges between researchers coming from different horizons?

Metz: Completely different? No, because the topic and even the title of the conference already indicated a specific orientation, and not a 360-degree general survey. Of course, empiricism and positivism, for example, were not represented, neither was 'salon' criticism, etc. But there were diverse points of view, and sometimes they were reasonably distant from my own point of view, despite indisputable common areas. I am thinking, for example, of what was said by Marie-Claire Ropars, Asanuma Keiji and others.

Marie: Do you think that the contract presented by the title, the confrontation between your works and film theory, was respected in this diversity?

Metz: I wouldn't say *all* of film theory, because today it is a very large machine, but a notable part of it was, yes. Unfortunately, as with every international gathering we should also make note of the researchers we were counting on who were prevented from coming for practical reasons: Mary Ann Doane, Kaja Silverman, Edward Branigan, Stephen Heath, Yuri Tsivian, Gábor Szilágyi, Dana Polan, Eliseo Veron.

2. Semiology and Other Disciplines

Marie: In the last twenty years, film theory has seen a rather remarkable expansion, albeit very uneven in certain domains. Semiology, semio-pragmatics and narratology have been significantly developed, but this is much less the case for historical and sociological approaches, what I would generally call the human sciences – the non-literary, non-linguistic disciplines, of a somewhat 'harder' type, or a little less soft, than the habitual discourse on literature. These approaches do not seem to have adopted the cinema as an object of study, to have really taken stock of it, in particular on the institutional level. How do you explain this uneven development? This is also a question that, roughly speaking, poses the problem of the relationship between semiology, theories of cinema and their interdisciplinarity.

Metz: Firstly, on the fact itself, I would be less absolute than you. In the domain of history, there is the work of Ferro, Sorlin, Janet Staiger, Douglas Gomery, etc.

As for the causes, I do not have an explanation. Nobody does. Everything that is presented here or there as a cause is, in reality, a *circumstance*, which sheds light on the issue but does not explain it.

To start off, this question should be asked of historians and sociologists. I would simply say, limiting myself to what I know, that, in France, toward 1963, there were circumstances favoring semiology, which had no equivalent for the other approaches: namely, the presence around Barthes (and Greimas, in a different way) of several young researchers, in a landscape that also contained Lévi-Strauss and Benveniste.

In any case, in order for a genuine history of the cinema to be created, somebody has to start. That is how it worked for semiology, and that is how it works for everything. It is possibly only the immediate cause, as it would be necessary to understand why this somebody began something at a certain time. But it does not prevent this from being the efficient cause.

Marie: Yes, but, at the same time, there is the formidable expansion of the 'new history' movement. And yet, this produced practically nothing on the cinema...

Metz: What about Marc Ferro? Is his work not a typical product of the new historians? He was the secretary of *Revue des Annales* for a long time...

Marie: Yes, but his work on the cinema remained very peripheral, while his books on more strictly historical subjects, such as his recent work on Philippe Pétain, are of an entirely different scope.

Metz: I would not say 'peripheral', but, this aside, I have observed something that confirms your remarks: namely, that, for us at the École des Hautes Études, among the so-called *Annales* historians, there are fewer specialists on the twentieth century than there are for earlier historical periods.

Marie: How has it come about that literature departments, in the very general sense of the term, have been more open to teaching film, and not history departments? I can suggest an initial answer: I believe that 'modern literature' represents a discipline with vague contours and an unrestricted methodology. It is a disciplinary field that differs greatly between the different campuses, above all if we compare it to linguistics or history. And so, there was a certain permeability and openness.

Metz: As far as the institutions are concerned, you are right. It is true that there are advantages to the amorphous nature and elastic consistency of 'modern literature' – a little bit like French classes in high school, or

English departments in the United States, or 'comparative literature' pretty much everywhere – and that it permits innovations to overcome traditional resistances, which presuppose a hard, even dumb kernel. But this does not explain the uneven development of *research*, to the (manifestly provisional) advantage of the galaxy of semiology, psychoanalysis, etc., at least for the last 25 years or so – which is a long time as far as a dominant idea is concerned, but very short in terms of the history of the world...

Marie: I have a complementary element to propose: I believe that, for the disciplinary institution of history – its professors and research teams – the cinema is a futile, frivolous object; it comes within the domain of fiction and does not represent very serious material. This sentiment remains strong: historians study garbage bins, refuse, because they can learn a lot about consumption and living standards, but the cinema, even less noble than refuse, does not seem to teach them anything about society, or at least a lot less. Historians seem to judge that its mediatic importance and the set of discourses to which it gives rise are disproportionate to its real place in the economic circuit, in the evolution of contemporary societies. For them, it is merely a vast simulacrum to be demystified.

Another aspect, which, alas, plays a decisive role in France, is the inaccessibility of the archives (in terms of both films and written documents). Students who have supervisors that point them toward the archives often find a closed door, even when it comes to written sources. In the United States, most of the major production companies have deposited their archives in university departments. This attitude is inconceivable in France, because the production companies are still dominated by a secretive mindset, protecting their sources, or even destroying large swathes of the traces of their past. This is the case with Pathé, for example: it is very difficult to study the first twenty years of its existence, when the company had a dominant position in the global film economy.

Metz: This is unfortunately true. But the closely-guarded archives also could have deterred our pals in modern literature...

Marie: Not entirely, since academics in literature can work at length on a single film, whereas the historian needs whole series.

Marc Vernet: It is true that, in relation to other countries (the US, the UK, Belgium), scholarship in France is distinguished by the inaccessibility of the archives. That said, there are some encouraging signs, like the openness offered at the Arsenal by Emmanuelle Toulet, or at the Archives du Film by Frantz Schmitt (who has unfortunately just been dismissed from his post), or at the Centre National du Cinéma by the Councillor of State, Théry, who has opened the dossiers of the Commission de Contrôle for the first time. But all this does not amount to a general policy. They are individual initiatives, and when the individual moves on, you have to start from scratch.

Marie: The paradox is that it is academics like you, me and Marc – that is, scholars with more of a background in literature – who encourage and set up teams of historical research, while very few professional historians have done so before us, with a few rare exceptions (including Marc Ferro and our friends from the Association Française de Recherche en Histoire du Cinéma, where the non-academic researchers are by far the most numerous). In France today, there is still a genuine ostracism of film studies among historians of the contemporary era, which explains the role played, in spite of themselves, by literature academics in embarking on historical research on the cinema.

Metz: I would add one remark, somewhat oblique with respect to your comments.

The pre-eminence of the sciences almost makes us believe that the ideal preparation for a film scholar lies in the École Centrale, or a firm grasp of mathematics. We willingly forget that there is something common, beyond the mere word itself, between the humanities and the human sciences: how can we fail to see that the grammar of foreign languages – rhetoric laden with examples, reading comprehension as a sensitivity to the signifier and the acts of construction, narratology frequently practiced in the study of novels, art history and the commentary of great paintings – that all this, and plenty else, directly prefigures the various kinds of modern 'scientific' analyses, which include the semiological enterprise? This last wants more solid and, above all, more explicit theoretical bases, but *it speaks about the same things*.

Of course, all research, as Jacques Aumont reminded us at Cerisy, when responding to me, deserves the name 'scientific', to the extent that it is neither a novel, nor a poem, etc.: if you use the term in this sense, there is nothing to discuss. But I prefer to speak of 'research' without an adjective, since this mirage of science, in our field, is the source of too many illusions for certain people, and of too many impostures among other people.

3. Writing – The 'Crisis of Theory'

Vernet: It is often said that theory, especially in Europe, has run out of steam, and that the major bodies of theoretical work have disappeared into obsolescence. For my part, I think that this is wrong. Simply put, theory is being developed along new axes, and possibly, above all, in new forms, new ways of writing. You yourself have known at least three different writing regimes: that of the *Essais*, that of *Language and Cinema* (which you specifically sought to be consolidated into a technique, from A to Z), and finally that of *The Imaginary Signifier*, with a much more literary, fluid, sometimes almost transparent style. What is your position today on this matter?

Metz: I agree about my three 'ways of writing'. As far as theory running out of steam is concerned, I do not believe this any more than you do. We are often fooled by the spectacular side of things (all the more so when, in this case, it is infinitely sad): the disappearance, one after the other, of several major figures: Barthes, Lacan, Foucault, the Althusser tragedy. Of course, this results in a huge void. But if you direct your gaze elsewhere, you will notice, for example in our domain, that there has never been such a large amount of interesting and solid work being done as there is today. When we speak of 'theory', we have in mind, as the expression indicates, a corpus, a set of research areas, and not only one or two giants (this is why my response would be totally different if you asked me about the major personal œuvres).

Another element has changed: theory, today, is no longer in fashion. But this tells us more about fashion than it does about theory.

Marie: What is in fashion now is the theme of the crisis of theory... (*laughter*).

Metz: As far as new ways of writing are concerned, they seem to trace a rather clear evolution over the last thirty years or so. The idea of the human sciences may well stretch back to the nineteenth century, but their actual, socially visible development dates primarily from the Libération. In the end, this is quite recent. At the beginning, it was implicitly admitted that, since a text was scientific, it could accommodate a rather rough or relaxed writing process, or even give a technical sense to every word used, so that this was all that was needed to express oneself. People took themselves for chemists, they sketched out formulae. (I note, however, that the 'greats', as if by chance, wrote beautifully: especially Foucault, Lévi-Strauss, Lacan, and Barthes, but this was not a concern shared by everyone.) And then, as the social sciences gradually established themselves, they were also subject to a common process. Researchers once again became sensitive to the basic, prejudicial demands of intellectual exchange: texts that were too poorly written, devoid of the minimum amount of skill and style, began to bore us, to leave us with a feeling of carelessness or shoddiness. A striking corollary is that authors, on the whole, write better than they used to. Either they have evolved without being aware of it, or they have a conscious will to respond to expectations. Of course, it is not that writers have become better, but that they have a greater respect for the reader.

Vernet: In the late 1960s and early 1970s, there was a unity at the École des Hautes Études that included Barthes, Genette, Bremond, and yourself. Today, this unity is no more, and yet there still seems to be repercussions of this past history. I wanted to know what your feelings about this are.

Metz: To the names you have just cited, we should add, for that point in time, the names of Ducrot, of Todorov, and of Kristeva (outside the École but not outside of our group), and of Julien Greimas, who, back then, seemed to us to duplicate or refract, in somewhat enigmatic fashion, the figure of Barthes. You are right to speak of a quite strong unity: this is what happens in situations that bring together a mentor with young researchers, who are yet to have real autonomy. Subsequently, in classic fashion, there was a diaspora – everyone chose their own path. Some of us really did part ways, such as Ducrot and Kristeva, or, later, Bremond and Todorov. Greimas and Barthes distanced themselves from each other. Then Barthes died. But it seems to me that of this geography dating from 1963, which lasted a further four or five years, there remains a partial affinity between Genette's work and my own, for example surrounding the notion of diegesis or narratological problems. By the way, Genette's approach, like my own, has something obsessive about it: in book after book, he calmly charts the terrain of poetics. I am, like him, not very permeable to those absurd 'important' or urgent matters (formerly 'ideological', now 'epistemological'), which we are incessantly deafened by, and which change every morning.

Vernet: In her intervention at Cerisy, Marie-Claire Ropars[1] interrogated you on the relationship between semiology and its 'outside'. Can we imagine semiology establishing relations with other disciplines and movements?

Metz: I have yet to study Marie-Claire Ropars' intervention in its written form. At Cerisy, I was struck by several points in which I was in agreement with her. In any case, I will give you my answer. Firstly, semiology, which is itself 'interdisciplinary' without shouting this out from the rooftops, has already established relations with other fields: ideological critique, psychoanalysis, feminism, textual analysis, structural history (see Jens Toft[2]), education sciences, etc.

As for more profound relations, like the notorious 'articulations' that people comically insist on researching, I do not believe in them. It is normal for semiologists to do semiology, for critics to do criticism, etc. If they manage to do their own work *well*, this is already a lot, and it does not happen that frequently.

It is true that the outside of semiology is immense, just as the outside of history or any other field is immense, for the simple reason that these disciplines are numerous, and the 'outside' of each one is constituted by the sum of all the others. Real competence, the formation of the mind, mental know-how can only be acquired within a disciplinary framework, because, as their name indicates, disciplines correspond to formations and not objects. Interdisciplinary undertakings can be interesting when each person involved sufficiently knows *both disciplines* in question. Otherwise, we bear witness to methodological psychodramas or metaphysical duels, as we all know well: the two approaches intensely stare into the whites of each other's eyes, and question each other on the place from which they are speaking. Interdisciplinarity must be above the respective disciplines, and not below them.

Marie: These last ten years have been characterized, during your relative silence, by the sensational appearance of Gilles Deleuze's two books on the cinema, which are now very much in fashion among certain academics and large numbers of students. Deleuze has often reaffirmed his numerous misgivings about semiological approaches, or those inspired by linguistics, but paradoxically he frequently refers to Peirce. How do you perceive his work? Is a dialogue, or a bridge, between your current project and his approach possible? Deleuze cites a large number of films, and reiterates the major classifications dedicated to the history of the cinema, which you rarely do. What do you think of him?

Metz: Firstly, the reference to Peirce. It is not really a reference, because many of Peirce's concepts are (avowedly) distorted from their original meaning, or even retroactively invented (and noted as such: see the 'rheume' [*reume*] supplanting the 'rheme' on page 80 of the first volume [*Cinema 1: The Movement Image*, trans. by Hugh Tomlinson and Barbara Habberjam (University of Minnesota Press, 1986)]. Deleuze could have written the same work without invoking Peirce. He had no 'need' of him (it is a different matter for Bergson). But it is common to bring up Peirce when you want to attack Saussure; Peter Wollen already did it in his first book, Bettetini did it, Eliseo Veron is still doing it.

As far as the numerous films and 'schools' that the book comments on are concerned, this is one of the qualities that make it such a rich and interesting work. It is also quite normal, if you think of what Deleuze himself said about his books. Deleuze clearly stated that he wanted to write a 'natural history' of the cinema. His objective immediately led him to films (the great, hallowed films), schools, filmmakers, etc. In a way, it is a vast film society of legitimation, with a dose of talent added: an almost Bazinian return to the cinema as amorous totalization. For my part, I will willingly go along with it.

Moreover, contrary to what I sometimes hear, I in no way think that his book is a war machine [*machine de guerre*] against semiology. Of course, third parties have used it for this purpose, but that is another matter. And of course, Deleuze is opposed to semiology and psychoanalysis – and he says this explicitly. But I fail to see where the war machine is. The work has nothing polemical about it; it is not a 'coup'. On the evidence it is very sincere, it is an endearing book where the author says what he thinks without bothering with other people too much. This is why it was somewhat meteoric.

Marie: And yet he cites a lot of journal articles, and not always the most interesting ones. He also creates a total impasse, not only with respect to semiology, but also to the great film theorists like Arnheim, Balázs, in short all of film theory.

Metz: Of course, but this is clearly a fundamental choice for him, and not a maneuver or a mark of sloppiness. It is easy to discern that he has decided to refer only to texts that speak directly about films. Moreover, he does not force us to make use of them. He does not adopt the posture of a specialist, even though he has seen a lot of films. He does not hide the fact that he has carried out a kind of 'raid' (and a raid of great scope for that matter).

His way of thinking is profoundly foreign to my own (there is no bridge between us), but I found his work to be very beautiful, a work of extreme intelligence. My 'response' is a warm esteem. I have never understood why books should have to 'match', because people in everyday life never match, and they are the ones who write books.

4. The 'Semiological Regime'

Marie: You just spoke of Roland Barthes as a mentor. This is a role that you have always denied or refused for yourself. And yet, if it is true that you enjoy the exterritoriality of the École des Hautes Études, this does not prevent you from lending consistent support to your old students.

Metz: It is the least I can do! I do not see any connection between helping people out and playing the role of mentor. It is a deformation of our profession to see subtle scientific politicking when it is often just everyday acts like helping a friend in need.

Marie: So, I will ask you a somewhat brutal question that other people have also asked, like Guy Hennebelle for example: is there a semiological regime within the university institution?

Metz: Of course, semiology has a certain (modest) influence, as is the case with any movement that has caught on. But it is funny to take umbrage at it, when you think of the massive, overwhelming power, in the same institution, of disciplines like English, History, Physics, etc. The university is a big house, very old and very complex, and becoming familiar with it is difficult. 'Power' does not lie in books doing well, but in the committees, the budgets, the hallways.

To return to the small upsurge of semiology, for the most part it has been beneficial, because it has contributed, along with other factors, to assuring (after many tribulations) the position of an entire generation of scholars, those who are about forty years old today. It has also contributed to film studies being admitted into academia (we had already tried this before, but without success), and not just semiological film theory, such that others have also benefited, which is good for them.

Now, on the crux of the matter: I never wanted to establish a School, or even to personally edit a journal, which would have immediately put me in the position of a boss. I do not wish to deny the reality of my position, the symbolic effect attached to my books, my notoriety abroad, and, above all, perhaps, my seniority (I was the first to take this path, and I am also the oldest member of the group). Of course, I had an intellectual and moral influence – as soon as you start writing, this is the risk, whether little or big. But it does not oblige you to *act* as a mentor, to tyrannize everyone, to condemn the work of others, to be haughty, to drape oneself in a stuffy solemnity.

Marie: Who, then, in your opinion, are the scholars directly extending your work?

Metz: At Cerisy, in my 'speech' on the last day, I proposed a threefold partition, which I have since reconsidered. But I would still adhere to it. There are the scholars outside of semiology (in its many forms), for example Jean-Louis Leutrat and Jacques Aumont, who are of great importance to my pluralist temperament, because they show that my enterprise has in no way *clogged up* the landscape. There are the 'other' semioticians – the non-Metzian semioticians, shall we say – like Marie-Claire Ropars or John M. Carroll in the United States. Finally, there are those who, more or less beginning with my propositions, have opened up new paths. I will not speak of the fourth group, those who are content to recapitulate my ideas while twisting them in all directions (at one point there were a lot of them): they are supposedly my 'disciples', but I recognize myself more in the third group. Moreover, I do not like the notion or the word disciple, which is reductive for the disciple, and burdensome for the 'mentor'.

II. The Unpublished Works

Vernet: While you have not published any books since *The Imaginary Signifier* in 1977, since that time you have worked on two major objects: the first is on the joke [*mot d'esprit*], for a book that remains unpublished because unfinished; the other is on enunciation, for a book which you are in the midst of completing.

Metz: Yes. But first a few clarifications. As far as the joke is concerned, my book is in fact 'finished' but, in its present form, it does not satisfy me. It was refused by two publishers – Seuil and Flammarion – after contradictory discussions between several readers, and, re-reading it, I appropriated this hesitant and finally negative judgment, which relates not to the subject matter but to the structure of the work (= useless digressions, awkward delineation of the chapters, etc.). So I put it to one side, with the idea of resuming it in this perspective, possibly in two years, when I retire.

Now, for my current book, it is true that I have written about two thirds of it, but I have had a lot of projects blocking its path, so I still need a year or eighteen months to complete it.

1. On Jokes

Vernet: What motivated your passage, after *The Imaginary Signifier*, to a purely psychoanalytic work on jokes?

Metz: To tell the truth, it is just as much a linguistic work (and even phonetic, for those quips that play on sounds). It is not a work that relates to the cinema, but only to written or spoken jokes. And also on Freud's famous work on the *Witz*, for which I have a profound admiration, along with various objections.

In spite of appearances, this manuscript is situated as a direct extension of *The Imaginary Signifier*, or at least the second half of that book, the very long text on metaphor and metonymy, where I was already quite distant from the cinema.

Each of the patterns of thinking (what Freud calls 'techniques') that produces a series of quips of the same mechanism, consists of a 'psychic trajectory', a 'symbolic path' that is primary in principal and then made more or less secondary. For example, following Freud, and in partial disagreement with him, I study the technique he calls 'deviation' (*Ablenkung*) – deviation of thought, of course. It gives rise to an immense, very widespread family of jokes and funny stories: a painter introduces himself to a farmer and asks if he can paint his cow. Answer: 'No way! I like her as she is!' At the airport, a woman asks how long the Paris-Bombay flight takes. Consulting his schedule, the desk clerk says, 'Just a minute, madam'. Satisfied, the woman answers: 'One minute? That's great. Thanks a lot!' Two friends are chatting. The first one says: 'Did you know that in New York someone has an accident every ten seconds?' His buddy says: 'Oh, poor guy! What rotten luck!', and so on.

All these quips relate to *slippages*, to displacements in the Freudian sense. These slippages are absurd, preserving something of the primary process (whence our laughter), as well as being made true-to-life, domesticated in order to accede to social exchange and become capable of passing into language. To this end, the invention of a joke allows for a kind of turnaround. For example, the double meaning of 'to paint' [*peindre*]: 'to represent on a canvas' and 'to daub with color' (it is thus necessary to be in accordance with the resources of the language in question, or in other cases with the discourse). Along with the turnaround, the joker needs to 'play' on two very uneven, unbalanced probabilities: in the context, the only acceptable meaning is 'to represent on a canvas', to the extent that the listener does not even think of the other meaning (this is what the joker is counting on). Thirdly, we must find a phrase that, while remaining simple and plausible, has the effect of resuscitating the meaning that had been implicitly excluded, or merging the two meanings. Thus, these familiar tales, outwardly facile, rest on sustained and precise abstract operations. I have studied about fifty of them, roughly thirty of which had already been discussed by Freud, from a corpus of about a thousand examples. In all instances, they are *itineraries*, typical pathways of thinking between 'plots' put into place by the joke itself. They are often similar to metaphor, metonymy or synecdoche in the broad sense of the terms (as defined by Jakobson and then Lacan). For example, lexical double meanings ('*Tous les sots sont périlleux*')[3] exhibit in a nearly pure state the work of condensation: two different ideas fuse into a single, identical audible syllable.

Vernet: Could you give some indications why you are opposed to certain aspects of Freud's book?

Metz: Yes, two things. In detail, many of the clarifications are marked by numerous contradictions, linguistic errors, approximate definitions, textual slip-ups, etc. (Freud is sometimes very slapdash, very hurried). Additionally, something more central: this very fine book was written in the wake of *The Interpretation of Dreams* and *The Psychopathology of Everyday Life*, when Freud was still struck by his major discovery, the unconscious. Hence, he is not always attentive to the discrepancies in the degrees of secondarization (even though the idea, on a basic level, is his), and he exaggerates the proximity of mental thought with the dreamwork. He does not take into account the tremendous constraint exerted on the joker by the waking state, socialization and the 'linguistic state', where one is dependent on a non-psychological machine. It is language, as much as the joker, that creates quips. The unconscious manipulates it, but within certain limits. Without the polysemy of the word '*peindre*' in the French lexicon, there would be no joke about the farmer's cow. The primary process only creates humor if it partly quietens down. Freud does not say the opposite, but he hovers uncertainly over this important point.

Vernet: Do you think that a real enrichment of psychoanalytic reflection through a better knowledge and understanding of linguistic mechanisms is possible?

Metz: No, I do not think so, although it is an obsession for French psychoanalysis. We should make an exception – which is actually pretty obvious – for the psychoanalytic study of objects that *are* linguistic, like the written or spoken joke, literary works, etc., that is, a certain field of study of applied psychoanalysis. But in psychoanalysis proper (which we always forget about), therapy, the process is more language-based [*langagier*] than linguistic in nature. In order to 'understand' the words that the analysand produces, it is clear that a theoretical knowledge of the syntax of the language or its phonological system is not what matters. It is more a matter of sensing, through the process of transference/counter-transference, what is functioning in the Freudian slips, contradictions, stammering, or the overly-assured phrases of the patient. This is still language, but it is not that of the linguist (Benveniste said this emphatically, and very early on). In a word, it is '*lalangue*', in the Lacanian sense, and not language as we commonly understand it. The former digs its twisting tunnels, its warrens, in the density of the latter, but they remain profoundly different, as if they were foreign to each other; their constant proximity does not lead to any resemblance. Moreover, psychoanalysis is intended to heal people – whatever the (Parisian) great minds may say – and, on this terrain, it is subject to the harsh competition of the striking progress made in neuropsychiatric chemistry, which it is absurd to denounce. Rather than be burdened by linguistics, or permanently sacrificing itself to the Desire of Literature, psychoanalysis would do better to reflect on its probability of surviving beyond the year 2000, and on the new role that it can play alongside medication, if it possesses the wisdom to accept this.

Vernet: Does your work on the joke have anything to do with the Lacanian formula according to which the unconscious is structured like a language?

Metz: Yes, plenty. But on the condition of avoiding an excessively frequent misunderstanding of this formula. The 'language' it invokes is '*lalangue*', which I just spoke about. Lacan utterly refuses any, let us say, iconic, figurative conception of the unconscious. The unconscious, in his view, is relational, ideographic, its space is like that of the rebus or the grapheme, not that of the photograph or the image, whence the reference to a 'language'. All the same, it does not resemble a language-system [*langue*], with a clear exposition and diurnal logic. Lacan is thinking of the depths of the machine, where poetry, Freudian slips and the abracadabra of dreams reside. Conversely, those who considered Lacan's formula as outrageous and provocative have unwittingly shown that they had turned language (in the eyes of linguists, and everybody else) into a particularly threadbare conception, entirely reduced to the secondary process, because they judged that the unconscious differed from it in such a radical and self-evident fashion. However, the study of metaphor and metonymy, in my work on the 'imaginary referent', has permitted me to measure the importance of the *primary part* that remains active in the most common figures, and in the very constitution of the basic lexicon, reputed to be non-figurative but whose terms often owe their meaning (their specific meaning) to an old figure that was then 'used up', as traditional linguists are fond of saying: this 'using up' strongly resembles the progressive secondarization of what was initially a rather disruptive outpouring.

Hence, to reply to your question, jokes all result from a twisting of *lalangue* on and with *language* [*la langue*], and it is the various possible imprints of this minor convulsion, this 'smiling scar', that I have tried to study, after, with and sometimes against Freud. Lacan's formula can serve as an extension of this work, even if, in the joke, the unconscious motion only acts, for the most part, in its preconscious state. Since Lacan, certain psychoanalysts willingly present puns as pure products of the unconscious to the fourth degree, targeting depth and manifestly crafted with great lashes of culture and labor. But this difference concerns the psychic 'milieu', more or less close to the primordial haze, and not the specific design of typical trajectories, like for example the 'turnaround' I just mentioned. As a characteristic itinerary, each one of them can be realized to various levels of secondariness; this is why, as we can see, jokes are not all absurd to the same degree, although they necessarily must have an ounce of absurdity in them.

2. Filmic Enunciation

Vernet: As for your current work on filmic enunciation, I would also like to ask you what motivated this transition to this object, which is in the framework of what we today call narratology, and which has precisely been developed while you were working on the joke. Genette has already indicated the manner in which narratology was the extension of semiology, but what interests me today is to better understand how this term can designate reflective thinking on relations between pairs of concepts, concepts that we sometimes consider as finalized (often when we take them in isolation), but which, for the most part, are really difficult, because matters are still not resolved. The first pair is 'history/discourse', the second 'enunciation/narration', the third 'conversation/projection', and the last is 'deixis/configuration'.

a. *History/Discourse*

Vernet: In his *Nouveau discours du récit*,[4] Genette said that he would have done better to sprain his wrist the day that he had hastily interpreted Benveniste's formula, which claimed that 'history seems to tell itself', by misjudging the importance of the world 'seems'. Are you carrying out a similar revision today? Do you think that Benveniste's formula has been applied too brutally? And if this is the case, does it not also imply that we again reflect on the position of the spectator, which would look both at history and discourse, and would thus show itself to be less affixed to the imaginary, and more devoted to the "belief in the spectacle," to adopt the expression you use in an interview with the journal *Hors-Cadre*? [see Chapter 9].

Continuing in this relationship with the double-barreled term 'history/discourse', I am struck by the fact that narratology has not worked on the position of the actor, despite the fact that we see actors throughout the entire film.

Metz: There are multiple aspects to your question. Firstly, narratology. My study of enunciation significantly overlaps with this enterprise, but departs from it at other times, because I am also concerned with non-narrative films, experimental films, television news, or historical programs, etc. I will return to this point later.

Secondly, my motivation. Without realizing it, you have answered your own question: while I was elsewhere, immersed in Freud, many interesting and solid works were published on narration and enunciation. Jean-Paul Simon began work on this matter very early, as the title of his book on the comic film does *not* indicate.[5] There was issue number 38 of *Communications*, in 1983, which you are well placed to know, and many other studies. After having surfaced and familiarized myself with this research, I set myself the task of systematically studying how far behind I was, what I had read too quickly, a bit like someone who goes through the newspapers upon returning from a distant country. I spent an entire year familiarizing myself with these analyses, and I found them interesting, I wanted to enter into the debate. Therefore, it is not the logic of my earlier work that led me to this new study, it was the work of others.

Now, 'history/discourse'. There is, first of all, the position of Benveniste himself. I am persuaded that he truly thought that history *did* tell itself (phenomenally, of course, not really). It was through simple prudence, to avoid lazy misunderstandings, that he added the verb 'seem'. It does not, however, settle the question, for we are not forced to think like Benveniste. As for me, in a text entitled 'Story/Discourse (A Note on Two Types of Voyeurism)' and published in a collective work dedicated to Benveniste [republished in *The Imaginary Signifier*, pp. 89–98], I go in the same direction: "it is the 'story' which exhibits itself, the story which reigns supreme" [p. 97] (= the final words of my article). The context indicates that we must take the idea in a psychoanalytic direction; just before that, I had described film as "the seeing of an outlaw, of an *Id* unrelated to any *Ego*" [p. 97]. The entire text, incidentally, has a lyrical and strongly 'personal' character, it is a form of prosopopoeia (at least that was the intention) of cinematic transparency, of the classical American cinema that I loved so much, that I exalted in, whose character I magnified without going into details. Nonetheless, I recognize that this article, if readers do not contribute a dose of finesse and sensitivity, or if they dispense with comparing it to my other writings, can indeed lead to confusion, because it does not clearly abstain from being a scientific text. As for what I have said elsewhere, it is that, very regularly, history is also a discourse, or that it has a discourse 'behind' it, etc.

Marie: So you no longer believe in transparency at all?

Metz: Yes, I do believe in it, but as being itself a type of enunciation, in which the signifier actively works at effacing its own traces (in this spirit, I have dedicated an entire passage of *The Imaginary Signifier* to it). In the same sense, my article on special effects, which dates from much earlier, recognized two different forms of pleasure (here, I am in entirely in agreement with what Marc [Vernet] has just said): the pleasure of immersing oneself in the diegesis, and the pleasure of admiring a nice toy, to rhapsodize before the cinema-machine. Whence those self-contradictory but very common reactions, like for example this strange phrase: 'What a great effect, you can hardly see it'. Whence also my idea of a 'belief in the spectacle', which Marc has just recalled.

Today, I think that enunciation is an instance with which we must *always* reckon, but that sometimes it is only 'presupposed' (= implied by the existence of the utterance), while it is itself 'enunciated' (= inscribed in the text). I have borrowed this distinction from Francesco Casetti without changing a thing, I think it is excellent.

However, the term 'marker' [*marque*] suggests a localized sign, which would for example be in the top-left corner of the screen, whereas what 'marks' the enunciation is most often the construction of the combination of image and sound. This is why I have spoken about 'configurations' (apart from motivated exceptions) rather than markers.

By way of example, here are some of the enunciative configurations that I have distinguished: the on-screen voice talking to the camera, the look-at-the-camera (the two often go together, as Casetti and yourself, Marc, have observed and commented), the written address (through a title-card), secondary screens (doors, windows), mirrors, the film in the film, the laying bare of the device, the numerous forms of subjective images and sounds (the semi-subjective image, perspectival sound, the notion of the 'underneath' that you defined...), the character's I-voice [*voix-je*], the oriented objective image (an equivalent to the 'intrusions of the author' in literature), etc., etc., without forgetting the neutral image, which, by the way, does not exist, but which, like the number zero in arithmetic, is indispensable for placing other enunciative regimes in perspective. In fact, we have not asked often enough that they should all be defined in a negative manner, like deviations from a point of reference that would be, precisely, neutrality: to consider off-screen sound as notable (which everybody does do) equates to implying that on-screen sound is in some way more normal; to isolate the look-at-the-camera as a particular figure is to consider that it is less striking for the character to look in a different direction.

In sum, enunciation is everywhere. Simply put – and this is where we come back to 'transparency', which it is absurd to deny as a *spectatorial impression* – it happens that this instance is done very discreetly, it asymptotically tends toward 'neutral' images and sounds, or at least neutral for a given period and genre.

Marie: So you are in radical disagreement with Bordwell, when he says that in classical films, there is no enunciation?

Metz: He says that for all films, not only classical films.

No, I am not in disagreement with him. He rejects the concept of enunciation for the mortal sin of linguisticity, but he adopts the concept of narration which, when the film is narrative, designates exactly the same thing (we will return to this matter). Whence my resolute assent to many of Bordwell's propositions and analyses. The 'disagreements' of this kind are chimeras that are deliberately exaggerated in order to occupy positions. I have never liked these labeling games, which only serve to mask real convergences and differences.

Vernet: So it would be a disagreement about the terms used? What strikes me when listening to you is that enunciation tends to be a much vaster territory than what was initially attributed to it. And that, in fact, in the past, the semiological and narratological work on enunciation owed much to a sort of nostalgia for the notion of the author. Through the work of the structuralists, we told ourselves that there remained a personal point of origin, and we in fact attempted, by studying enunciation, to recover something from this point, whereas your current position transforms it into a much more diffuse instance, which must be understood on two levels at least: what Paul Verstraten would call diegetized enunciation and, in contrast, the origin of the film-utterance [*énoncé-film*].

Metz: Yes, except that the former is merely one of the manifestations, or one of the avatars, of the latter: the origin of the utterance is diegetized by the fiction (in both senses of the word).

It is true that, for me, enunciation has little to do with the author, or even with any kind of 'subjective' authority, regardless of whether it is a real or imaginary person, a character, etc. Enunciation, as the suffix indicates, is an activity, a process, a *doing*. I have never understood why narratologists, after having banished the author with unnecessary violence (when it was necessary to keep the author as a concept, because it is the source of style), conceive of their so-called textual authorities in a perfectly anthropomorphic model: implied author, narrator, enunciator, etc. One could say that the author, ejected through the door, has come back in through the window. Now, it is either one or the other: in terms of Reality, it is the author and the author alone (the true, empirical author) who has created the work. And within the work, that is, in terms of the Symbolic, you only find enunciation. If the work depicts the film's director, as in *Intervista* [1987] by Fellini, it is once again this doing that does it. Enunciation is at work in each segment of the film. It is simply the *angle* from which the utterance is enunciated, the profile it presents us with, the orientation of the text, its geography – or rather its topography. The film can be presented – and always by means of fiction, even in documentaries – as being told by one of its characters, as being told by an unnamed voice, as gazing upon its diegesis from below, as itself being gazed upon by someone else, as containing another film, as 'really' addressed to the public by means of a title-card in the second person, etc. Enunciation is a landscape of creases and hemlines across which the film tells us that it is a film. It says only this, but it has a thousand ways of saying it.

Vernet: Has narratology not forgotten an element of the cinematic institution: a narrative film is not only made to produce a story, but also to produce an 'author', an image of the author as a figure of the artist in whom we trust. Every director of fiction films seeks to assure both the progression of the story and the progression of his career, by assuring that he can make another film.

Metz: I am skeptical, as I have just explained, about crypto-authorial authorities (whether enunciative or not), and even more skeptical when they are multiplied. There is nothing between the author and the act of enunciation. But there is something *alongside* them, an extra-textual authority that is not, however, 'real' (narratology sometimes confuses the two things), an imaginary author, or more exactly an image of the author that the spectator creates on the basis of certain qualities in the text refracted by their phantasms, their external knowledge about the filmmaker, etc. Edward Branigan is right to allude to this, and also to note that a text, strictly speaking, gives *no* indications about the author: it is situated in another world, in another 'frame', and if it contains (for example) fervent confessions in the first-person, only a knowledge about what is external to the text [*le hors-texte*] allows us to decide the strategy or spirit of sincerity in which these confessions are made.

By the same token, filmmakers can only make their films by fashioning an equally arbitrary image of the spectator 'for' whom they are working.

As for the filmmakers targeted by your question, they are guided by a concern for combining textual indices that they sow here and there with the character of the spectator that they have dreamed up, in the hope that the former will lead the latter toward the imaginary author that they wish to embody... And it is true that this case is very frequent.

Vernet: Before moving on to other matters, there was one final point in my question, concerning the position of the actor.

Metz: I must say, first of all, that nobody, to my knowledge, has spoken of the actor from the perspective of enunciation, except for yourself in the last part of your article in *Iris* no. 7 on the film character.[6] Theorists, because they are theorists, are used to seeking more or less subjacent structures. If they do not adequately perceive the actor, this is because the actor is too visible. He is dissimulated to them by an authority that has the advantage of being invisible, the character, who both conceals and is 'represented' by the actor.

As far as enunciation is concerned, it seems to me that there are two major types of actors, with, of course, intermediate or mixed cases. If the actor is unknown, he will necessarily function to the benefit of the character, because the spectator cannot detach him from the character in order to associate him with other characters, or a private life talked about by the gossip magazines – in short, he is not associated with anything else. So he 'sticks' to the present character, he has no other reality.

Marie: There are very fine things said on this issue in the article by Jean-Louis Comolli on *La Marseillaise* [Renoir, 1938],[7] counter-posing Pierre Renoir, who plays Louis XVI, to the almost unknown actor (Edmond Ardisson) who plays the young Marseillais Jean-Joseph Bomier.

Metz: When the actor is well-known (with the star being the limit-case), he imposes on the spectator the need to interrogate the reasons for his choice, reasons which are sometimes obvious and sometimes enigmatic. A film with Danielle Darrieux immediately orients us in two directions: it is going to take place in 'society' and it is going to be 'French'. And then, another result of enunciation, which Marc has spoken about in his article, is the fact that the well-known actor – that is, and I will come back to this, *well-known elsewhere* – will import into the film the echo of other films he has played in, he will instill his character with a multiple, virtual, fluctuating quality, he will make it vacillate, sometimes to the point where his identity is questioned. In *Les Bas-fonds* [Renoir, 1936], for example, who is Louis Jouvet? Can we really believe he is a Russian baron bankrupted by a passion for gambling? Is it not obvious that we are in the presence of genial, superlatively French thespian called Jouvet, who is neither a Baron nor bankrupt?

Vernet: This is what Michel has also shown for *Le Mépris* [Godard, 1963]. The actor, like the auteur, must have an imaginary status for the spectator.

b. Enunciation/Narration

Vernet: To turn to the pair 'Enunciation/Narration', Genette, if I recall correctly, sees a sort of equilibrium between the two. Narration relates to the mode, enunciation to the voice. In my work, I follow this division somewhat, with narration on the side of the nature of the story (the regulation of the delivery of information about the diegesis), and enunciation referring more to an extradiegetic authority, to the status of the text itself more than the diegesis. In your work, it seems the enunciation ends up single-handedly invading the entire terrain, dividing itself between a diegetized enunciation and an enunciation *tout court*.

Metz: No, I do not think it is like that. For Genette, the voice and the mode both relate to narration, whereas enunciation only concerns the idiom that is the 'basis' of the novel. For me, there is no such thing as enunciation *tout court*, or else it is permanently '*tout court*'. But it is true that it is expressed through figures that can be diegetic, extra-diegetic, juxta-diegetic (like the I-voice), etc. (this list is not final).

Jacques Aumont has clearly formulated one of the great 'challenges' of narratology: to study the explicitly narrative construction of the text. But in a narrative film, *everything* becomes narrative, even the grain of the filmstock and the timbre of the voices. This is why it seems to me that, in stories, enunciation becomes narration, provisionally abolishing a more general duality. Actually, I would define enunciation as a discursive activity (this is the literal meaning of the word: *act of enunciating*). Consequently, in a scientific documentary, scientific enunciation is at work, in an activist film militant enunciation is at work, in educational television didactic enunciation is at work, and so on. But, for narrative enunciation, whose anthropological importance is exceptional and whose social diffusion is vast, there is a special word whose homologue is absent everywhere else, the word 'narration'. We thus dispose of two nouns, and we have a tendency to look for two things, forgetting that for all non-narrative discourses, we do not even pose the same question. Before a geographical documentary, we do not attempt to distinguish the enunciation of some kind of 'geographization'. This is because this latter, in fact, does not have any social existence. So we say (very reasonably) that enunciation is geographical.

We also forget something, which is that the terminology was principally established in reference to *linguistic* narration, in particular, novels. There, the narrative codings are superposed onto a primary layer of strong rules, those of language; it is for them that we speak of enunciation, because the term is a linguistic one. Conversely, as an effect of this we can, if necessary, reserve 'narration' for the higher level. But the narrative film *does not rest on anything*, it does not pile up on some equivalent to language; it *is* itself, or rather it manufactures everything that, in it, would come within the term 'language'. Just as enunciation becomes narrative, narration takes responsibility for all enunciation.

To sum up, I think that enunciation is distinguished from narration in two, and only two, cases: in non-narrative discourse, which is nevertheless an enunciating instance; and in written or spoken narrations, where it is permissible to consider as 'enunciative' those narrative mechanisms that relate more to the idiom in which they are conveyed. (But the problem reappears: their *usage* inevitably conflates enunciation and narration, as we see with the deictics of novels.)

Marie: I think back to what Marc said earlier, that the spectator took pleasure in the tale related and in the narration as a narrating instance. For me, 'enunciation' designates the general *dispositif*, valid in any production of messages, and 'narration' designates the specific part of this *dispositif* concerning narrative messages.

Metz: Yes, except that narration, when there is one, mobilizes the entire *dispositif*. We should, in any case, be precise: 'inasmuch as there is a narration', because there are partially narrative films, partial to varying degrees. But this changes nothing in our debate: in a means of expression that does not involve language, narration, on the patch of terrain that it occupies, assures the totality of discursive regulations. Moreover, when we think of the figures that everybody considers as enunciative, we notice that frequently they are also inseparably narrative: the diegetic narrator, the non-diegetic narrator, the character's look to the camera, the off-screen voice, etc.

But it is still true that 'enunciation' is more general, because the term (and the notion) are also suited to multiple non-narrative registers, and consequently to the *dispositif* itself, before being specified.

Marie: What also deceives us, and what we tend to forget, is that for literary narratology there is a homogeneity in the material of expression, of such a kind that the character who narrates speaks with the same words as the book. For there to be such a reduplication in the cinema, the character would have to be filming the scene. If he speaks or writes, the textual functioning is no longer the same.

c. *Conversation/Projection*

Vernet: The other narratological pairing is 'Conversation/Projection'. Perhaps, it is true, one cannot measure the gap between the conversation situation described by Benveniste, which is the basis for his theory of enunciation, and that of the spectator faced with a film to which he cannot respond, and which is not supported by anybody. Conversely, however, is the manner in which Benveniste represented the conversation correct, and as simple as he says it is? It was critiqued in two of the talks at the conference, by Marie-Claire Ropars and Roger Odin.[8] The latter argued that, in conversation, we do nothing but hold discourses, which never have an enunciative source. Marie-Claire Ropars, meanwhile, asked if, by denouncing the mirage of the enunciation in cinema (= the quest for an author-character), you are not taking it outside of the film. What is your position, today, with respect to what could be an imperfect link between the conversational situation and the situation of a film screening?

Metz: As far as conversation is concerned, what I believe above all is that we have not sufficiently been aware of the specific and 'exceptional' character of this situation. Specific by its nature, by its status, and not, of course, by its frequency (it is precisely the latter that obscures the former). With Benveniste and Jakobson, the theory of enunciation is narrowly constructed, it is a configuration that is not generalizable. A great number of pragmatic situations are 'monodirectional' in Bettetini's sense of the term: reading a book, listening to the radio, a lecture, a seminar, watching a play or, better still, a film or television program, etc. In all these cases, the discourse is more or less prefabricated (sometimes integrally), more or less immutable (sometimes entirely), and the reactions of the addressee cannot 'feedback' on the machinations of the 'addresser': in sum, it is the exact opposite of a conversation.

Now, you say, could the conversation reveal itself to be more complicated than in Benveniste's descriptions (already not all that simple)? Yes, certainly. Do we not exchange discourses? That too, certainly; I said something along these lines in issue no. 1 of *Vertigo*.[9] But as complicated as we may suppose it to be (and psychoanalysis would rightly make it complicated), it does not modify the quality that radically opposes it to monovalent discourses, and it does not suppress the alternation between the *I* and the *you*. It also does not prevent the verbal tenses from being evaluated on the basis of the speech act. If my interlocutor declares 'I was ill', it is because this illness, in his view, is prior to the phrase uttered; by the same token, 'I will come back soon' informs us of a return that will come after the information act. On the contrary, the first effect of film – solely due to the fact that nobody can respond to it, and that it can be projected at times and places that are infinitely variable – is to 'unhook' all these terms from their strong meaning, and to limit their action to a fictional, de-situated space-time. The deictics, for example, in spoken words or on-screen texts, become 'weakened symbols', to use Käte Hamburger's terms. Hence, enunciation, for me, has nothing to do with the *I*, and the spectator has nothing to do with the *you*.

The first studies of enunciation, in the late 1970s and early 1980s, carried out research on the role of deictics. This is also what linguistics was doing, before pragmatics revealed the omnipresence of enunciation, which goes far beyond grammatical *persons* (enunciators and enunciatees). It was normal and necessary to initially explore this path; you cannot skip the stages.

In any case, as far as 'primary' research is concerned, I think that we must recall that enunciation has given rise to two kinds of explorations, which are, at the end of the day, quite separate: enunciation in the 'technical' (or pragmatic) sense, which was the great subject of the 1980s, and enunciation in the psychoanalytic sense (= identification, scopic regimes, divisions in belief, the male gaze and the image-woman, etc.), which was foremost in France during the 1970s and which is now only being studied by Anglo-Saxon feminists, who have carried out very important work in this field.

Vernet: You have just cited Käte Hamburger. What is your relationship to her thinking, and to her book?[10]

Metz: It is a dual relationship. On the one hand, I have difficulty in tolerating the brutal and arbitrary aspect of her work. For example, her affirmation that the cinema is part of literature, under the sole pretext that it is fictional, and without even thinking that it is not always fictional. Or her claim that her whole book is based on linguistic notions, when there is not even a shadow of linguistics in any of it. Thus, her definition of the utterance as the act of a subject saying something about an object is extremely vague, and even comes close to being trivial, as her study of lyricism shows clearly, where we see an 'object' that is both present and absent. She also has the gall to affirm – in 1957 and once again in the 1968 edition – that linguists have shown little interest in enunciation, whereas Benveniste's classic articles (which she did not know about) appeared between 1946 and 1959.

But what intelligence this wild woman had! What strength there is in her thought, notably in the definition of epic fiction! And then, to return to our domain, I essentially find her manner of situating the cinema (narrative film) between the theater and the novel perfectly just. Film is described as a mixture: characters accede to fictional existence through their own words, as in the theatre; but they are images, thereby escaping the all-too real limitations of the stage, and are capable of showing everything that the novel can describe, of being able to do without characters and speech for long passages, such that the fiction is also materialized outside of the protagonists, through an exterior intervention. I had sketched out somewhat similar ideas in a Spanish article, then at some lectures in Australia, and I will now re-open the question, this time with the 'help' of Käte Hamburger (and several others), in the context of an upcoming seminar where the enunciative regimes of the novel, the theater and the poem will be contrasted with each other, considered from the point of view of the cinema, and, so to speak, 'from' the place of the cinema. In sum, it will be a comparative study.

Vernet: Do you agree with this idea of a false enunciation, and of deictics deflected from their primary usage in narrative, or, more precisely, in fiction?

Metz: Yes, what Käte Hamburger says about these matters is enlightening. She shows that the preterite does not express the past, but the present of fiction: 'He was sad' signifies that, *at this moment in the story*, he *is* sad. So this 'past' is accompanied by an adverb in the present tense: 'This evening, he was sad'. I think this is very strong.

d. Deixis/Configuration

Vernet: The last pair in narratology, or in my primitive typology of narratology, is 'Deixis/Configuration'. Whereas deictics had occupied a decent share of the work done on narratology or 'enunciatology' (?), I note that you now speak of 'weakened deictics', and also of 'enunciative configuration', as if we have passed from a study of taxemes to a study of expositions, of more diffuse networks and heterogeneous constructions rather than units fixed in a kind of lexicon.

In this perspective, has the work of Edward Branigan been of any importance for you, and has the passage of deictics to configurations led to revising notions of the text and the impression of reality, insofar as the spectator who feels this impression operates on an enunciative material that is more complex and labile than the view, the image, or the visual field would be?

Metz: What makes the deictic conception of enunciation difficult is, to begin with, a fact that has often been noted but whose importance has not been adequately taken stock of. At the stage of transmission there is nobody, there is no person, there is only a text; the enunciator does not exist, it is a figure that is constructed on the basis of the text. At the stage of reception, on the contrary, there must be a person, a virtual spectator (much as Genette rightly talks about the virtual reader), a spectator who will become real through (at least) one other person, the analyst, or in any case, someone who has seen the film, because without him the very instance of reception disappears.

If someone at the pole of reception is necessary, this is because there is no text there, and if the pole of transmission can do without a symmetrical human presence, this is because the text compensates for it. We do not go to see the filmmaker, we go to see the film; but this *we* who goes to see it is not another film, it has to be somebody. The pairs of symmetrical terms, like 'narrator/narratee' and all the others, refer in reality to the conversation (again!), and they are more deceptive for the film or for the book, because they mask this basic, inaugural dissymmetry: the artist transmits his work to its place, while the spectator, who has nothing to emit, is himself displaced. *There is no exchange*. On the one hand, there is an object that removes the person; on the other hand, there is a person, present, deprived of an object.

I will add one thing. In my opinion, we should not cede to a permanently threatening latent confusion between textual pragmatics and experimental (psycho-sociological) pragmatics. The former furnishes no indication of the various empirical audiences. If we want to know them, we must go to see them, and thus leave the text (we must also leave semiology, which cannot do everything by itself). It is dangerous, even if it is partly a matter of words (see Francesco Casetti), to speak of the enunciative instance as an 'interface' between film and the world. Textual analyses will tell us, for example, that in sequence seventeen, the film 'positions' its spectator in such and such a location. This is true in the symbolic order (= of the film). But the spectator in the movie theater can position himself wherever he likes, he is the one who decides, and the film ignores this choice entirely.

In a soliloquy, the enunciation, dissociated from interaction, can only mark itself out by a *metadiscursive* path, that is, by unfolding the utterance in order to say that it is a discourse. It seems to me that the metadiscursive register contains two major variants, reflection and commentary. Reflection: the film mimes itself (screens within the screen, films within the film, showing the device, etc.). Commentary: the film speaks about itself, as is the case with certain 'pedagogical' voiceovers about the image, to use Marc's expression, or in non-dialogue intertitles, explicatory camera movements, etc. You are right to note that the notion of the text is displaced, or reworked, at least in relation to what it was in *Language and Cinema*, where I still presented the text as a rather smooth surface, even if I admitted that analysis could striate it along several axes. But at present it is the text itself that appears to me to be permanently stirred, crumpled up and torn into two by its own production.

It is indeed true – I will come back to your question, which has spread out even more – that enunciation, for me, ceases to be 'affixed' to privileged and relatively narrow textual zones (whence my hesitation about the term 'marker'), in order to be diffused over the entire discursive network. Deep down, *enunciation is the text*, but the text considered as production, not as a product. Alternatively, it is the text considered in everything that, within it, tells us that it is a text. This idea appears in the work of Marie-Claire Ropars, Pierre Sorlin, François Jost, and maybe some other people who I have momentarily forgotten. In my work, it has become the backbone for all of my reflections on the matter.

Now, for your question on Branigan. Yes, I am interested in his work, and our 'theses' overlap on several points, notably the idea of narration as an activity without an actor, or as having a status as metalanguage with respect to the narrated object. It is not by chance that I referred to his work not too long ago.

On the impression of reality, finally, I cannot give you an answer because, although it is one of my favorite topics, I still do not know if is affected by my new ideas on enunciation.

For Roland Barthes

Metz: Out of friendship, and fidelity to myself, I would like to finish up, as we did at Cerisy, with some thoughts on Roland Barthes, who was my only true mentor. This declaration will perhaps be surprising, for (alas) my work is not very similar to his. Linguists, film theorists, and even (later) Freud, have more visibly influenced me. But to have had a mentor is something else, it assumes a proximity in the daily exercise of the craft, an almost physical contagion, lasting many years, of a certain number of practical attitudes, ways of acting, and this is something that no book can do.

Roger Odin, in his contribution, remarked with much finesse that, although very concerned with theory, I was not that attached to theories, that I changed them according to my needs, without even pausing to think that they could be competitors. This is one of the traits that I share with Roland Barthes, with its effect on one's conduct, one's way of 'handling', we might say, the works of others.

This practical philosophy, which he transmitted to me more than taught me, is a kind of ethics; it is the will to set up, in the midst of carrying out research, an amicable, tolerant space. This is rather rare, for intellectuals are no more intelligent than other people, and they are often tense with each other. With Roland Barthes, his tolerant, unaffected manner was due to the quite unique combination of kindness (which everybody noticed in him), an attentiveness to other people, and a total freedom of mind with respect to established ideas, often borrowed from the physical sciences, that guide our field, such as Methodology, Result or Research Coordination. In this regard he was incredibly tranquil; he knew that there were misunderstandings, distortions and bluffing in the expeditious commodity of the great disciplinary divisions – 'post-modernity', 'structuralism' and their ilk – or even in the guerrilla war of projects that aim to oust each other when, so often, they are not responding to the same question and are in reality unrelated to each other. He saw different languages there, more or less apt in each case to *speak* about such and such an object. There was nothing discouraging about his skepticism, rather, he expressed a calm and confident belief that we could work differently.

I owe to him this level-headed conception of our profession, as he was an example of it before my eyes. I have constantly taken inspiration from it, or at least, I have constantly tried to. I am not the head of a school or the 'Pope of the audiovisual' (!), as the stupid stereotypes, without having read me and without knowing my work, sometimes have it. On the contrary, I am very wary of the imperialist forms of semiology, of those formalizations that are more complex than the object that they are 'explaining'. Semiology, for me, must remain one approach among others, well-adapted to certain tasks, but not all of them. Moreover, a concern for people, helping them out in the profession (there are minor distresses, and sometimes major ones), a meticulous respect for the expression of their thinking when citing them – in a word, amiability – founded on a constructive agnosticism and real (that is, modest) advances, all this seems to me to be more beneficial to research than any epistemological or proselytizing rigidity, even in the case of semiology. This is what Roland Barthes 'taught' me, without ever saying as much. And today, to pay back the favor, I cherish being able to say this to other people, to all those who would like (to re-use a turn of phrase that he liked) to understand me beyond my words.

Conversation recorded on September 23, 1989.

Notes

1. [Marie-Claire Ropars-Wuilleumier, 'Christian Metz et le mirage de l'énonciation', *Iris* 10 (1989), pp. 105–118.]
2. [Jens Toft, 'Pour une théorie sémiotique de l'histoire du cinema', *Iris* 10 (1989), pp. 177–181.]
3. [An untranslatable pun: '*tous les sots sont périlleux*' literally means 'all fools are dangerous', but the joke plays on the homophony with '*saut périlleux*' (somersault). Trans.]
4. [Gerard Genette, *Narrative Discourse Revisited*, translated by Jane E. Lewin (Ithaca, NY: Cornell University Press, 1988).]
5. [Jean Paul Simon, *Le filmique et le comique: Essai sur le film comique* (Paris: Éditions Albatros, 1979).]
6. [Marc Vernet, 'Le personnage de film', *Iris* 7 (1986), pp. 81–110.]

7. [Jean-Louis Comolli, 'Un corps en trop', *Cahiers du cinéma* 278 (1977), pp. 5–16; translated as 'Historical Fiction: A Body Too Much' in *Screen* 19, 2 (1978), pp. 41–53.]
8. [Marie-Claire Ropars-Wuilleumier, 'Christian Metz and le mirage de l'énonciation', *Iris* 10 (1990), pp. 105–118; Roger Odin, 'Christian Metz et la linguistique', *Iris* 10 (1990), pp. 81–103.]
9. [Christian Metz, 'L'énonciation personnelle ou le site du film', *Vertigo* 1 (1988), pp. 13–34.]
10. [Käte Hamburger, *The Logic of Literature* (Bloomington, IN: Indiana University Press, 1973).]

11. Christian Metz: Interview

André Gaudreault

Buckland, Warren and Daniel Fairfax (eds), *Conversations with Christian Metz: Selected Interviews on Film Theory (1970–1991)*. Amsterdam: Amsterdam University Press, 2017.

DOI: 10.5117/9789089648259/CH11

Abstract
In this short interview, published in 1990, Christian Metz praises his mentor, Roland Barthes, but also points out the problems and issues associated with being a mentor. He also discusses the role of theory in studying film, names a number of Québécois filmmakers, and ends by discussing the importance of the International Association DOMITOR, which studies early cinema and held its first conference in 1990.

Keywords: Christian Metz, film theory, Roland Barthes, DOMITOR

'Christian Metz. Entretien'. André Gaudreault. *24 Images* 49 (1990), pp. 63–65. Reprinted with the permission of André Gaudreault. Translated by Warren Buckland.

Since the late sixties, Christian Metz has enriched film theory with major works including *Essais sur la signification au cinéma*, *Langage et cinéma*, and *Le signifiant imaginaire*. From 7 to 13 June [1990], a conference on early cinema will be held in the city of Quebec, thanks to which Christian Metz will make his first trip to the city.[1] To mark this long overdue visit, we publish this interview with Metz by theorist André Gaudreault (*Du Littéraire au Filmique*[2]), conducted during another conference held in June 1989 in France, focused entirely on the work of Metz.

24 Images: You mentioned in your closing remarks at the end of the Cerisy-la-Salle conference that Roland Barthes was your mentor. What was your relationship with Barthes? Moreover, what do you think now that this relationship is reversed, where you are the mentor of other researchers? And what do you think, in general, of this famous relation to 'the mentor'?

Christian Metz: A multi-part question. ... Barthes was indeed my mentor, and he was also a friend. So it is a little complicated. Yet, in practice, it was very simple. He was very kind and extremely considerate with everyone, a famous man with the complete beginner, as I was when he recruited me. I received only good things from him, great loyalty in friendship, indispensible support for my career. My memory of him, even today, is vivid. When he died in 1980, I had a nervous breakdown that led me to the hospital.

Now, the reversal of which you speak, in which I am, in my turn, the mentor. I will not deny that it has pleasant aspects. But that is obvious. What is generally less well known are the very substantial downsides. First, the increase in demand with all its consequences (overwork, mail, etc.); also, the mental stress: some people turn you into a Superman, a burdensome image that is not pleasant (the exaggerated praise sounds like mockery); and then we are called to intervene at any moment, we must coddle everyone, etc. Second disadvantage: the position one occupies subjects us to attack without provocation, by third parties who simply do not tolerate our fame, or are not happy, etc., and do not shrink, on occasion, from insults or lying. It does not happen to me often, but it is very unpleasant.

More generally, I would say that there are two different things. 'Being' or not being a mentor, that is for others to say, it is not up to us. But *to play* the mentor, to adopt an authoritarian attitude, etc., that depends on you, no one is forcing you. If we do it, then we can be held responsible. I find this type of conduct detestable.

24 Images: You have answered two parts of my question. There was a third. I have not sufficiently stressed your student relationship to Barthes, and your situation as mentor in regards to your own students. ...

Metz: These two types of relationships are not comparable. Barthes was my teacher in an important but limited area: how to behave in the day to day part of the job, in the workplace, how to conduct a seminar, talk to students, to support a hypothesis, instill confidence in anxious young researchers, etc. But he was not my teacher with regard to research, except in terms of some very general methods (or, rather, attitudes of mind), which were very valuable. The only thing that really interested him was literature. He had little taste for cinema. He knew it better than people said he did, but not as a specialist. This did not prevent him from considering it an important area requiring investigation. He was waiting for someone who could take it on. That is how I started in 1963, working with the small group preparing the *Communications* journal's fourth issue.[3] He often repeated in meetings or thesis defenses that, apart from the literary field, which was favored because of its established tradition, film semiology was the only semiology that really exists; it forms a 'field' in which people meet, complement each other, criticize, have a certain degree of autonomy, etc. But ultimately, he taught me, above all, the importance of 'friendliness' and civility in working relationships, and their importance, too, for the research itself, which is an intellectual activity whose conditions of possibility are non-intellectual. Controversy, bitterness, and arrogance can derail the work itself.

24 Images: You have influenced people, but how have you influenced the development of theory itself? Your own, of course, but also future scholars?

Metz: In the field of cinema, which is traditionally a bit insular (or peripheral), it is true that I have some influence. I can see it in invitations I receive to distant conferences, in the fact that my texts have been translated into 21 languages, etc. Raymond Bellour explained this influence at the beginning of the [Cerisy-la-Salle] conference better than I can myself.[4] I will summarize approximately what he said: the important thing is not the theses I supported (film has no double articulation, it has no equivalent; enunciation is impersonal rather than anthropomorphic, etc.), because those who support the opposite view belong to the same world as me, to a world in which such questions are asked. And conversely, for a traditional film critic, double articulation is neither present, nor absent, it does not exist as an issue. In short, my 'influence' is not in what I said, but the fact that I was the first to speak in a certain way, which also allows others to argue with me. I placed discourse on cinema, which was still 'underdeveloped' despite some brilliant exceptions (Eisenstein, Bazin, etc.), in the sphere of the social sciences, as well as the humanities (which differ less than is claimed), but also within an approach constantly focused on precision, rigor, and level-headed thinking. There is nothing else, but that is enough. Of course, one can say that I brought together linguistics and psychoanalysis. But they were only catalysts for renewing discourse, the vectors of culture.

24 Images: For you, what is the future of film studies? Do you think it will decline or grow?

Metz: Grow, probably (I speak of research), since it has constantly done so for several years, and it is still a 'young' discipline that has not yet reached its zenith. It follows that new areas of film theory, created pretty much everywhere in universities, will produce researchers. Of course, this says nothing about the quality of the work, or its orientation. We see emerging today major strands mobilizing many people, narrato-enunciative pragmatics, the construction of a theoretical history, early cinema, but I think, frankly, we cannot draw any conclusions about the future.

24 Images: Now, a question that is perhaps impossible to answer: In your opinion, what is the significance of film studies for the cinema?

Metz: My answer is simple: no significance. Cinema can work very well without us; it has done so for decades, and continues to do so in 99 cases out of a hundred. We are theoreticians, which implies a way of thinking and a type of culture that is foreign to the world of cinema, which often instinctively hates theory, without understanding it. It is almost a problem of elitism. I never believed in the clichés about the enrichment of filmmaking by theory, etc. Of course, when I look back at the conference, I see that a filmmaker such as Alain Bergala, who has long followed my seminar and Barthes' seminar, etc., 'placed' in his filmmaking many things that emerged from those seminars. But what do we make of all the Bergalas, who are marginal figures in the cinematic institution, which is a big business, with stars, 'power', etc.?

24 Images: So, the purpose of film studies lies elsewhere.

Metz: It is located in knowing, in analyzing, in the effort to understand how things work. (To speak pretentiously: it is located 'in the realm of knowledge'.) When studying Greek mythology, its purpose is even less, for studying it only serves to know Greek mythology itself. It is not true that all disciplines can be 'applied', and it is pure demagoguery to say so. Some can be, like chemistry with medicine, and others not, such as filmology (and many others: philosophy, literary history, music, etc.). We must demand the right to disinterested studies; that is to say, to refuse mind-numbing technocracy.

24 Images: You will soon come to Quebec for the first time. Is there something in Québécois culture that interests you in particular? Or in Québécois cinema?

Metz: I am not really in a position to reply. I know the same Québécois filmmakers everyone knows: [Michel] Brault, [Pierre] Perrault, Claude Jutra, Gilles Groulx, Denys Arcand, Gilles Carle, the French speaking part of the ONF [NFB: National Film Board of Canada], etc.

24 Images: Which Québécois films have you seen?

Metz: Many, inevitably, during the 42 years I have been going to the cinema. But recently, *Un pays sans bon sens!* [Perrault, 1970] (I missed it on its initial release), and also *Le déclin de l'empire américain* [Arcand, 1986]. I loved Perrault's film for its way of intermingling fiction and documentary, and also for its humor. For example: the failed maturation of the small Québécois mice, the Québécois people's 'genetic gift of the gab', etc. There is also a lot of poetry: toward the beginning of the film, when the biologist and a friend go to see the ducks that populate a protected area in their thousands, at the seaside (or St. Lawrence?), and they evoke their childhood, their memories tied to this place. Images of snow, and of large ships slowly moving up river, Jacques Cartier's journal; all this is beautiful. The film is also very joyous, and made me laugh throughout. The mosaic construction worked well, and is very convincing. As for Denys Arcand's film, which wavers between a live theater act and a brilliant creation, it is nevertheless an irreplaceable record (even if it exaggerates), a record that is both intentional and unintentional on many things: the chatterbox, intellectuals, sex, relations between men and women, between teachers and students, remnants of fashionable modernity (in this case Susan Sontag, [Fernand] Braudel and [Barthes'] *A Lover's Discourse*). We would appreciate a little more tact, but the guy has a real force. On the other hand, the film awakens (for the French) a fairly common misunderstanding. We are shown obvious errors such as a university professor who has a property worth (back home) three or four million francs; his French counterpart earns 20,000 francs per month. The Québécois debate (ten or fifteen years ago) was freely self-deprecating, whereas for us, it is a rich country, while 'English' Canada (as Perrault said amusingly, because they are not English but Canadians) is even richer. Obviously, I know that this is relative: my Argentine friends think we are rich in France, and rightly so. ...

24 Images: The main reason for your trip to Quebec in 1990 is your participation in the DOMITOR symposium on 'Early Cinema and Religious Institutions'. What do you expect from this conference?

Metz: I think the DOMITOR initiative is very important. I was the first, as I learned later, to submit my application form and my membership dues, at the founding of the Association. Early cinema, at one time called 'primitive', was rarely studied, and mostly studied badly. The factual data, the basic information available to us thanks to inspired enthusiasts such as [Georges] Sadoul, [Jean] Mitry and others, are very often false. The DOMITOR project will enable us to learn more about early cinema, and also about the cinema itself, because early cinema marks for the first time the birth, genesis, and self-definition of an art. This is the only time where film history has merged with theory; you have written an article to explain this merging (thinking back, I also said something rather similar at the beginning of my article on the impression of reality in the cinema[5]). The beginning of an art, or a means of expression, is the time where theory is created in conjunction with its history; thereafter, both begin to separate.

As for the final paper that has been asked of me for this conference, I will do it from my perspective, that of a theoretician and semiologist. I am not a specialist of early cinema, which is a genuine profession that cannot be improvised; it is historical scholarly work based on the numerous and detailed viewing of films. To me, who is outside of this field and who has no desire to feign an imaginary competence in it, what is interesting is to say to early cinema specialists what they bring to *other* areas of research; for example, to the issue of the shot – a single shot film or a film with several shots where each functions autonomously, etc. Also, what do they bring to the theory of montage, editing, and narrative? That is what I plan to do after watching the films. I am very pleased to participate in this large gathering.

NOTE: The International Association DOMITOR aims to lay the foundations for genuine cooperation between researchers in order to promote the development of a rigorous and documented historical understanding of early cinema. The symposium entitled 'An Invention of the Devil: Moving Pious Pictures' will be held at the Museum of Civilization in Quebec June 7 to 13 [1990].

Notes

1. [However, in the end Metz was unable to attend the DOMITOR conference or visit Canada. Trans.]
2. [André Gaudreault, *Du littéraire au filmique. Système du récit*, Paris/Québec, Méridiens Klincksieck/Presses de l'Université Laval, 1988.]

3. ['Recherches Sémiologiques', *Communications*, 4, (Paris: Seuil, 1964)].
4. [Raymond Bellour, 'Le cinéma et ...', *Iris* 10 (1990): 15–35; 'Cinema and ...', *Semiotica* 112, 1 /2 (1996), pp. 207–29.]
5. [Christian Metz, 'On the Impression of Reality in the Cinema' in *Film Language: A Semiotics of the Cinema*. New York: Oxford University Press, 1974, pp. 3–15.]

12. Twenty-Five Years Later: An Assessment. An Ethics of Semiology

Interview with Christian Metz by André Gardies

Buckland, Warren and Daniel Fairfax (eds), *Conversations with Christian Metz: Selected Interviews on Film Theory (1970–1991)*. Amsterdam: Amsterdam University Press, 2017.

DOI: 10.5117/9789089648259/CH12

Abstract
In this interview published in 1991, Christian Metz looks at the last quarter-century of a discipline that he made a significant contribution to founding. He successively examines the role of linguistics (which is not to be confused with film semiology), the reactions raised by the emergence of semiology, the relationship between cinema and cinéphilia, and the question of research and teaching. He then distinguishes three groups of researchers in semiology, only one of which is directly descended from semiology, before speaking about his current work and paying homage to his only mentor, Roland Barthes.

Keywords: Christian Metz, film theory, semiology, cinéphilia, Roland Barthes

André Gardies, '(Vingt-cinq ans après. Un bilan). Une éthique de la sémiologie. Entretien avec Christian Metz'. *CinémAction* 58 (1991), pp. 76–94. Published with the permission of André Gardies. Translated by Daniel Fairfax.

André Gardies: 25 years later, how do you, as a founder of the field, perceive the evolution of film semiology, and how do you situate your own work with respect to this development?

Christian Metz: You have just used the word 'founder', but I would prefer to say 'initiator', because there existed, well before my intervention, approaches which, although they were not semiological, manifested rather similar preoccupations. I am thinking of the Russian formalists, Eisenstein, etc.

But I will answer your question. It seems to me that the issue of film semiology, even today, after 25 years, is sometimes poorly posed from the beginning. It is often understood as, or purported to be understood as, an application of linguistics; this then becomes a point of contention, a kind of blockage that holds some people back. It is also a flagrant distortion of the truth. Applying linguistics to the cinema would entail treating it as a language system [*langue*] or as analogous to a language system. However, my first in-depth article, from 1964, generally considered as the point of departure for my work,[1] said exactly the opposite: the cinema is not a language system (whence the title of the article). So we are not concerned with 'application' but with *taking into consideration* some elementary concepts like 'syntagma', 'code', etc. These concepts, incidentally, are for the most part not even truly derived from linguistics (I will come back to this point). Hence, notions like 'prefix', 'declension', 'optative', and many more, specific to language systems and them alone, have never been invoked in my studies of the cinema. I have only retained the most general concepts, *and consequently the least linguistic concepts*. This is what is sometimes poorly understood.

Gardies: But do semiologists of written or oral texts not encounter the same problem in discursive analysis? Was there not, at a given point in time, a conjunction of problematics, which, while referring to different fields, have ended up somewhat abusively becoming confused with each other in their common attempt to escape the linguistics of the sign?

Metz: I agree. The semiologists of the novel, for example, or of speech, were in an even more difficult position than we were, because the materiality of their object was linguistic in nature. The Soviet researchers were clearer on this point, with their distinction between 'a primary modeling system' (= the idiom) and secondary modelling systems like mythology, folklore (in fairy tales), the rules of literary genres, etc. Every poem, for example, is inscribed in a given language, but superposes on it an additional structural level. This bipartition is a little brutal, a little simple, but it was useful in its time, it helped us to escape from the minor awkwardness that you evoked.

On the same topic, I would like to once again say that the expression *cinematic language* is neither my own invention, nor that of any other semiologist. It comes from film critics and journalists, who also speak, in the same way, of 'musical language', 'visual language', etc. I found the word in critical articles from the 1920s, and it subsequently became widespread (it was the title, for example, of books by both Marcel Martin and François Chevassu). As for the 'arm-twisting [*forcing*]' on the term *language*, which some people attribute to me, it was provided by the film vocabulary around me and before my time.

I tackled the problem from the other side of the coin: because everybody used this formula, which links film and articulated language, I wanted to get to the bottom of the metaphor (the expression comes from Roland Barthes, when he commented on my undertaking), to measure its exact importance, to *explain* how the cinema resembled language and how they were different. And the differences, of course, were far more prevalent. But to know how and to what extent they differed, we need a minimum of linguistic investigation. We cannot compare two things by remaining ignorant about one of them.

Linguistics: A Stubborn Misunderstanding

Gardies: Was there not, at the same time, another form of pressure: the pressure exerted by the cinema's normative approaches, such as attempts to establish 'cinematic grammars'?

Metz: Certainly. If we restrict ourselves to France, there was Berthomieu's 'grammar', Robert Bataille's, and still others. But I cannot say that they exerted any pressure on my project. They were a little puerile, they never had much credibility.

Gardies: Indeed, but in several manuals on film language from the 1950s and 1960s we regularly find affirmations like: 'The low-angle shot expresses domination', 'The close-up translates the feelings of the characters', etc. This kind of norm, which tends to fix meaning, nonetheless belonged to the language of the era.

Metz: In this sense, yes, I was caught between a rock and a hard place. On one side there was the spontaneous, libertarian ideology of certain filmmakers and critics, for whom creation did not allow any constraints, organization, or plans (and who even became irritated at the activity of analysis itself, regardless of its content). On the other side, a false linguistics, which sought the cinematic equivalent of the imperfect subjunctive, and which closely followed the model of scholastic normative grammars, arbitrarily referring to a tiny number of languages (French, Latin...), and alien to modern research in linguistic science.

I thus found myself the target of reproaches for 'transplanting linguistics'. This may have been abetted by a material circumstance that produced the misunderstanding: shortly after my first publications, in 1966 (and up to 1972), the École des Hautes Etudes, my 'employer', asked me to deliver a course in general linguistics. This course, which was also called 'linguistics for non-linguists', responded to a strong demand at the time (which today has diminished, as you know) from students and researchers in other disciplines, and our institution at the time only had very 'specialized' linguistic seminars (Chinese syntax, etc.).

I certainly do not make any mystery of my intense interest in linguistics, but you can love something without 'applying' it to something else. When I speak of the cinema, linguistics becomes, in my view, a comparative tool, a kind of *support*, nothing more (and nothing less, for in this very limited role, it is irreplaceable). Through the search for common features and, above all, differences, it clearly illuminates certain aspects of the cinema (I insist on saying 'certain aspects': one cannot speak about everything at once).

Gardies: I believe that the strength of your work lies in the fact that you were able to choose the key concepts, the most productive concepts, on which a theoretical construction was possible. You chose the most pertinent concepts.

Metz: It is not for me to say, since then I would be both judge and defendant. What I can discuss, because it is not self-evident, is the great parsimony of my linguistic harvest. Linguistics is a rich, pluralist, respected science; it wields hundreds of concepts. And yet, I have only retained a handful of them, while the researchers who followed me added only another handful; we only have to look at the number of entries figuring in the excellent lexicon in your special issue.[2]

This little toolkit is rather modest if you think about what other disciplines of modern research assemble. I understand that people could take fright at it, but this does not mean that we are more ridiculous, merely that we are not familiar with 'scientific' approaches in general.

Furthermore, there is the slippage I just spoke about: notions like 'paradigm/syntagma', 'text/system', 'code/message', 'diegesis', etc., are of interest to general semiology, that is, the sum total of signifying phenomena. There is nothing especially linguistic about them.

But linguists (and others) have often provided definitions of them: this is the source of potential confusion, even though linguists themselves declared that some of their concepts, far exceeding the scope of studying language systems, were not linguistic: this, for example, is the explicit, unchanging attitude of Hjelmslev (and it is already present in Saussure).

Now, this changes everything, because although it is understandable that people have wanted, so to speak, to 'distance' the cinema from the sphere of language systems, I do not see how it can be excluded from the sphere of semiology, because it is quite obvious that the cinema is a means for transmitting – and above all creating – meanings.

Gardies: Was the fundamental questioning of the sign also a source of confusion? The sign was on the frontline during the first battles waged by film semiology. It was vociferously attacked, was it not? And yet, your work has convincingly shown that meaning in the cinema was not only the work of the sign.

Metz: I do not know if I have shown this *well*, but my voice has become hoarse saying it. I already did so in my 1964 article, with the assertion that the cinema is not a system of signs. Then, in 1971, also an early date, in *Language and Cinema*, with the 'critique' of the sign and the refusal to prejudge the size of the units, their form, the very presence of a fixed signified. I have not changed my outlook since then. I could summarize my work, on this point, with a quip: "Signification does not signify the sign."

Gardies: It would be interesting to undertake historical research on how such a distortion came about: what led to this narrow-minded reading of your work?

Metz: Sometimes the reading is worse than narrow-minded: it can happen that people have read the *opposite* of what I wrote, notably on the question you raised: the book patiently explains that there is no such thing as a [filmic] sign, and yet I am reproached for having said that there are signs; if needed, they will show you very seriously that there is no such thing...

Nonetheless, this blindness was not universal, for if semiology has sometimes been poorly understood, it also won over numerous adherents almost immediately...

Gardies: Yes, but since the misunderstanding, at a certain point in time, was so widespread, it is not simply a case of inadequate interpretation. Were there other events at play?

Metz: I have the beginning of an answer, or rather several beginnings. Firstly, to go back to the misunderstanding: it was not as generalized as you say;

I feel you are exaggerating its scale a little. Of course, my writings were the target of some bitter attacks [*boulets rouges*], but this is the fate of any well-known writer, it is almost automatic, and largely independent of the content. It is a social mechanism. On the other hand, the confusion you spoke about did not arise among scholars, nor did it surface in journals like *Image et Son* (as it was called at the time) or *Cahiers du Cinéma*, etc.

That said, I agree that the lack of understanding was very common. There are malevolent people everywhere. There are also fools, who do not understand what they are reading, or who get everything muddled up. These factors are often forgotten due to their triviality, but this does not prevent them from being pertinent, for us just as for anybody else. To this extent, it is the very success of semiology among certain people that prompted attacks from others (a classic phenomenon), and which has also attracted those who, not being well prepared, choked on it – like a potion without much of a magical effect – whether this was with an unruly, frightened sympathy, or with the unruly feeling that it was a *must*. My 'emergence' [*apparition*] (!) provoked enthusiastic and animated support, which left me stunned. My work generated a feverish hope (= finally, we will understand *everything* about the cinema, now that we have a miracle-gadget!), and sometimes even a genuinely 'groupie'-style behavior – which was quite embarrassing if you are not inclined to play the part of an Elvis Presley. This is the inverse aspect of your question, but it refers back to the same reality, which is the immaturity of the field.

Nevertheless, this is not the main thing. I believe that *within* the semiological approach there is something profoundly unusual, something that confronts old habits. When we speak of studying the cinema, everybody thinks of the biographical details of the great filmmakers, of the content of films and their plots, of a knowledge about technical credits and dates, of the evolution of the film industry, etc., but nobody gives a second thought to the mechanism of signification, without which all the rest would not even exist. It is just like everyday life: we are concerned with what people say, but not the machine, with its rules and inventiveness, which allows them to speak. Psychologically, socially, ideologically, the metalinguistic attitude (the attention paid to the *how* of signification rather than its concrete content) is always deviant, a little transgressive, and spontaneously unpopular. It sets you apart, makes you appear to be something of a fanatic. If you add to this the 'technical' difficulty (or austerity?) of semiological writing, and taking into account the almost elusive 'flimsiness' of the object of study (that is, meaning), rather than focus on the apparent growth of linguistics, then I think you can understand that film semiology has only been understood by a fraction of the public. In any case, this is how things are for all theoretical movements in their initial moments.

A Demand for Rigor and Precision

Gardies: Yes, of course, people could have not listened to you, but they did listen to you, because you often had your own words thrown back at you, but in a deformed way...

Metz: I see in this deformation a kind of minor hallucination. People project onto your text what they have in their own heads, they make you say what they would have said in your stead, or even, depending on their emotional disposition, what they would hate to hear. Furthermore, you should not forget that the reader of a book simultaneously 'reads' the other books of the same type – namely, all those books that were grouped into the same basket called 'structuralism'. Even if I did say (without being the only one to do so) that the sign was not the most important issue, the whole debate at the time revolved around the sign, the word itself kept on recurring, and therefore that is all that the inattentive reader would recall, without specifically remembering whether it was discussed in a positive or negative light.

This is the consequence – a 'warped' consequence, but a consequence all the same – of what we spoke about at the beginning of this interview, that is, the *attention* paid to the contribution of linguistics. This was a common trait of the era, of course, but all systems of ideas are inscribed in history. By means of this new orientation, semiology targeted something else, something that rather resembled (from afar) what Cohen-Séat's filmology had earlier attempted to achieve – but without truly attaining its goals, and using a method that I find both admirable and yet too scientistic.

As far as this group of precursors is concerned, I would like to honor the memory of Ed Lowry, an American scholar who died at a very young age, around thirty, a delicate, sensitive man, to whom we owe the only serious book dedicated to French filmology, a remarkably researched and intelligent work.[3]

Semiology, therefore, through this refocusing of attention, demanded of film theory precision, culture, rigor, and nuanced restraint – in short, sophistication; from which, on the whole, it was very remote, despite the André Bazins, Jean Mitrys, Edgar Morins, some journal articles, etc., which pointed the way, and from which I have drawn sustenance. I wanted film texts to have the maturity to link up with the whole of contemporary scholarship in the other sectors of what we somewhat abusively call the 'human sciences', or the 'social sciences'. What seems abusive to me is the word *science*, for we are not (or not yet?) at that stage, and I have never claimed I was either. I would simply speak of serious, or rigorous, research. This is already a lot, if you can imagine how provincial and unenlightened a lot of film writing was, how it was marooned on an autarkic island that the major currents of thought avoided.

Gardies: Was it not precisely in the wake of all this that the fundamental project was initiated, which was to constitute the cinema as an object of study? That is, to free it from an empirical, pragmatic vision, dominated by journalistic discourse, for example? As far as your own approach is concerned, when reviving for your own purposes the distinction introduced by Cohen-Séat between the filmic fact and the cinematic fact, in order to question this distinction, is there not the declaration to constitute the cinema as a scientific object, so as, in effect, to articulate a discourse on it, at the same as this discourse constitutes it as an object?

Metz: I would not have thought of formulating it the way you do, in particular in the last thing you say, but hearing you out, I agree. As for the word 'scientific' (I will come back to this), you use it in a provisional sense, in order to designate a goal, rather than a result that has been happily attained. In that sense, I could also use the term, and indeed I occasionally do, even if only to distinguish analytic essays from literary works. What exasperates me is the use of the word 'scientific' in an exclusive, totalizing sense, in order to pronounce excommunications.

Conversely, I will latch onto your allusion to journalism in order to express an opinion which, coming from me, may well shock those readers who are beholden to stereotypes: namely, that journalistic discourse, which on a concrete level very often turns out to be mediocre, is in no way despicable in and of itself (there is also, indeed, plenty of mediocre theoretical writing). The 'format' of the newspaper, its rhythm, the *speed* that it induces, can give rise to remarkable writing (I am obviously thinking of Serge Daney here) and texts that most scholars, not least myself, would be incapable of writing. To put it simply, journalism and scholarly writing are two different things, two discursive categories that do not have the same demands. Each has its own specific utility (I already said this in 1964, when speaking about newspaper film reviews). Among my friends, a few scholars are also good journalists, or have the potential to be, including: Raymond Bellour, Jean-Louis Leutrat, Dominique Noguez, Francis Vanoye – perhaps I am forgetting one or two others, but not a large number.

The Reproach of Zealotry

Gardies: In sum, under the common appellation 'cinema', we speak about different things. Semiology should thus constitute its cinema-object.

Metz: Absolutely. But I insist on repeating my wariness toward hierarchies that consider genres *en bloc*, like 'journalism' or 'science'. Every category has its good and bad side, which is a different problem entirely...

Gardies: Not totally, perhaps, because semiology has been so frequently accused of zealotry, of wanting to monopolize film discourse while despising other approaches, that this fact needs to be questioned. I believe there is also a kind of misunderstanding. You, yourself, willingly recommend moderation and courtesy; you have never, whether in your public speeches or in your written work, formulated a phrase that could be mistaken for zealotry. So it may be shocking that semiology has been put on trial like this. In your opinion, is there any justification for this? Apart from yourself, were there any attempts at zealotry, or was this the tenor of the period? Here, I am thinking about the militant discourses published in the journal *Cinéthique*.

Metz: I do not think that we should exaggerate the importance of this 'trial'. Reactions were divided, they varied widely, and changed all the time. *Cinéthique*, for example (because you bring it up), considered me to be the only worthwhile scholar in the field, but at the same time vigorously critiqued me on the political level.

Nonetheless, it is true that semiology was often accused of zealotry. You ask me why. Well, an important element to my answer would be that I do not know everything that is done and said in the name of semiology, and perhaps even in my own name. There are 'zealots' in every movement. It can be supposed without much risk of error that during the period that semiology was in fashion, it must have given rise, just as other theories do, to little local chieftains who spoke ineptly. The initiator of a movement is often less excited, more relativist, because he has found a certain appeasement in advance, by the very act of 'creating' the theory. All the same, it is quite true that I have never attacked anybody. I find polemics sterile, particularly when they become violent. When I was attacked, even insulted in some cases, I never replied. This is a principle, as well as being an advantage of my position. And when I lost my temper in public (this happened to me three times), I immediately regretted it and gave my apologies.

To return to what astonished you, there is another element that could explain it, which I have directly borrowed from Roland Barthes. It is an idea that courses through his entire œuvre, the idea that every position that is even a little bit intellectual or intellectualist, every objectifying position that is detached from 'lived experience', provokes violent reactions expressing a kind of populism [*poujadisme*], or even, to use the Italian, a kind of *qualunquismo*. We are reproached for not speaking like the ordinary man (not, of course, Jean Louis Schefer's ordinary man[4]), of not speaking 'just like everybody else'. This is a profoundly demagogic position. It forgets that the virtuous indignation of the ordinary man on the street magically disappears when confronted with the extravagant gibberish of sports reporters, whom nobody would dream of accusing of 'jargon', or even when they come across the hundreds of rare words that blacksmiths and carpenters use to designate their tools and techniques.

The Discreet Passion for the Cinema

Gardies: This specialized vocabulary is, in fact, linked to a spirit of rigor and precision. I think that a number of scholars working close to you, or even at a distance from you, owe a lot to this essential quality: the demand for rigor and precision. This is where you have been completely successful.

Metz: Well, it is not for me to judge whether I have been successful, but it is true that they are the values I believe in. As for the result, I would not, for my part, employ the word 'completely'. Perhaps I have succeeded in infusing a certain number of film scholars with this taste for precision, and this number may not be negligible – far from it – but it is not immense. There are, of course, important extensions of my work in other countries (my texts have been translated into 21 languages), but in each country they reach a rather specific public...

Gardies: Perhaps it is the fate of research groups to be numerically quite small...

Metz: I agree. What I said was an observation, not a regret. I cannot see myself whipping crowds up into a frenzy...

Gardies: What is more, your influence in film studies has, I feel, far exceeded the sphere of the semiologists. I think that, through your exemplary concern for rigor, through your manner of observing the film-object, describing it, taking stock of it, constituting it, you put lazy researchers in their place, so to speak.

Metz: As far as my indirect influence on other tendencies is concerned, I would like, if you will, to return to this matter at a more leisurely moment, because your insistence on the idea of rigor makes me recall, through the association of ideas, what I would call an exemplary lack of rigor, to which I have occasionally fallen victim: from time to time, I have been accused (by Louis Seguin, for example, with a somewhat inexplicable excess, because he does not know me) of never having watched a film. This is, of course, because I cite the titles of very few films in my writings. But this gives no indication whatsoever of the films that I have seen or not seen. And yet the advocates of this type of argument cannot seem to fathom that, when I see a film (I see about four per week and, right after the screening, I take lengthy notes on each one), I do not feel the need to tell everyone who cares to listen, to declare myself a cinéphile, to spout out lists of credit sequences. This is one of the petty infantilisms proper to the film world: actually doing something counts for little, you have to sing it from the rooftops.

Well, since it must be said, this interview provides me with an excellent occasion to say it: yes, I am a cinéphile, and I even have a certain MacMahonian bent that my reason tempers with great effort. Yes, I was raised on film noir. Yes, I am one of those who melt at the sight of Humphrey Bogart, who never tires of Welles, Fellini, Stroheim, Murnau, Ozu, Dreyer, etc. Yes, I love films, many films, and it took me 25 years to understand that I had wronged myself, in the eyes of some, by remaining silent on this matter through what was for me a simple concern for discretion and restraint. One should not hurl one's tastes and actions in the faces of other people. Can you imagine Genette declaring 'I love Proust'? And yet...

Gardies: I believe that what is not perceived is that semiologists, due to the nature of their work, generally only speak about a limited number of films, or even film sequences. But in order to do this, they must have already seen a large number of other films, precisely in order to nurture their painstaking work. Critics, by contrast, because their primary function is to inform the reader, must refer to the vast 'corpus' of current releases. The two objectives are different.

Metz: Yes, we are in agreement on this. I would add that, when a critic has talent, he can, when informing the reader, do more than just inform...

Influence on Criticism

Gardies: Absolutely. Given that the objective of semiology is to better understand both the cinematic fact and the filmic fact, it might be surprising that it has not had more of an influence on criticism. Is this not the sign of a partial failure?

Metz: On this point, I would go even further than you: semiology has had no influence on criticism, except, as I said earlier, for *Cahiers du Cinéma* during a certain period, and in a more intermittent, more superficial fashion, in some other journals: *Image et Son, Jump Cut, Wide Angle* ... (I am leaving to one side, of course, the theoretical journals like *Screen, Camera Obscura*, and so on, where my influence has, on the contrary, been considerable). You asked me whether, as far as criticism is concerned, this is a failure. Of course, we can always say that the lack of influence is a failure. In one sense, this is true. But personally (and in opposition to, I should clarify, some of my close friends), I do not feel it to be a failure. I am not affected by it in the slightest. In effect, everything depends on the goal we assign to semiology, and more precisely on the *social surface* that we wish to see it occupy. I have little concern for proselytism, and I spontaneously share the radical views of Lévi-Strauss, his skepticism toward applied sciences, and the very project of applying them: the 'human sciences', he effectively said, do not need to be applied, the objectives of knowledge, analysis and intellectual curiosity alone suffice. In short, to give a more direct answer to your question, I do not think it is indispensable for film criticism, which has its own requirements, to be semiologized, or even that anything whatsoever should be semiologized, apart from semiology.

Gardies: All the same, with the institutionalization of film, which has become an object of learning, has semiology unavoidably entered the era of its application?

Metz: We have not understood each other properly. Firstly, teaching. Film does not necessarily (or not only) mean teaching film semiology, it also means teaching film history, the major rules of the film industry, etc. Secondly, the didactic activity you allude to – notably, analyzing films for students with the aid of video cassettes – does not constitute an 'application', it is the transmission of knowledge itself.

Gardies: Precisely, is it not at the level of discourse that this problem presents itself? Of semiology itself, as a discourse? In sum, is it perhaps more a fundamental question of ideology, rather than the application of techniques? Is there an ideology of semiology? Does it secrete its own ideology? In other terms, does it adopt a fundamental stance in relation to the cinema-object and the film-object?

Metz: On a question as 'profound' and complex as that of the *stance*, which would require a whole interview on its own, I believe that every semiologist has their own answer. I can only speak in my personal name. I started out in phenomenology, which was triumphant at the time of the Libération, when I was studying, and to which I remain very attached. In one of my articles, 'Le perçu et le nommé',[5] I have tried to show that phenomenology is the necessary, prerequisite condition for all of semiology (Greimas already said this before I did). In my *khâgne*,[6] Jean Beaufret was my philosophy professor. When André Bazin presented films in the ciné-clubs of the Latin Quarter, I went to listen to him with passion. Later, Mikel Dufrenne published my first book. Dufrenne, who I often quote, is a great aesthetic theorist, and he is a man whose generosity of spirit and openness toward others are exceptional. In the same book series, he also published Lyotard's first book, and yet Lyotard, too, used phenomenology as a point of departure to go in other directions (in that book, he found the exact words to pay homage to Dufrenne, and I have taken advantage of the circumstance to associate myself with it).

In short, I started out in phenomenology [*départ dans la phéno*] (this would make a great title for a crime novel!). And as far as films are concerned, everything began (as an adolescent, of course) with an intense, insatiable cinéphilia. In the provincial town where I grew up, I was part of the group that ran the youth ciné-club, then I co-organized with a friend the *khâgne* ciné-club at the Lycée Henri IV, in Paris. Then, with a different friend, I ran the ciné-club at the Rue d'Ulm campus of the École normale supérieure. Subsequently, for a few months in 1955–1956, I worked for Georges Sadoul, who was looking for a sort of secretary and possible successor (our temperaments, which were at odds with each other, soon ended this attempted collaboration, but without any conflict between us).

But all these activities did not provide me with a profession. At the same time, I was pursuing classical studies, in the style of the time (I did my *agrégation de lettres*, etc.). For several long years, I simultaneously 'lived' in both of these two universes. They are truly very different. The humanities were already paving the way for the 'human sciences', much more than we care to admit.

I would go to pieces emotionally when admiring Marlene [Dietrich] in *The Scarlet Empress* [1934] and, once the emotion had passed, consider the film, its star and my own emotions as facts that could be questioned and analyzed with passion. For analysis, too, is a passion, it is *the other passion*, and the greatest passion is to question one's own passion. The opposition between the heart and the mind is the most absurd of them all, at least in its simplistic form, which is too often what is emphasized.

Analysis is also a Passion

In short, the education I received – with the minutiae that is the underlying principle of translation exercises, with the complexities of the extinct languages, etc., with the implicit 'moral' of the matter, which requires calm, attentiveness, wariness toward being overly excited – led me to a 'spontaneous' practice that was, in reality, acquired from this education, a practice of objectification, including (*especially*) when it came to those things that I most dearly treasured. The semiological project is born (for me) from this conjunction. When I read articles on Hitchcock that were limited to saying, in an exclamatory, feverish mode, 'I love Hitchcock!' I was dumbstruck, in spite of my own, very ardent, liking for the films of Hitchcock.

My way of doing things is also related to the fact that film semiology was a belated choice for me, which came when I was about thirty years old, and which was preceded by a wide range of different activities. For example, I was a translator from German and English specializing in historical and theoretical works on jazz music, for *Cahiers du Jazz* and the Payot publishing house. When you do several different things, each one tends to 'objectify' the other.

Gardies: Is this need for objectification also at the origin of your work on the 'imaginary signifier'?

Metz: Absolutely. My point of departure is that there is no contradiction, no incompatibility, between emotional affect and 'intellectual' analysis. It has often been observed that reflecting on our feelings does nothing to change them (they are stronger than this). Fellini's *8 ½*, which I have studied a lot,[7] still moves me every time I watch the film.

Gardies: Objectification allows us to invent a discourse (I will come back to this) while holding onto these emotions.

Metz: Yes. And even, if it is appropriate, an 'autobiographical' discourse (without all the useless probing into personal lives): my fascination for Ava Gardner is not unrelated to a familial lack that I can feel, and that I can talk about more or less clearly...

The Cinema as an Object of Teaching

Gardies: Something really strikes me about what you have just said: namely, the presence of this essential Barthesian stance according to which the fundamental human activity is discursive activity. That is, we must find, invent and produce the right discourse, the discourse that allows us to talk correctly about certain objects while constituting them as such.

Metz: I would add: the right discourse on what touches us the most. Take the objects of Barthes' discourse, for instance: Racine, Michelet, *Werther*, the photograph of his mother...

Gardies: Is there not a link between the emergence of a possible objectifying discourse and the present development of teaching cinema at the university?

Metz: The question could, in fact, be posed as follows: how has it come about that the cinema, today, is taught in several French universities, by a significant number of teacher-researchers, the majority of whom are quite respectable, whereas twenty years ago there was only a tiny number of them?

This surprisingly rapid expansion has, in my opinion, been the result of three contributing factors, which are partially independent of each other (it is their conjunction that has advanced matters). Firstly, there was the relative mental liberation of the university after the explosion of 1968, a partial but real drop in the level of naivety. Then there was the indefatigable devotion of a few individuals (Michel Marie being a prototypical example), who had a taste and a flair for organization, and who created the necessary networks. Finally, to return to the subject of our interview, the presence of a *teachable* 'corpus'. (Michel Marie again, and Roger Odin have said very interesting things on this matter[8]). For love is not something that is taught. The always renewable complicit pleasure of watching the obvious codes of the classical Western in action, the passionate admiration for Bresson's 'Jansenism', Rossellini's Franciscanism, Louise Brooks' famous bob, Mizoguchi's framing, Renoir's dialogues, etc.; all these points of fascination that I have in common (yes, I do indeed...) with the film critics of my generation, all this cannot be taught, it is an imprint of our feelings, a valuable piece of baggage that is both collective and, for each individual, intimate, fetishized.

Gardies: Does this mean that with the 'teachable' we have entered the era of knowledge [*savoir*]?

Metz: That word is perhaps a bit strong. I would prefer to say: the transmissible. And, by the same token, we have seen the formation of a small group of scholars who have in common, if not their 'ideas', at least some principles of discussion, of theoretical proximity, precision, a 'separation' between criticism and attack, etc.

Gardies: Perhaps there has also been the specific development of semiology itself? At a given moment, research carried out in neighboring fields, or outside academia, was able to establish exchanges and meeting points with what we could call the primary core.

Metz: Of course (and fortunately!). It should also be clarified that this transmissible 'corpus' I spoke about was not provided by semiology alone, except right at the beginning. The role of semiology has more been to shake things up a bit, and unleash a more diverse movement.

Gardies: Previously, the transmissible, institutionally recognized discourse – the first teaching positions, created in the immediate aftermath of 1968, attest to this – was that of film history, or general aesthetics. At the time, did semiology allow for an extension and a diversification of this discourse?

Metz: Yes. But film history remains an essential task. I have sometimes been wrongly criticized by those who condescendingly adopt the mantle of History, who do not see that there are distinct projects which *do not match up with each other* (the mania for 'articulating' everything with everything else is absurd). This is why I would never allow myself the inverse (and corresponding) dishonesty that would consist of despising historical research and teaching, or foisting semiological methods on them. We have to put a stop to this pointless bickering, which annoyingly shows up the underdevelopment of the field of 'film studies' to everybody (and I do mean to say 'the field'; this is not a question of individual flaws, but the result of a history, the history of this discipline, its marginality, etc.).

Gardies: But, at present, after this exponential expansion of the teaching of film studies, is there not the risk of academicism, or even a fossilization of scholarship, as the price paid for success?

Metz: It is more than a danger, it is the actual state of things. But this is a specific aspect of those movements that become well-known. See, for example, pseudo-Derridean deconstructionism in certain French departments in the United States, which is a form of scholasticism, like bad semiology.

Because you have broached this point, I will add that I am in no way an advocate of indefinitely extending the teaching of film studies. It has its place in the University, where we offer a large number of specialized disciplines, but if we imagined, like certain enthusiastic reformers, integrating it into basic education, then we would also end up having to include music, painting, three living languages, architecture, audio-visual studies, physical education, etc. So we would end up with a nonsensical list, whose only merit would be to remind ourselves that the function of mandatory schooling is *actually* to transmit the major tools of thought, which are small in number, and not to explore everything that is '*learnable*'.

But I will return to what you said about the perennial possibility of fossilization. When this occurs, we cannot do anything about it: how can we foster inspiration and initiative in a sclerotic scholar – that is, a sclerotic *person*? Where we can act is 'around the edges', thanks to those who have retained a freedom of mind, whether they are semiologists or not.

The Film Studies Landscape

Gardies: Indeed, today it seems that film semiology has spread to other domains, that it has created zones of specificity that the 'first generation' had not explored.

Metz: Yes, semiology has introduced – *either directly, or as a backlash* – a breath of fresh air, a general renewal of film studies (I am only speaking of theoretical studies here), which goes well beyond purely semiological writings, and which has resulted in a large number of specialized publications.

In this rich outpouring, I would distinguish three categories, or, in any case, three categories that are of interest to me, that have enriched, completed or modified my initial contribution rather than repeated it while distorting it in all directions. This does not include those who have definitely headed off for new territories. As you see, I do not count on annexing them to my own work, but they do participate in the overall movement over the last 25 years.

At Cerisy, in a few days [the colloquium 'Christian Metz and Film Theory', held at the Cultural Centre of Cerisy in 1989], I will cite the names of scholars (including yourself) while trying to briefly situate the work of each one – close to a hundred of them in all. But it would be overly fastidious to write this all down, so I will limit myself to a few particularly clear examples, without any thought of creating hierarchies or awarding prizes, in order to try to let it be understood what my three 'groupings' consist of. Roughly defined, they would be formulated as follows:

1. Those who were originally 'Metzians', and who have added something to Metz's work, inflecting it or extending it, or transcending it to go further, etc. The clearest example here is Michel Colin, an exceptionally creative mind, who tragically died, and whose memory should be acknowledged with the utmost respect. But I am also thinking of the advocates of semio-pragmatics, or certain forms of narratology.
2. Non-Metzian semiologists; that is, explicitly semiological undertakings that are independent of my work, if you exclude the inevitable interferences due to the climate of the era. The prototype here is Marie-Claire Ropars and her theory of *écriture*. Or even, in America, John M. Carroll and his psycho-linguistics of the cinema.
3. Extra-semiological works, which are very important to my unrepentantly pluralist eyes, because they show that the emergence of semiology has not impeded the development of the rest of the discipline. Here, I would immediately point (in France) to Michel Chion, Pascal Bonitzer, Dominique Noguez, Jacques Aumont, the three Jean-Louis (= Baudry, Leutrat, Schefer) and a few others.
4. Finally, to refine these classifications, there are intermediate positions, like those of Raymond Bellour and Thierry Kuntzel, who are at once 'Metzian' and fiercely independent.

The work of the Anglo-Saxon feminists, which I find very interesting, would also occupy a specific place: they often owe a lot to my book *The Imaginary Signifier*, while critiquing it on certain points.

Another clarification: when I speak of general renewal, I do not mean in an absolute or dramatic sense. There have been other renewals in the history of film theory, whether before my contribution (for instance, the first incarnation of *Revue de Cinéma* and Jean-George Auriol), or afterwards, with Deleuze's extraordinary intervention. In my mind, we have a *dated* renewal effect, as is also the case with the others. I was always astonished by those cataclysmically-inclined minds who see every book as refuting all the others, of such a kind that the anguish of divisive choices and revisions knows no end.

Refusing the School Mentality

Gardies: A classification such as your own could be surprising, because you have integrated both people who work in a manner quite close to semiology and people who are external to it. Since semiology cannot be the criterion for selection, what criteria are pertinent for you in making your selection?

Metz: My criterion is an open semiology, alien to any school mentality, refusing to condemn everything that happens outside of such a school, and focused on peacefully pursuing one's own projects. Schools, in our disciplines (and perhaps in all disciplines?), are instruments of power, 'terror' and rejection, they are machines automatically manufacturing schisms and other heresies, sometimes even hatred. Every week I receive up to twenty (and sometimes even more) professional letters, occasionally accompanied by a written project, coming from France and abroad, and I am well placed – by this and by the very diverse range of people attending my seminars – to see the ravages caused by Schools, which sometimes paralyze the best writers with the anguish of orthodoxy, while inciting among other people the childish hope of finally having the universal key, *the* method, etc.

I would also like, by means of this cavalier overview, to react against a confusion I have seen at work here and there, the confusion between 'film semiology' and 'the works of Christian Metz'. It evidently relates to the fact that I was the first one to begin this work (I am also, let's not forget, the oldest member of the gang). But it has an absurd side, because it would be impossible to call me the initiator of something if nobody had followed me, if I was all alone in the landscape, that is, if there was nothing for me to have 'initiated'. This is an absurd confusion, and what is more, it is unjust: unjust for all the film semiologists who are working today in various different countries, and unjust also, or at least inaccurate, in another, less obvious but no less serious, sense: blinded by labels, some people fail to see that around a fifth of my writings, the equivalent of a whole book (texts such as my article on *8 ½*), are only partly semiological in nature and, whether good or bad, essentially consist of 'studies' of a classical type, rather similar to longer articles that film journals occasionally publish.

To come back to the point, or to summarize what I have been saying, I would like to show *both* that semiology, for its 25 years of existence, has played an important role, and that it was not alone. I think any other position is inexact and, in the end, dishonest.

Gardies: Independently of their fundamental options, for what reasons are the works that you evoke 'good objects' in your eyes? In other terms, what qualities do you expect of a work in order to recognize some value in it?

Metz: It should be serious, rigorous... The qualities one expects of any intellectual work... The standard of writing, of course...

Gardies: Being serious and rigorous, here we come back to...

Metz: Not only being serious and rigorous, but also the novelty of the contribution, the exploration of little known terrain, the filling in of a gap...

Gardies: In other words, the three qualities you have constantly mobilized in your own work.

I believe that what is also important, but you are unable to say it, is that this rich, diverse, thriving activity exists because you have never had any desire for being exclusive. This is both a deontological and scientific position that is totally opposed to the sectarianism and zealotry which semiology has too often been accused of.

Metz: I do not see for what sake one could pronounce an exclusivity for our research where the 'truth' is evasive, multiple and admits several different perspectives (which does not, however, mean that any idiocy should be validated). Way back in 1964, in the final pages of my first long article, I took the effort to explain in detail that 'my semiology was unable and unwilling to replace the other approaches toward the cinema (criticism, history, etc.)'. I hoped for a calm and courteous insertion *alongside* the existing and future orientations. I added that it should go back over the entire past of film theory (I was still naïve and I had no idea that at this time I was virtually the only one, along with Jean Mitry and two or three others, to know this past...). On the whole, little attention has been paid to these concluding pages, or it has been felt that they were just there to be polite, whereas in my eyes they were of the utmost importance. And all of a sudden, despite such a precautionary statement, I had whipped up a hurricane, with people rallying 'for' and 'against' me, like in a rugby match. I was turned into a living God, or into a Great Satan. All this is quite amazing, and I was largely powerless before the sporadically catastrophic sociology of the intellectual and academic machinery.

But not entirely impotent: confronted with this turn of events, I have striven, for more than fifteen years, to '*break up*', through passages published in prefaces or interviews, not (of course) the idea of semiology and less still the works of numerous scholars of quality who surround me at varying distances, but to break up semiology as a dogma, or as a superego (= a school, once more). And I fully intend to continue to do so, just as I have done in this very moment.

Gardies: Something else. Whereas the terms '*sémiotique*' [semiotics] and '*sémiologie*' [semiology] are given as equivalents, or sometimes competitors, which of the two do you prefer?

Metz: I prefer *sémiologie*. Because *sémiologie* means Roland Barthes, Saussure, the European tradition, which does not separate semiology from philosophy, from general culture, from the literary tradition.

Sémiotique clearly orients toward other forms of thought: the rational empiricism of the Anglo-Saxons, or on the contrary the vast edifice established by Greimas. I do not underestimate these phenomena, but they are alien to my way of thinking.

My Current Work

Gardies: What if we spoke about Christian Metz now, about his work, his projects? We have had the habit of expecting books written by Christian Metz, but it has been a long time since you published anything. I imagine that there is a reason for this.

Metz: Yes, I have been silent for a long time. Firstly, as a result of personal issues, which are now over. And right afterwards, because I worked a lot on a manuscript on the joke, a literary and psychoanalytic study, the joke in Freud, as well as more generally speaking. It was finished, but I was not satisfied with it, above all its structure, its mode of exposition, uselessly long and weighty. In short, I put it to one side, 'in the cooler', in order to return to it in my retirement. In our circles, it is customary not to speak of our failures (this is another superfluous taboo), but I find this custom quite idiotic: do we hope to make other people believe that we have never failed at anything?

As for my current work – 'current' meaning that it has occupied my attention for the last four years – it relates to the notion of enunciation, and more specifically enunciation in the cinema. I am preparing a book, about which I will not say too much, for my two articles recently published in *Vertigo* have already given an idea about it.[9] The subject, by the way, is not original, it is in the air. There was the special issue of *Communications* (no. 38) in 1983,[10] the work done by the Italians, and many others; you yourself took part in this debate, in your article 'Le su et le vu', and in your book on African cinema.[11]

To simplify matters drastically, I can express the idea of this book in a single phrase: the conceptions of filmic enunciation that are often proposed appear to me to be too closely linked to the linguistic model, with deictics, enunciator/enunciatee, I/you, etc., whereas enunciation, in a *dispositif* without an interlocutor, can only be of a metadiscursive type, folded in on itself, whose content is 'It's a film' more than 'It's me'.

Filmic enunciation is impersonal and is often confused with the very *place* of the film. As its 'markers' it has everything that, in a film, reminds the spectators that they are watching a film, or that they are in a cinema. On this basis, I give an overview of different 'positions' of enunciation more or less governed by rules: the off-screen voice addressed to the viewer, the dialogue title-card, the I-voice of the character ('voice-over'), the subjective image, extra-diegetic music, etc., with, in each case, various examples of shots and sequences drawn from the repertoire of well-known films (this will be a more 'concrete' book than the other ones, to put it bluntly).

The exploration of the deictic 'network' is, by the way, a normal and necessary approach in the early stages, as Jean Paul Simon mentioned to me, who theorized these problems very early on. And yet, the most deictic filmic constructions, like the off-screen voice directly interpellating the spectator, still stage a false deixis, or more precisely a simulated deixis, because the spectator cannot respond...

Gardies: Like the aside in theater?

Metz: Exactly. Incidentally, Vernet and Casetti have both made this comparison.

Gardies: In the midst of this discussion of enunciation, I note that we have not broached a question that is nonetheless important as far as semiology is concerned: is one of its major contributions its emphasis on the textual dimension of the film, thereby provoking a clear rupture with the discourse of the widespread *doxa* on cinema, 'The cinema is life, it is reality, etc.'? In a certain way, has semiology not adopted, without saying so, these words by a certain famous filmmaker, 'A just image is just an image'? Filmic enunciation, we have just said, has the specific function of designating itself as cinema, and hence of disturbing the transparency of the windowpane.

Metz: Yes, but to varying degrees and in different modes. If enunciation is never entirely 'effaced', it can happen, willingly or not, that it is 'marked' with a great deal of discretion.

This reflexive conception of enunciation, so to speak (the text that more or less refers to itself) has been prefigured, to my mind, in certain remarks made by Pierre Sorlin, Marie-Claire Ropars, yourself, and François Jost. In my case, it has become the guiding thread of my whole work. But I owe a lot to all those theorists – there are at least fifteen of them – who have studied this question, and who, by the way, I cite abundantly.

Gardies: I believe that you would not want to end this interview without paying homage to someone who was very important to you.

Metz: Yes. I am *unwilling* and *unable* to finish without a thought for my only mentor, Roland Barthes who, in 1966, assigned to me the task of taking care of film semiology in the École des hautes études. Of course, I inherited neither his genius nor his style (his way of writing books, but also his elegant and inimitable manner of managing the profession's day-to-day administration, which Jacques Le Goff evoked so well[12]). On many points, I have not adopted his ideas. But he taught me day by day for 24 years – from 1956 until his death in 1980, as I knew him when I was still teaching at a *lycée*. He taught me something that is just as important as any of his theories, and that I strive to put into practice with my own, obviously more modest, means: the meticulous attention one must give other people, and which is generally lacking in scientific exchanges; the bypassing of hardened divisions like 'structuralism', 'schizo-analysis', 'post-modernism', etc.; the refusal of all brash tirades and triumphalist boastings; the avoidance of all jargon, including the jargon of semiology; the necessary inscription of specialized research in a vaster, older culture, not through pedantic citations, but through tone, and a concern for style even in technical publications, the choice of the exact word even outside of the terms defined by theory; and above all, his amicability, which in his case led to a recognition of kindness and civility, spontaneously undertaken, day after day, to the benefit of the lowliest student who came to visit him, and this despite the fact that our crumbling universe, founded on *demand* and the self-engendered hysteria of the institutions, crushed him with fatigue and was the nightmare of his life. Amicability is not friendship (the latter is not commanded, it is encountered, and it would be absurd to wish to generalize it through some kind of precept), but it is an indispensable prerequisite, and is insufficiently perceived as such, for remotely normal relations between scholars, for the opening of a breathable space for agreements and disagreements, for discussions exempt from theatrical stiffness or anguished hostility, and, by dint of this, for more rapid progress in scholarship itself.

Conversation recorded by André Gardies (Paris, June 15, 1989).

Notes

1. 'Le cinéma. Langue ou langage?' in *Communications* 4 (special issue on 'Recherches sémiologiques', ed. Roland Barthes, 1964). Reworked version in Christian Metz, *Essais sur la signification au cinéma* vol. 1 (Paris: Klincksieck, 1968) [*Film Language: A Semiotics of the Cinema*, pp. 31–91.]
2. [Jean Bessalel, 'Onze concepts clés lexique'. *CinémAction*, 58 (1991), pp. 158–173.]
3. *Filmology: Establishing a Problematic for Film Study in France (1946–55)*, PhD, Austin, TX, 1982, p. 412 [Published as: Edward Lowry, *Filmology Movement and Film Study in France* (Ann Arbor, MI: UMI Research Press, 1985).]
4. [Jean-Louis Schefer, *L'homme ordinaire du cinéma* (Paris: Gallimard, 1980).]
5. In the collective volume entitled *Pour une esthétique sans entraves – Mélanges Mikel Dufrenne* (Paris: 10/18, 1975). Repr. in Christian Metz, *Essais sémiotiques* (Paris: Klincksieck, 1977). [Translated as 'The Perceived and the Named' in *Studies in Visual Communication* 6, 3 (1980), pp. 56–68.]
6. [A two year pre-degree preparatory class in literature and the humanities.]
7. 'La construction 'en abyme' dans *Huit et Demi* de Fellini', *Revue d'esthétique* 19:1 (January–March 1966). Repr. in Christian Metz, *Essais sur la signification au cinéma* vol. I (cf. note 1). [*Film Language: A Semiotics of the Cinema*, pp. 228–234.]
8. Michel Marie, 'L'enseignement du cinéma et l'hydre sémiologique', *Ça-Cinéma* 18 (1979); Roger Odin, 'Rêverie pédagogique', *Hors-Cadre* 5 ('L'école-cinéma', 1987).

9. 'L'enonciation impersonelle, ou le site du film (en Marge de Travaux Récents sur l'enonciation au cinéma)', *Vertigo* 1 (November 1987). [See Christian Metz, *The Impersonal Enunciation, or the Place of Film* (New York: Columbia University Press, 2016).]
10. 'Énonciation et cinéma', special issue edited by Jean-Paul Simon and Marc Vernet.
11. 'Le su et le vu', *Hors-Cadre* 2 ('Cinénarrables', 1984); *Cinéma d'afrique noire francophone. L'espace miroir* (Paris: L'Harmattan, 1989).
12. 'Barthes Administrateur', pp. 43–48, *Communications* 36 ('Roland Barthes', 1982).

Index

17W51725/ T2/ 9789089648259